# WOMEN IN EXILE

# WOMEN IN EXILE

MAHNAZ AFKHAMI

UNIVERSITY PRESS OF VIRGINIA
*Charlottesville and
London*

This is a title in the series
FEMINIST ISSUES: PRACTICE, POLITICS, THEORY

THE UNIVERSITY PRESS OF VIRGINIA
Copyright © 1994
by the Rector and Visitors
of the University of Virginia

*First Published 1994*

Library of Congress Cataloging-in-Publication Data
Afkhami, Mahnaz.
    Women in exile / Mahnaz Afkhami.
        p.   cm. — (Feminist issues)
    ISBN 0-8139-1542-2 (cloth). —
ISBN 0-8139-1543-0 (paper)
        1. Women political activists—United States—
Biography.   2. Exiles—United States—Biography.
I. Title.   II. Series: Feminist issues (Charlottesville, Va.)
HQ1236.5.U6A25   1994
305.42—dc20                                        94-7817
                                                        CIP

Printed in the United States of America

# Contents

# Contents

# Preface

This book is about hope. It is about women who keep the fire of hope burning despite the suffering and cruelty that pervade our world. The women whose stories make this book are not different from waves of women exiles and refugees moving across borders everyday, seeking protection and shelter in foreign lands across the globe. The overwhelming majority of the eighteen million refugees and the twenty million euphemistically called "displaced" are women and children. They are victims of hunger, disease, and rape. From Cambodia to Afghanistan, from Bosnia to Somalia, they are at the mercy of forces beyond their control. They all suffer, in most places they have no protection, and many of them despair. But most cope, some succeed, and a few, like women in this book, excel by not only pulling themselves out of the conditions of misery but also becoming leaders in the struggle for a better world.

The women in this book were forced to leave their homelands by political events beyond their control, and all but one came to live in exile in the United States in the 1980s. They represent a wide variety of socioeconomic backgrounds. They are Buddhist, Muslim, Christian, Jewish, and atheist. Their education ranges from the highest academic degrees to bare literacy. They have experienced displacement, coped with the circumstances of uprootedness, adjusted to a foreign environment, and forged a new identity for themselves.

When the change in their lives happened, some were strong, militant participants in events, some were completely apolitical and were caught by surprise, but they all managed to become leaders by example and by deed. Ho Ngoc Tran of Vietnam, in exile since 1978, is now a pediatrician and community activist. Alicia Partnoy of Argentina, in exile since 1979, is now a writer and member of the board of Amnesty International. Maria Teresa Tula of El Salvador, in exile since 1987, is a human rights activist representing Comadres in international forums. Sima Wali of Afghanistan, in exile since 1978, is now executive director of Refugee Women in Development. Marjorie Agosin of Chile, in exile since 1973, is now an acclaimed poet and professor at Wellesley College. Hala Deeb Jabbour of Palestine, in exile since 1981, is now a novelist and feminist activist. Florence M. Simfukwe of Malawi, in exile since 1964, is now a nurse and a member of the "Survivors" committee of Amnesty. Samnang Wu of Cambodia, in exile since 1977, is now a public health specialist with Montgomery County, Maryland's Refugee Health Program. Tatyana Mamonova of Russia, in exile since 1980, is editor of the journal *Woman and Earth* and author of a number of books on Russian women. Azar Salamat of Iran, in exile since 1982, is managing editor at a Public Service Agency. Ge Yang of China, in exile since 1990, is a writer and journalist. Fatima Ahmed Ibrahim of Sudan, in exile since 1989, is president of the International Democratic Federation of Women and recipient of the 1993 United Nations Human Rights Award.

The stories presented are based on oral interviews I had with each woman over many sessions. My training in oral history methodology had taught me to listen sympathetically, carefully, and intensely, but never to impose my own notions and interests on the interview situation. Early on, however, I decided that this was not to be—indeed, it could not be—a traditional oral history document. An exile myself, I had too much in common with my subjects and it soon became apparent to me that we shared too many experiences and feelings for an objective oral history project. Invariably, I became a participant in the life that evolved as each story unfolded. The stories in this book, therefore, are my rendering of lives and experiences that resemble mine and that I think I understand as my own.

The conversations were recorded over a number of sittings, ranging from two to six, each session taking from three to six hours. We met in informal surroundings, usually in the woman's home or at my office on a holiday. I tried to arrange the sharing of food. I felt that a more casual atmosphere lent itself better to recollection of memories that so often involve rituals of family and friends around the taking of a meal together.

In each case I described the nature of the work at length and explained that the subject was free to tell her story as she chose and to emphasize any portion of her life as she wished—that we were composing a work together and she was free to weave her pattern through the tapestry of our collected lives. I always began with offering my own story. The rapport that was established between us was due to many factors, but mostly it was achieved because I too was a woman in exile and the book was to represent our collective experience.

Our conversations were open-ended. For each woman the process involved a search for understanding and a summing-up as she composed a life and formulated an identity. Each woman herself determined the structure of her narrative through her choice of topic, the order of relating her experience, and the emphasis she chose to give each segment of her life. I tried not to interfere with choices and with the values assigned to various events. Summing up the hundreds of pages of transcript representing each woman's story was my task.

In each interview I made a number of queries and probings based on my own experience and knowledge of the stories I had already heard. In talking of childhood, for example, I always asked about the moment or the event that brought home to her what being a woman meant in her society and how she felt about that moment and event. In the few cases where it was not expressed, I asked about her feeling on leaving her country. In our discussions of exile, I tried to draw out the degree and type of attachment to the original culture by asking questions about the language used in dreams or in conversations at home. I asked about ceremonies of passage and holidays. Throughout the interviews I refrained from forcing the narrative into a preconceived mold by introducing set questions. I weaved my queries into our dialogue when it seemed appropriate.

For many of the women, the telling of their story was a new experience. It was the first time they related their whole life systematically. For everyone, it was an emotionally trying process.

I transcribed the tapes verbatim, often producing hundreds of pages of unedited text. I condensed the material quite freely, relying on the dynamics of our interaction during the interview, our contact and conversations outside the interview situation, and each woman's personality and reactions to and ways of dealing with exile. In a number of cases there was a hiatus between the first and the second set of interviews. This happened when after writing the chapter, I felt that as a reader I would want to know more.

Each woman read the text of her story and approved the contents, agreeing that the story represented the essence of her history. A few corrected names or dates or other factual matters. Each story is thus the product of a dynamic interaction between two women and two sensibilities, informed by a series of shared experiences. Yet the stories are in the end a record of the lives of vibrant, interesting, and powerful women. What we aimed for was not an objective but an intuitive rendering of the feel and meaning of our lives at home and in exile.

The life stories tend to bring out a sense of how it is to grow up a woman in each of the cultures represented, how each woman views herself within her society, when or how changes in her or her environment make it impossible to continue life at home, what specific events or feelings prompt the journey into exile, and what processes link the life known to the new life and reshape or help reinvent the personality within the new cultural context.

Every woman I approached was generous with her time and spontaneous and open in sharing her life. Only two women refused to be interviewed when I explained the project. One was a young woman from China who was preoccupied with the politics of Tienanmen Square at the time. Another was a South African woman who said she was not ready to relive her recent past as yet.

The interviews were all conducted in English except for two: Ge Yang's interview was interpreted by Xiao Qiang and Maria Teresa Tula's by Stephanie Willman. I am grateful for their generous contributions of their time and effort. A number of women whose stories are represented here are poets and writers in their own language. That the stories were told in a language not their own has undoubtedly affected their tone. I regret that I have missed the subtleties of their story in their own tongue.

I thank my sisters in exile for their generous and wholehearted support, for sharing their stories with me, and for helping to produce this collective biography of exile. Knowing them was a joy and inspiration which I will cherish always. I have written these stories of struggle, survival, and empowerment because of their inherent value as personal narratives, but, as a victim myself, I like to think that they will also bring to light some of the root causes of exile and encourage those in power to seek solutions to this devastating and escalating problem of our time. Most of all, I hope that the example of these women will embolden other women in exile to defy the odds, to endure, and to conquer—for themselves, for their children, and for the world.

## Preface

My friends and colleagues in Sisterhood Is Global Institute Robin Morgan and Marilyn Waring showed faith in this project from the beginning. Their support, especially in the initial stages, was most valuable to me. My literary agent Edite Kroll went beyond her professional duties to encourage and support me as a friend and a feminist through the process of writing and publication of the manuscript. My editor Nancy Essig of the University Press of Virginia was especially helpful with critical suggestions and constructive ideas as well as her enthusiastic support. I am grateful to them for their help. I would like to express my special appreciation to my colleague and friend Ezzat Aghevli, who has worked with me for two decades, at home and in exile, on all that I have done professionally, including this book.

My mother and sister, exiled women themselves, gave me the warmth and love that sustained me during these difficult years and helped me with ideas and comments. My son Bobby and my brother Hamid read parts of the book and offered useful suggestions. Their irrepressible sense of humor helped me keep the balance between pain and joy as I journeyed through the lives I have retold in this book.

My gratitude also goes to the directors of the Foundation for Iranian Studies who provided me with two travel grants and secretarial assistance and for their unfailing encouragement and support. I am grateful to Yaddo, the wonderful oasis that gave me a safe haven during two stays in 1991 and 1992. There I worked on this manuscript as I enjoyed the company of writers, painters, musicians, and other artists in a special atmosphere that made work a pleasure.

Of my husband Gholam Reza Afkhami I can only say that if I could conceive of a state of being "without him," I would have to add that this as much else in my life would never have been done.

# WOMEN IN EXILE

MAHNAZ AFKHAMI

# Women in Exile: A Prologue

No, you have not seemed strange to me, but near,
Frightfully near, and rather terrifying.
I understand you all, for in myself—
Is that presumption? Yet indeed it's true—
We are one family. And still my answer
Will not be any one of yours, I see.

—Amy Lowell, "The Sisters"

I AM AN EXILE. I have been in exile for fifteen years. I have been
forced to stay out of my own country, Iran, because of my work for
women's rights. I recognized no limits, ends, or framework in this
work outside those set by women themselves in their capacity as
independent human beings. The charges against me are "corruption
on earth" and "warring with God." Being charged in the Islamic
Republic of Iran is being convicted. There is no defense or appeal,
although I would not have known how to defend myself against such
a grand accusation as warring with God anyway. There has not been
a trial, not even in absentia, and no formal conviction. Nevertheless,
my home in Tehran has been ransacked and confiscated, my books,
pictures, and mementos taken, my passport invalidated, and my life
threatened repeatedly.

My life in exile began at dawn on November 27, 1978. I was
awakened by the ringing of the telephone. My husband's voice
sounded very near. It took me a while to remember he was calling
from Tehran. He had just spoken with Queen Farah who had suggested I cancel my return trip from New York scheduled for the
following day. The government was trying to appease the opposition

by making scapegoats of its own high-ranking officials. Feminists were primary targets for the fundamentalist revolutionaries. I had recently lost my cabinet post as minister of state for women's affairs as the regime's gesture of appeasement to the mullahs. It was very likely, my husband was saying, that as the most visible feminist in the country I would be arrested on arrival at the airport.

I searched for my glasses on the table by the bed and turned on the light, still clutching the receiver. I looked out the window at the black asphalt, glistening under the street lights. It must have rained earlier, I thought as I listened to my husband's voice, tinged with despair, yet somehow aloof and impersonal, as if this had little to do with him. Two months later when I would call to discuss the deteriorating situation and the need for him to get away, I would sound the same to him. The ties between a person and her home are such that even those nearest fear to intervene directly.

When I said good-bye I was wide awake but not clear-headed. What will I do here, I wondered. During the past few weeks my days had been spent negotiating with the United Nations' lawyers the terms of an agreement between the government of Iran and the UN, setting up the International Research and Training Institute for the Advancement of Women (INSTRAW) in Tehran. Evenings had been spent in meetings with groups and individuals trying desperately to affect the outcome of events in Iran.

Now it was suddenly all over for me. I could not go back home. I was left with a temporary visa, less than $1,000 in cash, and no plans whatsoever. I crossed the small room and automatically turned on the television to the Reuter news channel. The moving lines of the news tape were a familiar sight. In the last few weeks I had spent many hours staring at the screen, following the latest news, waiting for the inevitable items on Iran. When I looked up, the sun was streaming through the room.

Where would I go, I wondered as I dressed. I remembered I had planned to buy a coat that day. "What sort of a coat?" I asked myself. What sort of life will I be leading and what kind of a coat will that life require? Who am I going to be now that I am no longer who I was a few hours ago? I smiled at my reflection in the mirror. Need there be such existential probing connected to the buying of a winter coat? Even though I was far from the realization of the dimensions and the meaning of what had happened to me, my identity was already becoming blurred. The "I" of me no longer had clear outlines, no longer cast a definite shadow.

For a decade I had defined myself by my place within the Iranian women's movement. The question "Who am I?" was answered not by indicating gender, religion, nationality, or family ties but by my position as the secretary general of the Women's Organization of Iran, a title that described my profession, indicated my cause, and defined the philosophic framework for my existence. On that November morning in 1978, I realized that an immediate and formal severance of my connection to WOI was absolutely necessary. In those days of turmoil, when the movement's very existence was threatened, WOI did not need a secretary general who had become persona nongrata to the system and its opposition. I sat at the desk in my hotel room and began to write a letter of resignation.

"To the Central Council of the WOI," I wrote, and I pictured the faces of the women on the council. I feared that by the time the letter reached Tehran, members of the council might themselves be in gravest danger. I smiled to remember Dr. Alam, the president of the central council to whom I had given Kate Millet's *Sexual Politics* as part of a campaign to bring the council into contact with examples of feminist thinking in other countries. Dr. Alam was not well versed in English. She had shocked her conservative extended family by looking up from her book during a relaxed weekend gathering and inquiring loudly of a younger, American educated member, "What means fuck?"

"We have worked together and achieved much during the past decade," I wrote, and remembered the day when I stood in my office, holding the phone to my ear with both hands, trembling with excitement as my colleague reported from the Majlis that the Family Protection Law had just passed. I put the receiver down, joy bubbling in my chest, not knowing what to do to celebrate. I picked up the phone and called a woman who had complained to me recently about her powerlessness to affect her children's destiny after her husband's death. The previous law had required that in the absence of the father, they be placed under the custody of a grandfather, an uncle— in their case, an uncaring granduncle. I called her and said, "Afsaneh Khanom, congratulations, as of this hour you will have a say over your children's future."

"We have confronted many obstacles together," I wrote, and

recalled driving in the desert city of Yazd through the parched, dusty winding streets, defined by the high mud walls of houses. We had stopped to talk to a woman who was crying as she ran close to the wall, her shoulder touching the mud bricks from time to time, loosening bits of dirt and dust. She was the legal advisor of the WOI center, she said. Her husband had just battered her for her work on behalf of the organization and had forbidden her to set foot in the center. In Bandar Abbas a woman had allowed us to look under the hard, coarse surface of the "Borghe," a masklike covering pressed over her nose and eyes, to see the bruises and cuts it created as it rubbed against her perspiration-soaked skin in the 104 degree heat. In Esfahan a woman at a textile factory had told us she locks in her four small children in her one room home ten hours each day so that she can work.

"We have built a feminist infrastructure which will not be destroyed," I continued, and thought of the tens of thousands of women who had helped create a network of classes, childcare centers, consciousness-raising groups, and health care clinics throughout the country. In factories, villages, and schools women had repeated to us that the most important single need of women is financial independence on which depend all their liberties and capabilities. Without it, all rights and legal protection become irrelevant; with it, all else is within reach. I remembered the many discussions and meetings and one-to-one conversations out of which grew the concept of the Houses of Women. At the heart of each center were the vocational training classes. Around the classes grew other services such as childcare, job counseling, and family planning that made it possible for women to participate in classes and once trained to seek and sustain a career uninterrupted by unwanted pregnancies.

The centers' programs had grown to include lectures, discussions, and consciousness-raising gatherings. Although the activities were not political in themselves, they created a heightened sociopolitical awareness that culminated in the massive participation of women in the revolution of 1979. I recalled a meeting of the secretaries of the provincial organizations after one of the first demonstrations in Kerman in which masses of women in black *chadors* had marched. The secretary from Kerman had explained to us about the marching women saying they were "our own members—we have talked about mobilization and assertiveness and now they are mobilized and assertive and ask for the downfall of the regime!" And she was right. The phenomenon of millions of women participating in the uprisings would have been unimaginable in a society with a lower level of feminist consciousness. That the women were as mistaken as the intellectuals and the nationalists and leftists in their appraisal of the future does not detract from the significance of their extraordinary movement.

I returned to my letter, summarized our mutual accomplishments, summed up the reasons for my resignation, pledged my continued dedication to the cause, and wished the movement and the council victory against the forces of reaction. I read the text over the telephone to my assistant in Tehran, both of us fighting to hold back our tears, already thinking not of the decade fast fading into the past but of the dark years ahead of us. She told me about bomb threats to the centers in Zanjan, in Sabzevar, in Sirjan. She said that the day before they had to evacuate the childcare center at the headquarters twice because of similar threats.

I was reluctant to say good-bye, knowing that cutting the connection meant literally that—cutting my ties with my job, my cause, my country, and my home. Finally I put the receiver down, repeating to myself, "that's that," "so much for that."

During the next days I lived a refusal to believe, a denial of the event, an inability to mourn—a state of mind which for me continued for years to come. A flurry of activity related to making arrangements concerning the death is the surest means of keeping full realization of the fact of it at bay. So I plunged myself into a series of actions aimed at ensuring survival in the new setting. The first priority was obtaining permission to stay in the United States. You need this to get a job although sometimes you can't get it without having a job—one of the many vicious circles encountered in the life of exiles. Those who enter the country as exiles discover that what had been their natural birthright at home will now depend on the decision of an official who may, for any reason at all or none, deny permission, a process from which there is no recourse.

As soon as possible, I was told, one must get the necessary cards—driver's license, social security, credit card. These are to help one to assure the community that one exists and will continue to exist for the foreseeable future and can be trusted to handle a car and pay a bill. There is a certain excitement involved in all this. Finding a place to live, learning new routines, looking for a job, establishing new relationships—all within a separate reality, outside the framework of one's customary existence. It is possible to once again ask, "What do I want to be?" I contemplated whole new careers, from real estate to law, from teaching to opening a small business. They all seemed equally possible yet uniformly improbable.

All of this activity buys one time—time to assimilate the fact of loss and time to prepare to face it. You are told often that you must distance yourself from the past, that you must start a new life. But as in the case of death of kin—you don't want to move away, close his room, give away his clothes. You want to talk about him, look at pictures, exchange memories. You shun contact with all those healthy, normal natives who are going about their business as if the world is a safe, secure, and permanent place a piece of which belongs to them by birthright. You work frantically to retain the memory and to reconstruct the past.

When you mourn a loved one, you wish more than anything to be either alone or with others who share your sense of loss. I sought mostly the company of other exiled Iranians. Together we listened to Persian music, exchanged memories, recalled oft-repeated stories and anecdotes, and allowed ourselves inordinate sentimentality. We remembered tastes, smells, sounds. We knew that no fruit would ever have the pungent aroma and the luscious sweetness of the fruit in Iran, that the sun would never shine so bright, nor the moon shed such light as we experienced under the desert sky in Kerman. The green of the vegetation on the road to the Caspian has no equal, the jasmine elsewhere does not smell as sweet.

Like children who need to hear a story endless times, we repeated for each other scenes from our collective childhood experiences. We recalled the young street vendors sitting in front of round trays on which they had built a mosaic of quartets of fresh walnuts positioned neatly at one inch intervals. We recalled the crunchy, salty taste of the walnuts carried with us in a small brown bag as we walked around Tajrish Square, taking in the sounds and sights of an early evening in summer. We recalled the smell of corn sizzling on makeshift grills on the sidewalk. We remembered our attempts to convince the ice cream vendor, a young boy not much older than ourselves, to give us five one-rial portions of the creamy stuff smelling of rose water, each of which he carefully placed between two thin wafers. We knew that any combination of sizes would get us more than the largest—the five-rial portion. But the vendor, in possession of the facts and in command of the situation, sometimes refused to serve more than one portion to each child. We remembered walking past families who were picnicking, sitting on small rugs spread by the narrow waterways at the edge of the avenue, laughing and clapping to the music which blared from their radios, oblivious of the traffic a few feet away. We laughed about our grandmothers or aunts who sat in front of the television enjoying images from faraway places, around which they constructed their own stories, independently of the original creator's intention.

We recalled all this with affection and nostalgia. Yet we cursed ourselves and our culture and our habits and expressed our distrust, contempt, and suspicion of our compatriots. "Iranians are . . ." began an enumeration of our supposed national characteristics, confirmed, reiterated, and further embellished by each person present, provided that they were all from the same background and that there were no outsiders among them. These descriptions did not include the revolutionaries, around whose character a new set of myths had begun to accumulate.

During the first year of the revolution, the hostage crisis dominated our lives. Each evening we waited for a news show called "America Held Hostage." We watched with disbelief images of bearded, shouting, fierce-looking youth, brandishing machine guns and shoving blindfolded American diplomats in front of the ravenous television cameras that gorged themselves on these scenes, spouting them out every night on this and other programs, making it harder with each passing day to identify ourselves by our nationality in casual encounters on the street, in a store, or on a bus.

The next year brought a consolidation of the power of the clergy over the population and a systematic clamp-down on those they considered their enemies. Women were the subject of daily admonition, direction, or complaints in the government-controlled press of the Islamic Republic of Iran. Their dress, their manner, their duties at home and in society, their role as mother and wife, the danger of their seemingly irrepressible sexuality were discussed endlessly regardless of what calamity faced the country. War, famine, internal upheaval, international crises were each and all unable to push women off the front pages of the newspapers.

As months passed, women persisted in their novel and original methods of resistance. We heard and read how they let their veils slip back slightly off their foreheads, covered their legs in stockings that were a shade thinner than prescribed, wore raincoats that were belted at the waist, sunglasses that not only covered mascaraed eyelashes but indicated Westernized tastes and ways. All indications were that women were by no means under control. They pierced the heart and conscience of the mullahs and their adamant followers with their persistent forays into the margins of proper behavior. Women who had never worn makeup before began to wear it as a statement of their independence. That the numbers of women who followed these patterns seemed to grow instead of diminishing was a source of constant anxiety and frustration to the government. We read with disbelief and amusement the president of the Islamic Republic's dec-laration that the rays emanating from a woman's hair disrupt the composure of males in her vicinity—a phenomenon which he de-clared a justification for strict enforcement of the veiling regulation. The statement was followed by many similar dictates from religious authorities. The newspapers proudly carried news of guards stopping women on the street to admonish them for poor coverage of their heads and bodies. We heard accounts of women being dragged off to be questioned and flogged. We learned of cases where lipstick was wiped off with a razor blade and the scarf was attached to its proper place on the forehead with a thumbtack.

The media were mesmerized as the Ayatollah Khomeini issued decrees of death and destruction against individuals and groups within Iran and individuals, nations, and whole regions without. Pundits who had knelt reverently before him in the village near Paris before he arrived in Iran continued their objective, neutral coverage of his statements of prejudice, cruelty, and megalomania. I, who had experienced the camaraderie and support of the international femi-nist community, was affected more than others by their silence during the first few years after the revolution. Even when pregnant women accused of adultery or those accused of homosexuality were stoned, even when Ms. Farrokhrou Parsa, Iran's first cabinet minister for education, a doctor, teacher, feminist was executed on charges of prostitution, few commented. In fact, her execution did not even merit a mention on the evening news. The total absence of reaction or support made me begin to doubt my own perception of reality. Nearly a decade would pass before the announcement of the *fatwa* against Salman Rushdie once again would make it possible for Western intellectuals to have a clear-cut, strong reaction to Khomeini. The protest would come not on behalf of Iranian women, but in support of a British writer's freedom of expression.

During the early years I kept myself frantically busy with phone calls, lectures, meetings. Slowly, the life I had fashioned for myself in the new surroundings began to take shape. I now had a home in a suburb of Washington, D.C. Artist friends helped me collect a small selection of the works of Iranian women painters. A growing library of my old favorite books of poetry and fiction found a place in my room. The Foundation for Iranian Studies, a cultural institution that I helped create and managed with the aid of former colleagues, began to expand its activities. My family survived the travails and threats against them and all gathered near each other around Washington. Iran as a physical entity grew dimmer in our memory and more distant. But we remained obsessed with the events and processes that had led to our exile. All conversations, social occasions, and readings centered around what happened to us and more often than not ended in assigning blame.

As I went about building a life for myself in America, I learned through many encounters to simplify the spelling of my name, to mispronounce it to make it more easily comprehensible for my new contacts. I made small changes in my walk, posture, way of dressing to approach the new environment's expectations. In the process I drifted farther away from my self. The woman exclaiming about the weather to the sales girl at Macy's, calling herself Menaaz was not me. The original word, *Mahnaz,* had a meaning—Mah, moon, Naz, grace. Translating myself into the new culture made me incomprehensible to myself. I barely recognized this altered version of my personality. Frost once said "poetry is what is lost in translation." I realized that whatever poetry exists in the nuances which give subtlety to one's personality is lost in the new culture. What remains is dull prose—a rougher version, sometimes a caricature of one's real self. This smiling, mushy person was not me. It was my interpretation of the simplicity and friendliness of American social conduct. I embarrassed myself with it.

In public places I acted as if I were alone. In Iran, even in places where I was unlikely to meet someone I knew, I always acted "socially"—as if the people I met were potentially people I might come to know, people I might see again. I conducted myself with a consciousness of this assumption of possible further acquaintance, of a reasonable continuity of events. In America I acted totally isolated and separate, as if there were no chance that someone on the street might ever relate to me in any other way than as a total stranger. I caught glimpses of my American friends chatting with the owner at a restaurant in the neighborhood, greeting friends at other tables, talking about their plans, their homes, their professions, discussing the variations in the menu with the waiter, amazed that life went on as if nothing much had happened. I longed for this elemental sense of connection with my environment.

I kept on searching for the effects of dislocation on my feelings and reactions and spent much of my time studying my own mental state. The preoccupation had come close to neurotic proportions. Fortunately, in my work with the Sisterhood Is Global Institute, an international feminist think tank, I had become acquainted with a number of women from various countries who, like myself, were in exile. Gradually, through our conversations, I began to see that the only way to understand myself was to stand back from my own experiences and focus on someone else, that the best way to see inside my mind was to concentrate on another as she looked inside hers. It was in talking with them that the project "Women in Exile" began to take shape.

I met Tatyana Mamonova of the former Soviet Union, Sima Wali of Afghanistan, and Marjorie Agosin of Chile, the first three women I approached, through the Sisterhood Is Global Institute. Our initial informal conversations revealed that behind the varied events which brought us into lives of exile in the United States, there lay a pattern of struggle, fear, violence, chance, choice, loss, dislocation, puzzlement, restructuring, and adjustment. The idea of the mosaic of stories culminating in a collective biography of exile evolved from these initial informal exchanges. These conversations taught me that the telling of a life story by a woman, in her own way, through her own choices and assignment of values, is an alternate and valuable way of learning, teaching, and knowing.

I chose the other participants to reflect a variety of socioeconomic, political, religious, ethnic, and geographic backgrounds. I looked for women who had been forced into exile because of their political activities and philosophies or activities and philosophies of the groups they belonged to rather than for economic reasons. From among possible choices, I selected those with whom I sensed rapport and whose stories seemed to fit the mosaic that shaped our collective experience.

Marjorie led me to Alicia Partnoy of Argentina who introduced me to Maria Teresa Tula of El Salvador. Sima told me about Samnang Wu of Cambodia. Robin Morgan introduced me to Hala Deeb Jabbour of Palestine. Dorothy Thomas of the Women's Rights Project of Human Rights Watch invited me to join the project's advisory committee where I met Zhu Hong who gave me the name of another Chinese woman called Zhu Hong who lived in Boston. Zhu told me about Ge Yang. Azar Salamat I have known since childhood. Because of the prevailing situation in Iran and for security reasons, her story is the only one in the book that appears under an assumed name. I met Florence Simfukwe through Alicia Partnoy when she asked me to join her work with survivors of state violence. Fatima Ahmed Ibrahim was suggested by Abdullahi An-Na'im, director of Human Rights Watch/Africa. Ngoc-Ho I met at a mutual friend's house after the work was nearly finished. She later made a special trip to Washington from her home in Chicago to allow me to interview her. She encouraged me as did a number of others, by saying that she would do all she could to help because she thought of the book as her own.

Each of the twelve stories in *Women in Exile* begins with descriptions of a society's disingenuous ways of shaping the woman's personality to fit the patriarchal mold. Even those who are active participants in political movements are outsiders without the power to influence the decision-making process in their society. Political events beyond their control lead to upheaval. They are vulnerable and as caretakers of families their lives are most affected by disruptive and cataclysmic events. There comes a time when their own safety or that of their children requires them to take charge of their lives and make the decision to escape. They undertake journeys of turbulence and danger. They reach the United States only to realize that the physical dangers they have endured are the preliminary stages to a life of exile. Slowly they begin to absorb the full impact of what has happened to them. A period of bereavement is followed by attempts to adjust to the new environment. Along with the loss of their culture and home comes the loss of the traditional patriarchal structures that limited their lives in their own land. Exile in its disruptiveness resembles a rebirth for the women. The pain of breaking out of their cultural cocoon brings with it the possibility of an expanded universe and a freer, more independent self. Reevaluation and reinvention of their lives leads to a new self that combines traits evolved in the old society and characteristics acquired in the new environment. The women share the capacity to stand up to adversity and to rise from victims to empowered and independent individuals. Their lives are enriched by what they have known and surpassed. They are "damaged," as Sam-nang says of herself, but they repair themselves into larger, deeper, more humane personalities. Indeed, the similarities between their lives as women and as women in exile supersede every other experience they have encountered as members of different countries, classes, cultures, professions, and religions. A majority of them are forced into exile because of their individual political stance. Some like Samnang Wu of Cambodia, Ngoc-Ho of Vietnam, Hala Deeb Jabbour of Palestine and Sima Wali of Afghanistan are swept by a wave of cruelty and violence that makes it impossible for them to survive in their homelands. For some, the journeys are perilous ordeals that reinforce their belief in their own capacity to endure and to survive.

The life stories detail moments of such pain, hopelessness, and despair that the women's progress to a state of security, strength, and power becomes a heroic show of character. Some endured physical suffering, some more subtle forms of injury, but they were all thrashed about by forces over which they had little control—brute forces bringing devastation that often exceeded the boundaries of rational comprehension. Initially, the women point to others whom they consider stronger than themselves and credit chance, luck, solidarity with others as keys to their success. But as they compose their lives, they come to reaffirm the power and energy at the center of their own being that made their victory over the circumstances of their lives possible.

Samnang—who found herself one morning leaning against a tree, pregnant, exhausted, hungry, leeches feeding on her blood, staring helplessly at a Khmer Rouge soldier standing above her, ordering her to join his other wards on their meaningless march to nowhere—is today helping other Cambodian women to learn about life in the United States and about preventive health practices.

Azar once sat perched on a horse on a mountainous trail on the Iran-Turkish border, completely at the mercy of smugglers, protected by no government, sought by two. She is now an exuberant and energetic manager of a national project, mother of two healthy children, owner of a pleasant home.

Sima, once a vulnerable and fragile victim, held and interrogated by soldiers who had targeted her as the enemy, feeling alone, alien and uncomprehending in her own city, is now a well-known leader of an important organization dealing with Third World refugee women.

Ngoc-Ho was amazed by her own automatic response to authority after years of living with terror when she threw herself at the feet of a Filipino soldier following her six-day boat journey during which she lost her child. She is once again a practicing physician and a pillar of her family and community.

Maria Teresa, who was once beaten, raped, tortured, and imprisoned, now travels around the world, giving testimony on behalf of her organization Comadres and for the cause of human rights.

Florence, who once sat on the damp floor of a prison cell in Malawi, fearing she might lose her husband who lay sick beside her and anxious about her children's uncertain future, is now a successful nurse and a human rights activist.

Alicia, once one of the "disappeared," has now received her Master's degree, published a number of books, married, bought a house and continues her work in support of Amnesty International.

Marjorie, who felt she was "a woman without a country," marginal, irrelevant, powerless, has now gained recognition as a poet and as an advocate of Latin American women's rights. She teaches at Wellesley College where she is held in great regard by her students and colleagues.

Fatima, who spent many years under house arrest and in constant fear for her family's life, is now president of an international women's organization and a prominent spokesperson for African women.

Hala, who was once imprisoned within the strict codes of her family and culture and who felt threatened by the hostility in her adopted country, is now active on behalf of the Palestinian cause and seeks to bring understanding between Palestine and Israel by working with the women from each side. She writes and speaks on topics related to Third World feminism.

Tatyana, who anxiously paced her room in a third-rate hotel in Vienna after she had been forced by the KGB to leave the Soviet Union, fearful of her country's government and anxious about her own and her child's future in a strange environment, is now a writer, lecturer, and television producer.

The physical facts of the women's lives are less significant than the focused self-understanding, self-affirmation, and self-esteem that they exude as they give structure to the events of their lives and the choices that shaped their personality and their destiny. It is as if each woman has experienced a symbolic death and rebirth and managed to become a better person for it.

Their arrival in the United States presents them with a new set of problems, an arduous process of learning, adjusting, and evaluating, which they accomplish with great success. Through this process they discover that their ways of coming to terms with life differ significantly from those of the men in their lives. For a brief period, a twilight zone between the loss of the old cultural patterns and assimilation of the new, they break free from the bounds of patriarchal structures. Suddenly an abundance of choices seems available and a variety of life models appears attainable. They compose their identity and arrive at a sense of self and a level of consciousness that is liberating and empowering. Hala describes the feeling well when she says, "I began articulating my feminism. I felt free in this area as I had never felt before. I could be what I wanted to be, say what I wanted to say, without fear, without endangering my children, my reputation, or the honor of my family and without all the guilt that presses down upon a woman and a mother in my own culture. My feminism flowered—that's exactly how I feel—like a large, healthy plant which is given water and air and sun until it blooms. I began to feel unencumbered."

## A Prologue

Paradoxically, exile with all its pain and struggle brings an expanded universe that would not have been attainable within the old structures. Each woman is pleased with the new self she has created and the wider universe within which she has placed herself. The unspoken truth seems to be that the temporary break with patriarchal systems, gained at the cost of tearing the ties to one's familiar world, is the positive side of life in exile.

The majority of the women have either no male partner in their lives or have a revised and restructured relationship very different from that which they would have in their own countries. This requires fundamental adjustment. Those who are connected to men from their own cultures must help them as well. The men seem to have a harder time dealing with the change. Women come from one condition of marginality and powerlessness into another that offers them alternatives of empowerment. Hala says, "I was able to lead the family . . . because I am a strong woman. I had to fight my husband every step of the way."

Men apparently must deal with a more acute sense of loss of the fatherland. Women feel that to confront the men with their own new sense of liberation is too much of a burden for them to bear. They allow the men to save face, to sustain some of their traditional ways of expressing themselves. Sima articulates this when she describes her decision to keep a low profile in the politics of her community. She treads her battlegrounds carefully. As a strong leader and one of the most well known and respected Afghans in the United States, she nevertheless chooses to stay away from certain discussions, to steer a careful route and to avoid confrontation with her male compatriots. They respect her for that and are grateful, thus allowing her influence to grow unimpeded.

The women are aware that they have lost part of themselves through the loss of their homeland. They find substitutes for this loss. Maria says her work is her country. Marjorie considers her language her homeland. Ge Yang says her own country is lodged permanently within her mind while she borrows temporarily a country in which to do her writing. They echo each other when they say the world is their home and repeat wistfully that it means they have no home. Marjorie, Alicia, Sima, among others, talk of having gained identification with a more universal cause.

They appreciate the United States as a safe haven, a place which welcomes them and allows them to find themselves. They appreciate the relative freedom of women in this society. They are, however, conscious that the country is hospitable for the young and the strong. They fear the loneliness and fragility of the old and the weak in this country. They regret that they have lost the closer ties and more committed interpersonal relationships with the extended family they enjoyed at home. Yet they know that for women part of the price of having those close ties is loss of independence and freedom of action.

In the years since exile began for some of the women, conditions in their countries have changed, allowing them to return to their homeland. They discovered the irreversible nature of the exile experience even when it became possible to return. They realized not only that their country has changed but that they themselves are no longer who they were before they left. They learned that once one looks at one's home from the outside, as a stranger, the past, whether in the self or in the land, cannot be recaptured.

All of us have learned first hand that nothing is worth the suffering, death, and destruction brought about by ideologies that in their fervor uproot so much and destroy so many and then fade away, blow up, or self-destruct. Ge Yang foresees inevitable changes in her country. She notes that the leaders of China have declared that the cultural revolution was a mistake. She expresses our chagrin when she asks of everyone and no one, "Twenty two years of my life is wasted and they call it a mistake?"

We learned in looking back over our lives that nothing is worth the breach of the sanctity of an individual's body and spirit. The sharing of our narratives of exile made us conclude simply that we wish to seek a mildness of manner, a kindness of heart, and a softness of demeanor. When has a war, a revolution, an act of aggression brought something better for the people on whose behalf it was undertaken? we asked ourselves and each other. We have paid with the days of our lives for the knowledge that nothing good or beautiful can come from harshness and ugliness.

## HO NGOC TRAN

# Jade in a Bottle of Wine

*I met Ngoc-Ho at a friend's house in Virginia. Introductions imme-*
*diately revealed that we shared the experience of exile. This made it*
*possible for us to bridge the preliminary niceties and move at once*
*into the deeper intimacy that otherwise takes years of shared mo-*
*ments to achieve. She listened carefully as I described my work with*
*women in exile. She told me she and other exiled women she knows*
*have long had a yearning to articulate their experiences, and therefore*
*she considered this project as her own. She volunteered to come back*
*from her home in Chicago to tell me her story.*

*On a bright Saturday in June, I opened the door to see her kind,*
*smiling face and the small basket of flowers she held out to me. As she*
*told me her story I saw once again how close we all were to each other*
*and yet how far. When she first spoke of the Tet, the Vietnamese*
*festival of the new year, my mind registered the misbegotten military*
*offensive that preoccupied us in our university days. But when she*
*spoke of learning "to wrap and unwrap things," I understood imme-*
*diately that she was describing the delicate handling of the complex*
*web of interrelationships that stand at the core of civilization yet*
*serve to bind women to age-old, suffocating social structures.*

*We both cried helplessly when she evoked the scenes of her boat*
*journey and the death of her child. We beamed as she recounted how*
*she transcended her loss and built a life of purpose and meaning.*

*Ngoc-Ho has managed to learn about her new world and about*

*herself within that world. She has structured a new composite person-*
*ality for herself. She has devised a new set of rules for "wrapping and*
*unwrapping things."*

THERE IS A well known Chinese poem about the wonderful friendship between two people. On a moonlit night before they separate, they talk of the pain of separation, but take their consolation
from the beauty of their relationship, which they compare in its
purity and rarity to "a piece of jade in a bottle of wine." My name,
Ngoc-Ho, comes from that poem. The name has had an influence on
my personality. I have centered my existence on close friendship—
the kind that recognizes no boundaries.

I was born in 1947, when the communists and the nationalists
were fighting the French for independence. My birth coincided with
my parents' escape from an area controlled by the communists to the
territory under the influence of the nationalists. My mother gave
birth to me in a warehouse. There was no one to help her but my
father. My earliest memories are of unrest and chaos. When I was
seven, North and South Vietnam split, leading to a great exodus from
the North to the South. My father had to follow his business, which
took him to Laos for a number of years. My mother took me and my
sister and brother to the town of Dalat in the mountains by a lake, a
quiet, idyllic place, surrounded by wooded areas, where we played
with swords made of tree branches and shields made of bark. We
made houses out of leaves and gave tea parties with make-believe
teacups and teapots. We lived in one rented room and had a wonderful life.

I went to a French school. We were considered refugees from the
north, so we had to attend a special session at school in the afternoons. I was made to realize at an early age that even in my own
country I was different, second class, not quite accepted.

Finally, my father wrapped up his business affairs and joined us
and we moved to Saigon. There, I attended a private French high
school, where the main language was French and we studied a few
hours of Vietnamese language and history and culture each week.
The teachers were French. They gave every child a French name. My
name was Maryse. I hated the name, but French arrogance required

that we assume a French identity. I was so immersed in the French culture that I couldn't judge the French in any but the way they judged themselves.

I became conscious of my imprisonment within the French value system years later when I met my husband. In our intimacy we shared our views, values and visions of life. I learned, for instance, that our ideal model of a happy family life was very different from each other's. His image of a happy life was of a Vietnamese hut, close to a pond surrounded by bamboo shoots. Mine was of a snowy winter evening and an older woman sitting by a fireplace in a rocking chair, knitting. Even though I had never seen snow in my life, my image of peace and contentment and security required French scenery. My dream was to serve the people in Africa, not realizing that my own people needed more help than the Africans. My dream of serving humanity was also a French dream. I couldn't resent the French because I thought as the French thought. I only began judging them after my exile when I visited France as an adult.

My parents didn't have a happy marriage. My father didn't love my mother and they stayed together for our sake. My father always had a mistress. But although he was not good to my mother, he was good to us. He saw to our upbringing and schooling and was always with us at dinner time. This situation confused me. I couldn't sort out the ethical dictates of the society and the conflicting signals I received from the behavior of my father. He brought his mistress home. We all knew their relationship and realized mother's suffering. I was confused by the experience of a good father who did bad things.

Women in Vietnam were at the mercy of the men. There was no divorce. There was no way for women to survive without the support and protection of the men. Society was rigidly structured and hierarchical with clear-cut rules and regulations defining the limits of behavior, depending on one's age, sex, and class. For the woman there were the Three Rules: *Tai gia tong phu*—when a daughter, obey thy father; *xuat gia tong phu*—when married, obey thy husband; *phu tu tong tu*—when widowed, obey thy son.

They were four maxims of general behavior for women: *Cong*—engage in diligent work; *dung*—maintain a neat appearance; *ngon*—use appropriate language and voice; *hanh*—sustain proper moral behavior.

As a Vietnamese child, you learned how to act. At the table, you learned how to set the meal and how to eat it. But before you learned how to eat, you had to find out who you were. All your actions derived their rightness from your knowledge of your place within the hierarchy. As a child you ate with your parents. It was a privilege to sit with them. You waited to receive permission to eat and you ate what you were given. You had to learn how to speak, using the proper tone of voice and style of language. You had to learn how to wrap and how to unwrap things.

As a woman you learned to walk with deliberation—never too fast. It was important to avoid seeming impulsive and hurried. You learned to sit properly, your legs tucked under you and the tunic brought forward and draped and folded over your knees.

Our's was a traditional Vietnamese house—a large room with two pillars separating it into two sections. At the center was the altar of the ancestors. There was a large sofa like a large, raised platform, used also as the bed of the master of the house. When guests came, they sat on the borders of the sofa, the men cross-legged and the women demurely with their legs to one side, tucked under them. They shared tea. If they stayed for meals, men ate together and women ate separately in the kitchen. Children, when allowed to eat with the parents, were forbidden to talk at meals. Parents and children did not communicate openly.

Our greatest holiday was the Tet, the Chinese New Year. Tet is a time of renewal. The house was cleaned spotless. A special meal was prepared and we prayed to our ancestors to share the food with us and celebrate the Tet ceremony. For three days food was laid out for the spirits of our ancestors. Those who were poor and could do little to celebrate brought flowers into their homes.

During my childhood I was reasonably comfortable, although I was confronted with a double prejudice because of my father's Chinese ancestry. When I went to my mother's family, I was looked down upon because I was considered a member of the hated Chinese minority; when I went to my father's family, I was considered one of the distrusted Vietnamese.

All our childhood activities were centered around school and home. Our friendships were within the school. We went to school every day except Sunday. Once we returned home, we stayed home.

We didn't even ask whether we could go out. We didn't put our parents in an awkward situation. We knew our limits as obedient children. Our principal activity at home was reading and doing schoolwork.

After high school I went to medical school. The first years were quite ordinary, except that I felt I needed more diversity in my studies than the school courses provided. I spent some of my time reading Russian novelists and French poets. Gradually the war was intensified. Children were brought in with injuries from shrapnell. Cousins went to the front and bodies were returned in bags. Each night I was awakened a number of times with the sounds of the American convoys passing through the city. The news and movies were full of the war. But since all my life I had never known anything different, I took all of this to be part of normal life.

During the later part of my medical training I was witness to a scene that seriously affected my approach to my chosen career. In Vietnamese medical schools the more advanced students are usually placed on call at a hospital. Part of the time they are entirely on their own and often hold full responsibility for a whole ward. One day I was on call when a friend at another unit was called to the bedside of a child. She asked me to go with her. The mother waited expectantly. She looked at my friend with great hope and faith. Her whole body seemed to incline toward her with respect and trust. My friend examined the child with confidence. She prescribed medication. The nurse administered a shot. The child died.

I was struck by the thought that we do not deserve the kind of faith placed in us. The event did not change my friend's vision and view of her profession, but it changed my way of looking at my work. I finished medical school, but I did not want to practice. For two years I stayed home with my children. Finally I went to work at a pediatric hospital.

My husband was a surgeon. He was sent by the government to the United States and Europe in order to specialize in pediatric surgery. He returned to Vietnam to continue to work for the government. Because of the war situation, everyone who worked for the government had a military rank. My husband had the rank of captain.

When the communists took over Saigon, they immediately announced a reeducation program for all military ranks. There was to be a three-day reeducation camp for soldiers, a two-week period for personnel up to the rank of captain, and three months for those with ranks higher than captain. We were all trying to adjust to the new rules and conditions. We only wished to continue to work for our people and to return to a normal life. My husband prepared himself for his reeducation program, thinking he would have it over with and return to his work in a short time. We packed food and clothing for ten days.

Schools were designated as rallying points for the reeducation camps. I was staying with my mother at that time. I took my husband to the designated school, which was across the street from my mother's house. In the middle of the night I heard army trucks leaving the school. The next day my mother and I rushed there to see what had happened, but the place was deserted. It was just a vacant school building with no one to give information.

I had two daughters and was pregnant with my son. My preoccupation with the children and my instinctive urge to protect myself during pregnancy helped me to keep calm and control my anxiety. Ten days passed. There was no news of my husband. Months passed and no news. I was lucky to be an employed professional. Many women who had no job or specific expertise were left without any means of supporting themselves or information about what had happened to their husbands or when the men would be allowed to return home.

After six months letters arrived from the men, urging us to behave and comply so that they could return home safely and soon. We wrote to them urging the same. The new government pressured husbands and wives to demand from each other obedience to the government by holding up the hope that this would expedite their reunion. Rumors were spread that if the families behaved properly, the men would be allowed to return.

With the men gone, women had to take on extra burdens. I had to do the work of many people. The hospital where I worked was administered by an illiterate man who was the sole decision-maker on all matters, including dispensation of medication. If I needed plasma for a child, he would refuse to allow more than a bag, saying he thought one was enough. He would determine how much medicine a child was to receive. I saw fifty babies a day, ten of whom died within twenty-four hours of their arrival at the hospital. I remember a mother with a three-day-old baby who had so little flesh on his body I could not administer a shot to him. I asked her about the baby's diet and the mother told me she had fed the child only rice water and salt. I began to ask why she had not given him some sugar and stopped myself when I saw her face and body, all skin and bone. Then the image of my uncle came to my mind, my mother's cousin, a corpulent and well fed cabinet officer in the communist government, moving about in the company of his own doctor. He visited my mother from time to time. He came in a fancy car, bearing gifts of butter and chocolate. He brought with him his own personal physician who accompanied him everywhere. Once when he was hospitalized he declared he hated air conditioning, so he had a nurse fan him all night. Communist leaders had used the anticolonialist, anti-imperialist sentiments of the people to gain their support and to gain power. They had talked of the benefits people would enjoy once they freed themselves of foreign domination. As it turned out, they were only interested in material benefits and power for themselves and cared nothing for the people.

My husband was the only pediatric surgeon for the whole country, north and south. He had been trained in highly specialized surgical procedures, such as creating an artificial anus for children who are born without one. Sometimes these operations were performed in stages. He was taken away when some of his patients were at the end of the first phase. They kept him at the camp for nearly three years, no one caring what happened to him or to his patients.

During the years my husband was detained, we lived in constant fear. I was allowed to visit my husband twice during three years. The first time was eight months after he left home and the next in the second year of his detention. Each visit was limited to half an hour and a guard stood by and did not allow us to talk in private. Conditions in the camp were terrible. There were no sanitary provisions. There was no meat or fruit. Each day the detainees were given a bowl of rice, often with insects crawling in it. Disease was rampant. Some went blind from infection.

My third child was born a few months after my husband was taken away. It sounds so facile when I say the numbers and the words. But it seemed endless then with no sign of hope for the future. During those years our needs and preoccupations became purely physical. There was never enough food. Our thoughts were of food and how to find enough of it and how to get some to our family members in camp. Women who were suddenly left with the responsibility of children, parents, parents-in-law knew that the husbands were starving, and when it came time to visit wanted to take to them all they could. They did not want to let them know how poor they were and how hard the situation was at home. Sometimes they sold pieces of furniture or their clothes to bring food to the camp.

There was a limit to what we were allowed to take when we visited. There are many stories of the visits and the ingenious methods used to transfer food. One woman tried to take extra meat to her husband by tying the package under her stomach. When he saw her coming, bundled up as she was, he thought she was pregnant. He would not come near her and the woman underwent agonies of fear and anger and pity before she finally succeeded in letting him know without drawing the attention of the guards to herself that what she bore was only a package of food for him.

After my husband returned from the camp, he worked at the hospital for ten months. The rulers had discovered how much his services were needed and had become aware of his international standing. But we both came to the conclusion that it was impossible to be of use to our people under the circumstances created by the communists. There was no sense, no reason, no human consideration in the conduct of the affairs of the country. Every day we confronted the government's lack of reason and care in providing the minimum facilities for the performance of our duties. Medication and other tools of our profession had become politicized and their distribution and availability a function of the whim of some uncaring, irrational, and unintelligent party bureaucrat.

What's worse, the government "idiotized" the population. To sustain its power, the ruling party used methods of behavior-control that reduced people to the status of animals, automatons without the capacity to think or make decisions, walking about as if in a daze.

They split families by arranging endless meetings that members of the family were obliged to attend separately, each with his or her own sex and age group. They trained each group to discuss their problems within the group. The children were given rewards and encouraged to inform on their parents. They were asked to describe the family's lifestyle and the information was used to control the adults. Women were encouraged to complain against their husbands. Food was used as a means of control. Gradually, through importing and making available only a certain type of clothing, they forced the whole population to wear the same dark-colored uniform.

In a short time, everyone began to look the same. You ate what they wanted. You wore what they wanted. You said what they wanted. Gradually you came to think as they wished. Originally, people resisted celebrating Ho Chi Minh's birthday. But, eventually, through offering cheap colas on that day, everyone began to participate in the celebration. I found myself drinking the damned cola at the prescribed hour along with everyone else in the country. I realized the evil in this. Every day I felt more strongly the need to break free.

My husband was a patriot. He loved Vietnam and felt connected to the country. He had been abroad and knew what awaited us there. He knew what it meant to lose one's culture and one's values. But we realized that regardless of how we tried, it would be impossible to be useful to anyone under the communist government. More importantly, we realized that our children could not grow in that society, and we could not accept bringing up our children in an atmosphere with no possibility of growth. So even though we knew the dangers of an escape journey and the hardship that awaited us at the end of it, we decided to leave.

The life and future of our children were an important factor in our decision. My daughters were five and four and my son was thirty-two months old when we made the decision to leave. It was difficult to find a reliable channel because we couldn't trust anyone to give us information. We were not allowed to gather in any group larger than three. We were constantly afraid of being arrested on some pretext or other. When people were arrested, no one knew where they were taken and for how long. Every move was controlled. If you wanted to stay overnight at your mother's, you had to ask for permission and explain to the authorities the reasons for your request.

In Saigon there were fishermen living along the seashore. The fishermen had boats and fuel enough for their work. There was a group of smugglers who made a business out of transporting people in the fishing boats. They acted as intermediaries. We met a smuggler, a woman, through one of my husband's friends, another doctor, who had been with him at the camp. A woman had asked him for anti-nausea medication. He had guessed it was for a sea journey. He had asked to be taken along and the woman had agreed, thinking it useful to have a doctor on board. We contacted the same woman to make arrangements for our journey.

Rumors were going around that those who had been released from the camps would soon be taken again. It was typhoon season. We decided to take the risk. The boat on which we traveled was a two-engine vessel, three meters wide and twelve meters long. Originally, there were supposed to be forty five passengers. The woman had told us there would be food and water and fuel. We had the option of going to Hong Kong, Thailand, or the Philippines. The journey to Hong Kong was not the best choice at the time because the point of departure was located deep in the south. Passage to Thailand would be easier and shorter, but there was fear of pirates, who often stopped the boats on that route. The crossing to the Philippines was longer and exposed us to rough seas and the possibility of typhoons but avoided the risk of attacks by pirates. We decided to take the Philippines route.

She told us that whatever belongings we wished to take we must turn over to her. She would place them on the boat for us and we would avoid calling attention to ourselves as we left for the shore. The woman had a partner, but apparently they didn't trust each other. She had the compass. He was to bring the food and the extra fuel. The fishermen wouldn't have had enough fuel for the journey.

We left on a Sunday. In order to avoid suspicion, we each completed our rounds at the hospital before leaving. We started out at 7:00 P.M. It was getting dark. The woman who was our contact was very greedy. The man with the supplies hadn't arrived. She must have thought that the journey would not be so difficult with the small amount of provisions already on board and rushed the fishermen to leave before the food arrived. There were seventy-five on a boat with a maximum capacity of forty-five. My sister-in-law was with us. She and my husband each held one of the children and I held the baby.

In the afternoon of the first day the sea became very rough. The waves were several meters high. Time seemed endless. Soon we realized there were no supplies. We had left Saigon with nothing. My mother had kept telling me to take a bag of oranges with me because the baby loved them. But I had said no, there will be enough of everything on the boat. I have blamed myself endlessly for refusing to take the oranges. I had no way of measuring how much time had passed. I tried to keep track of nights and days, but thoughts were jumbled in my mind and all experience seemed one frozen moment of saltwater, dry throat, and rocking motion.

After some time I no longer felt the pain in my stomach and the dryness in my throat. I was numb. The baby clung to me. He kept whispering to me, "Mommy, I haven't done anything wrong, I have behaved." I prayed for rain. I looked at the sky and recited chants and prayed until I felt the soft wetness of the drops on my skin. Then I came to myself and realized that I had imagined the rain.

Six days passed with nothing but sickness, death, and thirst. And I pressed the baby to me, trying to hold on to his flickering life. He mumbled, "Mommy, I didn't do anything," and I chanted and keened and prayed and stared at the sky until my neck was frozen on my shoulder and I couldn't bring my head back to the normal position.

He was the baby born to me when my husband was at the camp. He was a good child. He was never a problem. He always behaved. On his first birthday I had not been able to find even a cookie to celebrate. In the boat he kept apologizing to me. The waves were so high we were always soaked through. I was chilled the entire time. In the morning of the sixth day a light rain began to fall. I saved a few drops in the palm of my hand and tried to pour it in the baby's mouth. But he was dead. I held his body in my arms and stared at the other two children. He had been so trustful. We had gone through all this because of the children.

They wanted to give him a burial at sea. I told my husband if they threw him in the water, I would go with him. In the afternoon of the sixth day we came to an island. We buried the child on the island. We had sold everything we had for the trip. I had sewn a diamond ring, the only valuable thing left to me, into the baby's sleeve. That was to be our capital in the new world. When we buried him on the island, I could not take the ring; I left it with him as a remembrance. I haven't been able to find where he was buried. It was on the seashore on some island. So it is just a story that ends here.

In the Philippines, a couple of soldiers came to direct us. When they approached, I fell to my knees and began crawling in front of them. They were just a couple of soldiers, but I was so conditioned by the government in my country that any symbol of power reduced me to an animal whose only urge was to survive.

I have since come to consider this—the reduction of the human essence to the basest animal instinct—the worst crime of the communist government. It is not right. It happened to me. I acted like a dog afraid of a master. I resent that day on the beach in the Philippines when I lost my sense of my human self. I don't believe in any isms. I don't follow capitalism, communism, any other ism. I only believe in the right of the people to be happy and free. I believe that no government has a right to do to the people what the government of Vietnam did to me.

The Filipino people were good to us, but the circumstances were difficult. I had to walk for forty-five minutes every morning from the seashore through the forest to the city to fetch the fish and vegetables for our meals in the camp. We slept on the sand. We walked for forty-five minutes to take a shower under an outdoor tap. I kept my clothes on because the people waited and watched. During the communist rule, I had lost my house, my clothes, my books—everything I had. I borrowed a pair of pants and tunic from my mother to wear to work. After the six days on the high seas and the six weeks in the camp, I felt I had lost my personality.

Finally, we were taken to Manila, where we stayed at another camp with two thousand refugees. There I witnessed how otherwise nice people—doctors, teachers, pharmacists—come to care for nothing, except a bit of something to eat. They fought over a piece of meat or a can of peaches. They planned their days around the acquisition of something to eat with no thought of tomorrow.

At the camp we met a man we used to know in Vietnam. He had also left on a boat. After days on the sea they had seen a ship coming toward them. The crowd on the boat, excited and happy about the prospect of being taken aboard, had stood on the side facing the ship. The boat had capsized and many had died, including the man's two children. When we saw each other again, he told us his story, but he seemed impassive and without emotion. Once we exchanged experiences, he made it a point of coming to my tent each day at twelve, I don't know why, perhaps that was the time of the incident, and he asked me questions and talked to me about my child and persisted until I couldn't control myself and burst into tears. He would say, "It's good to see you cry. I can't cry. Your tears are for my children too."

It took me five years to get over the death of my baby. Since then I have hated the rain. I waited and prayed for the rain and it did not come, not until my son was dead. For the first five years when it rained I became agitated. I did not want my daughters to see me upset. I took the car and drove somewhere to cry. I still feel him in my arms, and hear him apologize for the way things were.

Finally we came to California. We stayed with a cousin. The first day of my stay I noticed my cousin spreading a powder over the grass in front of his house. I asked him what it was, and he explained that in their neighborhood it was important to have a nice lawn. He was feeding his lawn with vitamins. I laughed until tears came to my eyes. This was the first of a series of ironies I have confronted in exile.

At first my husband, like the others, was in a state of shock. He was offered a job in a children's hospital in Chicago, where he had been in pediatric surgery before, but he wasn't quite ready. He worked as a social worker for the refugee community, earning a few hundred dollars a month. I tried to take the medical exams but could not concentrate. It took me a few years of doing nothing, taking care of my girls and supposedly studying, before I began to recover.

In 1980 my husband took the Chicago offer. I passed the required examinations and went back to the pediatric residency. It was an integrated program. I worked at three hospitals. One was a cool, distant setting, where concentration was on research. Another served the black population. The third was an ordinary white middle-class community hospital. I liked best working with the black community with whom I felt an affinity. I disliked the white middle-class setting. During this internship, one day I walked inside a room where I was supposed to examine a child. As I entered I noticed by the way the parents looked at me that they expected a different kind of person as their physician. They were very polite. But I realized that I was not wanted. Parents in this community would never trust me to provide the best care for their children. As a pediatrician I know that I must have the trust of the parents as well as the children to do my best.

I decided to go to my own community. Soon I realized that there too people had changed. In Vietnam, despite all the atrocities, I had felt fulfilled in relation to my patients. I had felt I was rendering a service that they needed and appreciated. Here in America the Vietnamese had the notion that the others, the Westerners, were better than we. They didn't seem to appreciate our services. I realized that I would be more effective in another capacity. The community needed help, especially in public health. So I changed my career and switched to public health.

I now realize that people cannot change as quickly as their setting. They transform themselves outwardly, but their essence does not change. The women who come here from Vietnam cannot adapt to the conditions here. In this country people have taken decades to change their mental habits. The Vietnamese women haven't had the time to evolve in line with the new ideas. If an American woman feels incompatible with a man, she gets a divorce and soon will seek the company of other men. The Vietnamese women have begun to think that the relationship between men and women is unfair, but when their dissatisfactions and complaints lead to divorce, as they sometimes do, they cannot go out freely and seek a new companion. We are faced with many conflicting cultural signals, and it is difficult to sort out, choose, and develop new values and behavior patterns.

I am concerned with cultural and health problems of the refugee population. Together with some friends we set up a nonprofit organization called Direct Aid to Refugees. We organize cultural activities. We celebrate the Tet festival and the children's festival. We try to help with adjustment of the refugees and alleviate some of the problems caused by intercultural conflict.

My family life has been influenced by attempts to adjust to life in this country. Being accepted into the American society has not been easy. When we first came to the United States, I tried to do for my children what was customary here. When their birthdays arrived, I sent out cards and invited their schoolmates to their birthday parties. No one came. It is hard to teach children to deal with this. I tell them they must not base their self-worth on the reaction of others. They must retain their identity independently of the signals they receive from the society. We can pick up American habits, eat fruit for lunch, drink coffee; we can even call ourselves American, but we are still products of our own cultures. We have to learn to respect ourselves even when we receive negative reactions from the American community. We have to know who we are and not change our basic nature because of the requirements of the new environment.

Now, after years of trying to adjust to life in exile, I have begun to feel comfortable with who I am. I enjoy both the Vietnamese community and the American community. Once you have your values clearly thought out, those who come to you come accepting what you are. After a few years, people in our neighborhood learned that we are doctors and professionals. So the children began to come to the birthday parties. I tell my children that it doesn't make a difference one way or the other. Those who appreciate you for what you are inside matter in your life, not those who will come to you because you have this or that profession or own one thing or another. I try to teach my children that if they link their identity to the response of others, there will always be some person or some group that may not like, appreciate, or want them. I told them they must understand me too. They must know that some of the things other children are allowed cannot be allowed them because their parents have been raised differently. We have to work things out together. Sometimes I change and sometimes they will have to. When I first went to their school and saw students and teachers in shorts, I was shocked. But now my own girls wear shorts to school. So it's not that we are inflexible. But there is a limit. They must know that they are not American. They were born Vietnamese and will always be part Vietnamese. They will learn the American ways, but will always find their roots in their own culture.

With my husband I have a relationship based on respect. If we had lived in Vietnam, he would have had a less tolerant role and he would have taken a more dominant position in our decision-making. He now sees me more as a person than just a wife. He sees me as someone with an independent set of values. I used to be obedient. I was young when I married. He was soon taken to the camp and was away for three years. Then we had a few short months together in Vietnam before we left. There was little time to judge and compare.

But here I have become more aggressive, he says. I can't know what I would be like had we stayed in Vietnam. Perhaps there too I would not have been obedient and submissive. But I think that I have changed for the better. Vietnamese women do change here. Some just imitate without internalizing the moral foundations of American women's behavior. That is not healthy. The men resent it and it doesn't help the women either.

The men came here at an age when it is very hard to adapt. They came at the peak of their career. My husband was forty-two. It was difficult to start all over again when he had already reached the height of his profession and was a valued and well-known pediatric surgeon in his own country. His manner of coping is to follow his medical profession but to devote every extra moment of time and ounce of energy to the cause of the future of Vietnam. I share his hopes and his aspirations. We talk all the time about home, about the past, and what life was like in our childhood. It is good for the children. They listen to us and ask questions and learn about our culture. My husband, being eleven years older, experienced the war more acutely than I did. His background was less mixed; therefore he is more attached to Vietnam. He knows a great deal about the customs and traditions. Our children consider themselves Vietnamese Americans. We celebrate all holidays, Vietnamese and American. We have the Tet as well as Christmas. Our life is richer for this.

I think about Vietnam. I used to dream I was there and woke up in terror and was relieved to find that I am in America. We eat Vietnamese food. We speak Vietnamese at home. My children read the Vietnamese paper. At meetings of the community we speak Vietnamese. But I still miss the language. It is so comfortable to be able to communicate easily. I sometimes imagine I hear the street vendors who used to sing out their wares. I have images of the green landscape, the pine trees, and the lake where I played as a child.

My close family are all here in America, so it is easier to distance myself somewhat from Vietnam. My mother lives with me. The children have learned that they must be very polite to her. They know that they must be obedient and respectful. The girls are American in their dress and behavior, but they are on the conservative side. I wanted the first years to be easy on them. I wanted them to absorb some aspects of the American culture. But now that we are all quite settled and have worked out who we are, I can be more strict about their behavior. Ours is a strange dialogue. I tell them, "You are good, you now know the difference between right and wrong, but now that I see you do, I have to tell you once again what is right and what is wrong."

I have grown so much through all that has happened to me. I look at my mother and I see that if I had stayed in Vietnam, I would have been just like her with my cares and thoughts and actions all pre-scribed for me. Her relationship with me is not what I want with my children. She never spoke to me. She never tried to understand me. Communication was not on the agenda for parents and children. But here women think about and analyze their own identity. The positive thing about being in America is that I can realize my poten-tial as a woman. Doors are open to women here that are closed in my country.

I miss the people. I miss the way of thinking and behaving that is familiar and comfortable. I still feel I don't belong here. I know I will never belong here. It is not one-sided. I think this society will never accept me. This is a very fair country. They believe in upholding the civil rights of the people. On paper, Americans new and old have the same rights. But the new Americans are not truly accepted as Ameri-cans. People are kind and feeling, but they withhold their complete acceptance. So even though I wake up frightened that I am back in Vietnam and am joyous that I am here, even though the Americans have been nice all in all, I know I will never feel completely at home here—or anywhere anymore. I don't even think about the future. I live day to day. It is important to feel at peace with yourself, to come to the end of your days feeling you have completed your life con-structively. I feel comfortable with myself. Perhaps more, now that I have had a chance to rethink my identity and arrive at a composite self, made of my own Vietnamese self and my American cultural acquisitions.

# Birds without Nests

*Maria Teresa is a sturdy woman. Her caramel skin is taut, her body compact and muscular. She looks strong. A lifter of heavy things, a long-distance walker. She would not run—she is too pragmatic and sensible to waste energy. She would walk, not for exercise, but to get somewhere she needs to go. She does not relish obstacles, nor is she afraid of them. She confronts them as they come along. Maria Teresa deals with actualities. She does not have the time for introspection, for self-analysis, for feeling her own pulse. Her presence brings me back to the practical, to the real. Exile to her means waiting to go home, and home means a nest. She wants little for herself—work, to close her eyes at night knowing she will not be awakened by men with guns, walking in the streets without being stopped and snatched away. She wants much for her children and for her people. She wants a land peopled by men and women of education, with minds enriched by knowledge of other cultures and languages. She wants for her children what she cannot have herself: good jobs, a comfortable home, and joy in life. She is willing to work for what she wants, and she has tested the boundary between the possible and the unendurable. Because her view of life involves an acceptance of what she cannot change, she does not wallow in the past. Her past is a weapon she will use to alter the future. I heard a prayer once which said, "Oh Lord, give me the patience to accept what I cannot change, the courage to change what I can, and the wisdom to know the differ-*

*ence." Maria Teresa is a wise woman. She begins telling me her story in strong, calm tones that betray little emotion.*

I WAS BORN IN Izalco, in the SonSonate province, eighty-nine kilometers from San Salvador. I come from a humble family. My mother never went to school. She was very young when she married my father. My grandmother, with whom I lived as a child, had never gone to school either. They had to work to live. My great-grandmother made chocolates to sell and my grandmother was a baker. She baked bread and also worked as a cook in our town. This was the business she taught my mother for her survival. My father left my mother when she was three-months pregnant with me. My father had grown up in the machismo culture. He had many women and that was a cause of pride to him. His machismo also affected the way he acted at home with his wife. He was rough and unfeeling. When he left us, my brother was three years old. I met him for the first time when I was seven.

I lived with my mother and her mother. My grandmother was very poor. My father's mother lived close by also, but there was such a difference between our ways of life. My grandmother's house was a humble wooden house without running water or electricity. The mother of my father lived in a brick house with light and water. It was very different from our house. I didn't understand why this was so, why there was such a difference between these two women's lives.

When I grew old enough to understand, it made me fear my father's mother and I didn't even want to meet my father. I was afraid of him without ever having met him.

When I was a year old my mother went to find a new life in a nearby town, taking my three-year-old brother with her. Since she couldn't work and take care of two children, she left me with her mother.

I went to school for one year. It was difficult for me to stay in school because my grandmother worked in the house of a middle-class family from six in the morning until ten at night. She earned about six dollars a month. She cooked for ten people, four cats, and four dogs. She did the washing and the ironing. After all this when she came home at night, she made chocolates so she could bring home some extra money. I helped my grandmother in the house where she worked. The six dollars a month was for both of us. My grandmother didn't know much about the ways of the outside world. She didn't have social security and all these years they never gave her a raise. They frightened her with her lack of security.

One time the social security agents came to the house to check on the employees. The owner of the house hid the three women who worked there in the bathroom and told my grandmother to tell the agents that she would only be there for three months and didn't need social security. She did as she was told because she believed that the owner was protecting her.

At breakfast, lunch, and dinner we served the entire family until all the food was gone and nothing was left in the kitchen except the pots. After an hour of serving them at the table, the lady of the house would put a little of the leftovers from the plates for me and my grandmother. If nothing was left my grandmother would get some beans or a piece of bread for the two of us. I didn't understand why it had to be like this.

I asked her why they didn't leave something for us, and she said, "You don't understand anything." She looked very sad when I asked her these questions. So, soon, even though I still didn't understand, I didn't ask her anymore.

She was paid a colon a day, thirty colons a month. She always had to get advances to pay for a bit of bread or some cheese for us, so she always owed the family money before the month started. There was no way she could quit. So we continued this life for a number of years.

My grandmother died when I was thirteen. I felt her loss with all my heart because she had been mother and father and friend to me. After she was gone my father and my aunt both wanted me to live with them. But I went to live with mother—because she was my mother. She made a living by selling tortillas. She had remarried and had children from the second marriage. We all lived in a room in a house with thirteen rooms, each rented to a different family.

I had a hard time adjusting to all this. A new city, this new home with all the strangers who were suddenly my next of kin. I didn't understand it at all and felt very depressed. A year later, for the first time in my life, I met a man. I began to hope that this man would solve all my problems. I thought he might take me away from my mother and her new family. Yet I feared him just as I feared my father and brothers. Now I laugh when I look back and realize my own ignorance. I had my first daughter when I was fifteen years old. The father left me when I was four-months pregnant and I never saw him again. So much for my savior! My daughter is now twenty-five and she has never seen her father.

I was fifteen with no money, no education, and a baby to raise. My grandmother had given me happiness, so I asked her spirit for guidance. I was depressed with life but I didn't allow myself to think of death. I went to the streets and sold the things my mother made— tamales, corn on the cob. While working I met the man who would become my husband and the father of my children. I was seventeen and afraid of men. I was particularly afraid of him because he was well educated and older than I. But soon I grew close to him and he taught me many things about life and about love. He also taught me about freedom.

He was a worker. He never let me know about his political activities. In 1978 he was taken prisoner, and only then did I realize the extent of his involvement in politics. He worked in a sugar factory that belonged to one of the fourteen most influential families in El Salvador. The workers in this factory formed a union and asked for better working conditions and higher wages. My husband told me he would take part in a demonstration by the striking workers in front of the factory. This was my first experience of political activism, and I was worried about the outcome. I took him his lunch at noon. I asked him what was happening, and he told me, "We are not working until we resolve our problems." "Are you sure they are not coming to harm you?" "No," he said, "we are not doing anything. We're only demanding our rights."

So he stayed behind the factory gates. I remember he had the flu. The next day I brought him soup and medicine. On January 30 at 10:00 A.M. the military forces arrived. I was standing there holding the parcel containing his meal when I saw the police, the militia, and, it seemed, the whole army arriving. The men started running, the soldiers started running, and I stood there silently as if I were dreaming. A commander from the national police stopped and asked me, "What are you doing here?" "Nothing," I said, "I am not doing anything." "Then get out of here," he said. "Why? I am just standing here on the street, minding my own business." He began shouting. "I gave you an order, I told you to get out of here. Now are you going to do what I ask?" "Look, I am not a soldier, so you can't shout at me like that. I am going to stand just where I am standing." He came up and pointed his gun at my chest. I had never thought of these things before and wasn't thinking very clearly then. I just knew he had no right to push me around, and I knew that I was not going to let him do it. Then another soldier came up to me and said, "Señora, please leave or he will shoot you and it will be for nothing." We stood and stared at each other for a while, then we each moved in a different direction.

I walked around the factory to see what had happened to my husband. I saw the workers were being pushed against the wall and their hands were being tied behind their backs. I saw my husband being pushed to the ground with the butt of a rifle pressed to his ribs. Then I saw a woman being dragged by her hair. Other women who had gathered were being pushed back with rifles held to their chests. The soldiers were holding grenades. The women were frightened. They were yelling and crying. None of us had ever seen anything like this before. I saw my sister-in-law in the crowd of women, and we started picking up stones and dirt and sugar cane and throwing it at the soldiers who were dragging the woman by the hair. Other women joined us. Soon the soldiers let the woman go.

This was my first experience with collective political work and my first encounter with women's shared experience and group action. I didn't know anything about the politics involved. One of the women took me to the union and there I began to learn about the politics of the situation, about relating to others, and about describing my thoughts and feelings. I learned then that 1,800 members of the union had been captured.

They were all allowed to leave by the end of the second day of interrogation. Twenty-two were detained, among them my husband. In the evening they were taken to San Salvador to the general barracks of the National Guard. For three days no one had any news of them. I later learned that they had been tortured with electric prods and beaten. After three days they were taken to the prison. When I went to look for my husband, I met for the first time women from the organization called Comadres. These were women who were trying to get information about missing members of their family. With them I found real group support and solidarity with women who shared my concerns and understood my life. At this point my life changed from a common life to a political one.

I found myself without a job, without money to hire a lawyer for my husband, without any friends to turn to for help. I began working with Comadres, visiting prisons, attending conferences, taking part in street activities. I realized I was not alone, that many shared my predicament and my concerns. In 1978 I traveled outside my country for the first time. I went to Costa Rica to attend a conference where a number of representatives from Central American countries gathered to discuss human rights in their societies.

When I was in Costa Rica, my husband was freed. My friends at Comadres told me, "Now your husband is free, do you want to go back or do you want to continue with your work?" I said, "Thank God he is free, but I have made a commitment and I am going to keep it." I stayed for eighteen days in Costa Rica, giving interviews, meeting women, building solidarity for our work.

My husband had a hard time adjusting to my new role. He was grateful that I had worked for his release, but he wanted me back in the house. He wanted my life to return to what he considered normal—cooking, washing, ironing, and taking care of the household. We talked about it. We didn't fight. We didn't argue. We had a dialogue. He said, "I don't want you to go out, I want you to stay home." I had a commitment to my work, but I didn't want a fight each time I went to a meeting. I decided to try a new tactic. I said, "All right, you don't want me to go out, I'll stay home." So I stayed home for two or three days. On the fourth day the women from Comadres came to the house. They asked what had happened to me and why I hadn't come to the committee. I said, "My husband seems to want me to stay at home and take care of him." The women looked at him with surprise. He was embarrassed. After all, we all shared common goals and all were dedicated to the same principles. He looked at me and said, "I thought perhaps you didn't want to go."

Later, when the women had left, he said, "All right, you have won." And so I continued my work with Comadres. I think he was afraid for me and worried about what might happen to me. But at the bottom of it there was the machismo, the male attitude that made him think I couldn't handle politics. In the end we reached an agreement that neither of us would order the other around. I had to make a point that either we worked together for our people or—if I had to choose between the work and the limited life I had led before—I would leave him. He understood then that I had changed. We lived together for thirteen years after that, both of us working for the same cause, but we never talked to each other about our work. We each learned from outsiders what the other was doing. In the house we talked about household matters and family problems but not about the work we were both dedicated to. He worked for the labor unions and I worked with human rights groups. Sometimes I would run into him on the streets during demonstrations. I didn't know he would be there. He helped me with housework and with the children, but he couldn't accept completely my independent political life. He never treated me like a comrade, equal to him in our work.

My husband was assassinated on June 20, 1980. They came for him around 7:00 P.M. the night before. It was a Thursday evening. We were in the house with the children about to have dinner. I was seven-months pregnant with my daughter Gisela at that time. It was a stifling evening and I shuffled around putting the dinner things on the table. Suddenly a number of men in civilian clothes appeared at the door. They asked for my husband, saying they wanted him to act as a witness to a robbery that had taken place on the street near our house. I lowered myself into a chair as I listened to my husband telling them he didn't know anything about a robbery. They told him to shut up and go with them. They tied his hands behind his back and pushed him toward the door and took him away. As I tried to go to my husband, they turned to me and shouted, "You—over there. Stay where you are." I remember as he was leaving he looked back over his shoulder and said, "Take care of yourself." I felt somehow that look was the last, that I would never see him again. The next day I went to look for him in various security offices. In each place they told me they didn't know anything about him. When I was running from office to office asking about him, my husband was already dead.

On June 21 I ran into a relative who asked, "Where is your husband?" I didn't want to tell her about him, so I said, "I don't know. I have been working." She said, "You really don't know then?"

and showed me the newspaper. There was a picture of my husband's body. She read the caption aloud: "An unidentified man was killed in confrontation with the police." When I saw my husband's picture, I put my hand to my forehead. I felt everything was spinning around me. My son Raul was with me and he asked, "Mommy what's happening?" I said, "There is a picture of your father. He seems to have been in an accident." I went home and took the other children and went looking for my husband's body.

No one would give me any information. Finally I went to the judge of the county where he was supposed to have died. He said he didn't know anything. I said, "You are the judge how could you not know anything." He refused to answer me. "Listen," he said, "I know you, you are from Izalco and so am I, and I'm giving you a piece of advice. Don't look for him." I said, "How can I not look for him? He is my husband." Finally I shouted, pounding on his desk, "Just as my husband has been killed, judges can be killed too. I may be powerless, but the people will take revenge." The judge was surprised. It wasn't what I was saying, but the rage in my voice that moved him. He hadn't expected me to shout like that. He took me to the cemetery. There I saw my husband's body with his hands tied behind his back, his clothes torn and his feet bound. He had gunshot wounds at his temples.

When we got back to the house, soldiers were standing at the door and all around the house. It was impossible to approach the house without getting caught. So we left for San Salvador with the clothes on our back as our only belongings. That is the last time I lived in my home. My life in exile had begun.

After my husband's death, life was very difficult. I had children to take care of and I was far away from my family. When you are in political life, friends and family want to stay away from you out of fear. I relied entirely on the help of Comadres. They arranged for me to take my children to Mexico. I worked in various Latin American countries with Comadres until President Duarte came to El Salvador with a platform of democracy and respect for human rights. I returned to El Salvador to live and work in my own country. But the situation remained the same, and I continued my work with Comadres. My life centered around my work and the care of the children. The only relationship I drifted into was a brief adventure that ended with me pregnant and alone as before. The only good thing about it was that I have Oscar as a result.

On May 6, 1986, I was captured as I was walking to the Co-madres offices at around eight in the morning. A man came up to me and grabbed me from behind. I turned back to see who it was and immediately felt a gun pressed to my ribs. He whispered, "Don't make a sound," and pushed me toward the open back door of a white car. They blindfolded me and shut the door and took off. Finally the car stopped and I was led up a staircase and into a building. I was taken to a room where I could distinguish a number of male voices. They sat me in a chair, tied my hands behind my back, and tied my ankles together. Then they began questioning me. They asked me where I was going. I thought they didn't know me so I said I was going to visit my aunt in San Salvador on the bus and I had missed my bus stop and ended up where they had found me. They asked me whether I knew those worthless women, the Comadres. I told them I didn't. They asked me a number of questions and I felt sure they had no idea who I was. They asked me whether I was married and how many children I had and where my parents lived. I kept telling them that I was a washerwoman and I was on my way to visit my aunt. Then one of them came up to me and grabbed my throat until I choked. He told me I was lying. He said they knew I knew all the Comadres and the houses where they keep their weapons.

Then one of them spoke to me in a soft voice, saying they wanted to help me. He said, "We will find you a house and help you get a job if only you give us the information we need and repeat on television that you are a terrorist and a member of Comadres." He removed my blindfold to show me an attaché case full of money. He said, "All this can be yours and you will go free if you cooperate." I said, "I am not a terrorist and Comadres are not terrorists. You are terrorists who have brought me here and are doing this to me." They asked again about my parents, my husband, my children. They asked where I lived. I lied for fear they would harass my sister-in-law with whom I was living.

The voices kept changing. One would say, "This is the wrong woman, we should let her go, there is no use keeping her." Another would be rough and threaten me. One would say, "The woman we are looking for is short and wears glasses." Another voice would call me terrible names and hit me hard across the mouth. A different voice would say, "Don't hit her, she is innocent." I realized that this was a game between them to gain my trust and get me to admit what they wanted. Then they started threatening they would bring my children and torture them in front of me. They played a tape of what sounded like children's voices. I couldn't tell whether these were the voices of my children. I was seven-months pregnant with my son Oscar then and feared for the baby. Then they untied me and raped me. I felt one of them drawing the edge of a knife across my stomach, saying, "I am going to cut you open like a watermelon." At that moment I wished with all my heart to die. But then I remembered my children and tried to recall the image of my grandmother and asked of her spirit to give me strength to endure all and to live. They pressed the dull edge of the knife harder on my stomach.

Then they told me they were going to let me go, but that if I told anyone what had happened to me, they would come back and take me and kill me. They took me to a car, threw me in, and drove for a while. I had no sense of the duration of the drive. Finally they stopped at a street corner, took off my blindfold, and let me out of the car. I couldn't see for some time. Once my eyes got used to the light, I stopped a woman and asked her for money for a taxi. The woman stared at me. I realized I must look half-crazed, bruised and bloody as I was. She handed me a bill and quickly walked away from me. I couldn't decide whether to go to the hospital, to my house, or to the office of Comadres. Finally I decided to go to Comadres. The doctor came to me and treated me there, so I didn't have to go to the hospital. They told me it was May 9 and that I had been gone for three days. I gave a public declaration. So on May 28 they arrested me again. I was crossing the street with an older woman. I saw a blue van with darkened windows. I said, "Antonia, look! There are the beasts." She whispered, "Hurry up Maria, run." I started running but then I remembered she was with me and stopped. I stood there waiting silently. They grabbed my arms, put a gun to my side, and shoved me into the van. I heard Antonia scream. I heard them tell the driver to go to "the big house."

They took me to an interrogation room. There they asked me about the contents of my purse. I told them I had cigarettes, identification papers, and money. They asked me why I had so much money. I said I had been selling crafts for the Comadres and I was taking back the money. They took off my watch, my wedding ring, a cross. They made me take off my clothes. They examined every part of my body to see if there were any signs from carrying weapons. They thought the strap mark from my brassiere was actually a mark from carrying a rifle over my shoulder. Then there followed the questions: name, age, where I was from, how much education I had, my husband, parents, children. Still I was blindfolded. I didn't know who they were and why they had captured me. After the interrogation they gave me a pair of short socks and a T-shirt. They shoved me from one toward the other and each hit me on my neck and shoulders. They threw me against a wall and made me raise my arms above my head. They continued hitting me on the back and shoulders. At that moment I heard a woman's voice. She whispered my name and said, "Maria Teresa, you are in the General Police Headquarters." Then I heard her being dragged away. They asked me whether I knew the woman and I said I didn't. But I recognized her voice. She worked in the office next to ours. We knew she had been arrested with other members of the human rights commission. This time they kept me for twenty-four hours. They hit me. They threw water over me. Some of them ordered me to do exercises. It was complete psychological and physical war. They gave me no food or water for twenty-four hours. The next day, it was a Thursday, they took me to another interrogation room. It was a long, narrow room with windows all across where you could see what was going on in other rooms.

They made me sit at a desk in front of a pale, skinny man with a thin moustache who never stopped smiling. He showed me a photograph of me carrying a bag of food to the Comadres offices. He said, "With this evidence it will be difficult for you to get out of here." Apparently they thought I had explosives in that bag. Then he said, "I am going to do my best to help you if you also try to be cooperative. To begin, you must tell me where the Comadres keep their weapons." When I told him the Comadres had no weapons, he said, "These people," pointing toward the others, "would rather kill you. I want to throw away these documents and let you go home, but you must not make it difficult for me." Then he showed me a picture of the woman they had captured. I recognized her. Her name was Violetta. She was the new secretary at the Comadres office. I said I didn't know anything about her, which was the truth. He nodded his head to the man who was standing behind me. I felt a blow to the back of my head so hard and so unexpected that I fell forward onto the desk. The man with the smile continued smiling and said, "What happened to you señora?" as if he were surprised. I said, "Nothing." He said, "Watch out, this man here is a wicked man, a torturer. It's better for you to be friends with me and we can work this thing out together." He kept smiling, and the man behind me kept hitting me. For a time they stood me up and hit me so that I was thrown against the wall and fell. Then they pulled me up and hit me again. I became quite numb. My head stopped thinking, my heart felt nothing. At some point they brought me a cup of water and a tortilla and beans, and left me alone. I was very hungry but I also feared being drugged. But the baby inside of me moved and my stomach was empty, so I ate the food and drank the water. In a few minutes I felt drowsy and closed my eyes. Suddenly I began hallucinating. I saw enormous walls from behind which huge animals jumped at me. I prayed that the interrogators would not come back just yet. I saw horrible images. Things I had never imagined before. I'm not sure whether drugs caused the hallucination or the state of my body and mind caused me to see these horrors.

They kept me for twelve days. There existed a law called Decree no. 50 that said a person under investigation had to be taken to a regular prison or released within fifteen days. On June 8, 1986, they took me to the office of the director of police and showed me a video where Violetta denounced me as a terrorist. On the eleventh they took me to a room, blindfolded me, and made me sign a document I was not allowed to read. On the twelfth a police doctor examined me and declared me in good condition and testified that I had not been tortured.

I was then taken to the women's prison. A month after I arrived at the women's prison, the judge's secretary read to me what they had forced me to sign. In this document I had affirmed that I was a terrorist, anarchist, and communist.

At the women's prison I was allowed to see the doctor at the clinic. After the beatings I had realized I couldn't hear very well. The doctor confirmed that I was deaf in one ear. This doctor was a stupid person. The women disliked him. There were young women there who had endured terrible experiences. They had been raped and tortured. They woke up screaming in the night. Sometimes they became hysterical. One woman told me how she had been taken up in a helicopter and made to watch while they threw a prisoner out over the wilderness. They had held her at the door, saying they would do the same to her. When she had crises in the night and woke up screaming, the doctor's diagnosis was that she was a young woman and her problem was lack of sex. It takes a very stupid man to think of the needs of women in those circumstances in that way.

While I was in the women's prison, eight babies were born. Some were conceived when the women were raped by soldiers and interrogators. Others were born of women who were arrested when they were pregnant. My son Oscar was one of the eight born during that time. He was a thin and colicky baby, but I was amazed that he was born alive and relatively healthy. There were twenty-seven children in all, aged newborn to seven years old. Those whose children were born in prison or were noted beforehand received a food portion. My daughter who was with me was not registered, so we got nothing for her. The food consisted of a tortilla each at breakfast, lunch, and dinner. Sometimes the children were given a piece of cheese or a cup of soup. Visitors brought food and women sold handicrafts and earned a little money for extras. But for the most part we were all hungry all the time. Sometimes visitors brought medicine, money, and milk, which was turned over to the committee of the political prisoners and distributed among the women. Most prisoners didn't have visitors. My relatives didn't come to see me. Once an aunt came and a few times my sisters-in-law visited. But my friends from Comadres came all the time. They proved to be my real family. They brought me things and I shared what I had with the other women. These women would say, "I need such and such a thing," and I would give what I had. That's how we did things in prison.

We organized a daycare where we would watch each other's children so that we could each get some rest. Since only fifteen of the eighty-nine women were literate, we attended literacy classes. On Saturdays we had assembly. We discussed political and economic and health issues and the news that drifted in from the outside. We told of our family problems and helped each other find solutions. We set up women's health and sexual education programs. At night we sat around a large table, and after dinner we sang songs and danced. On visiting days we acted out little plays for our visitors, trying to show them why we were arrested and what our life in prison was like. Many visitors didn't know why the women were captured and held.

Sometimes we had demonstrations to protest things that affected our lives in prison. For instance, we protested the police entering the women's space to spy on what we were doing. We protested the closing of a gate that kept us in after six. We protested any limitation on our movement and space. Sometimes we protested the way they treated our visitors. They tried to make the visitors register, or searched the women, taking off their underwear to see if they were hiding anything. We also protested beating or mistreatment of other political prisoners. Sometimes we protested because they wouldn't take a tortured woman to the hospital to get treatment. For all these things, we made demands. As prisoners we felt we had the right to life and respect.

Once they brought in an older woman called Josephina. Her son was in another prison. When she went to visit him, she was captured as a terrorist. They interrogated this woman. They took off her clothes and looked in her vagina to see if she carried anything inside. They tied her up and put a flashlight in her. She remained calm and retained her dignity and composure, not letting all this break her spirit. I learned a lot from women like her who had endured so much and showed such courage.

After my release from prison I stayed in El Salvador for a few months while the Comadres tried to make arrangements for me to leave the country. I went to the office infrequently and always in the company of another woman. I knew that sooner or later I would be detained again. Finally I found myself on a plane to Mexico with my youngest children, legal passports, and three hundred dollars. I was not happy to be leaving my country, but I took comfort in thinking, "My work is my home and I can carry that with me where I go." At the airport the Mexican officials questioned me for over an hour. My documents were in order, but they kept delaying my passage. My daughter Gisela began to get nervous and started to cry. One of the policemen whispered to me that it would cost two hundred dollars to let me through. I told them I couldn't afford that much, but they said surely a tourist can afford two hundred dollars. I paid them the money, they stamped my passport, and wished me a happy journey.

I worked in Mexico with Comadres until a friend arranged my

passage across the border into the United States. I knew I had no chance of getting a visa with a baby, a small child, and no money. So I had to cross the border illegally. From the Mexican side to Tucson I walked for five hours in the desert with Oscar in my arm and Gisela holding to my hand. In Tucson I stayed with a friend until I could arrange passage first to Los Angeles and then to Washington, D.C., where I continued my work with Comadres. Throughout all this I was torn between the feeling of relief to be safely away with my youngest children, but aware that with every move I was getting farther away from my oldest children and from my country. But the need to survive did not allow me to think much about the future or about the meaning of every act or every event. I have always lived one day at a time, but during the first months of exile I did not allow my mind to think beyond the next hour.

I applied for political asylum as soon as I arrived in the United States. But the State Department does not recognize that I and others like me are in danger in El Salvador. After six years I still do not have proper papers. My life here is not very different from before. After my husband died, it was as if I were living in a darkness where nothing pleased me. I never went to parties or the theater or attended a social event. I worked with Comadres, trying to make our case understood by other people so that changes could come about. I do the same here. I go from my house to the office and from the office to my house, or I pick up and drop the kids at school. The difference is mainly in that at least when I go to bed at night I don't fear that they will come in the middle of the night. I feel my children are safe. I sleep better.

Living in America is strange. At times I find it difficult to see that what we need so much in El Salvador, people throw away here. Dogs live in better houses here than many people in El Salvador. Even though there is poverty here, I don't often see people living under scrap metal and plastic.

We live like birds without nests. In the summer we are here and in the winter we go somewhere else. We have no home of our own. This is the life of a Salvadoran—to be here, to be there, because we can't be in our own country.

In the meantime I work for peace and hope that my children will go back and we will all work the earth and live in peace. The United States has given us a lot. We have learned much, we have experienced solidarity. When we go back, my daughter will speak English very well. She can become a translator. All that we learn we will take back to our country. A million and half Salvadorans are in exile all over the world. I think of all the languages our children are going to take back to El Salvador—English, French, Swedish, German. I think of what El Salvador will be like in a few years. Since many have married people of different nationalities, there will be a wonderful mix of people. In the future my children and grandchildren will live what I dreamed of, what I never had. Because of the sacrifices that have been made and the changes in the world, they will know peace and tranquility. We are now fighting for demilitarization. We will strive to convert all the missiles into peace, food, education and housing. In the meanwhile I am glad that my children are studying well. My older son Raul helps me by taking care of the others when I go on speaking tours. I am sometimes sad because my children don't have any diversions. We don't have the means for them to enjoy the distractions available in this country. But our life is not a normal life of diversion and forgetting. All my children want to keep studying as much as possible. They are willing to make the sacrifices our economic condition forces upon them. My son is smart. He doesn't take drugs, he doesn't smoke, he has no vices. He is honest and responsible. He still asks me permission to do things.

I work as I wait, and I believe in what I do. I know that change will come. I am a lucky woman.

# HALA DEEB JABBOUR

# An Answer Waiting
for a Question

*I had spoken with Hala on the phone a number of times before I met
her for our first interview. She saluted me with a warm "Salaam" in
her low husky voice which I knew from our many conversations. The
greeting quickly established our kinship as Middle Eastern women.
Her townhouse door opened and closed a number of times during
our talk as her children and their friends, young men and women in
shorts and T-shirts, walked in and out on their many errands and
social functions of a Sunday afternoon.*

*She served tea and sweets and bread and cheese with the typical
generosity expected and received in our part of the world. She is a
woman with sure, purposeful movements. She tells me about the
many stages of her exile experience. She seems to have charted the
course of her life carefully, making studied choices, paying the fair
price for everything she receives from life, reasoning herself into a
state of contentment, but unable to reason herself into happiness. I
know how it is to know that one has done the best one can, has even
had more luck than most, but in the struggle has lost the capacity for
genuine lightheartedness. The fear, the sadness, the questioning of the
value of all things are there to stay. "The bottom of one's heart is
clouded," Hala says—a saying I had often heard from my mother-in-
law in Iran.*

*Hala is an emancipated Arab-American woman. She has contem-*

*plated the characteristics required for this self-definition. To fit this definition, she has fought her mother, her husband, her community, and her own belief in the values in which she was immersed in her early years. The image suits her. She has no complaint about the price she has paid. She knows she has negotiated a good deal.*

I WAS BORN in Jerusalem in 1943 to a Christian family in Palestine. It is important for me to say this—it was Jerusalem, Palestine. I left Palestine in 1948. My memories are very hazy. I sometimes can't tell which of my images are my own and which I retain from pictures I have seen in later years.

My first image of myself is of a little girl of about three. I am on the roof of our house where my father kept a crowd of birds— pigeons, sparrows, canaries in a space enclosed with mesh wiring. It looked like a large cage. The birds huddled together, cooing and purring and rubbing against one another. Sometimes one would perch near the roof, hanging precariously, almost upside down. I felt the pent up energy of the birds confined to this small enclosure. I reached for the latch and tried to open the door, so that the birds could get out and have more room to move about. They caught me just in time, before I released the entire coop. I like to think this was my first reaching out to freedom.

My childhood in Jerusalem was quiet, ordinary and peaceful. I lived with my family in a house with two stories. My parents and I lived upstairs and my grandparents lived on the lower floor. Down the street lived uncles, aunts, and cousins. My early recollections are of crowds of people who were all related to me. A crowd meant family, warmth, security.

My next recollection is of the family at dinner: light, food, and chatter suddenly interrupted by bullets, screams, and explosions and my father pushing me to the floor and the smell of the dust from the carpet which felt rough against my cheek and the pressure of my father's hand on my spine forcing me to stay down.

The next image I have is of the family on a plane bound for Cairo. I knew nothing of what was happening. I didn't know who was doing what to whom. It was an outing, a trip, an adventure.

During the next few years we moved from Cairo to Amman,

Jordan, and on to Beirut, Lebanon. It was a period of dislocation and temporariness. Suddenly life had lost its anchor and we were afloat in a changing, moving world. In this new life a crowd meant strangers, the unexpected, and danger. It was safe only when we were alone.

My parents didn't tell us much about what had happened to us. Children in our culture were to be seen but not talked to. We weren't told why we had left our home. We didn't know that we were exiles. We weren't taken into our parents' confidence. We received some information by osmosis, through feeling the mood of the older people and hearing bits and pieces of their conversation.

It was in Amman that I became aware of the politics behind our personal moves. I began to realize what it meant to be a Palestinian. Awareness of my identity made me more self-conscious. I became aware of being a woman. My mother had an aunt who took care of us when my parents were out. She was a charming and likable person. One day she asked my brother, who was two and a half years younger than I, what he wanted to be when he grew up. My brother couldn't answer. I tried to help him by enumerating the options: "Doctor, engineer, pilot, teacher." He still couldn't make up his mind. Then I waited for her to ask me the question. I felt clever and important. I knew very well what I was going to be. But she never asked me. In years to come, I waited many times with a perfectly good answer for the question that was never asked of me. "Aunt Jamileh, aren't you going to ask me what I am going to be?" I asked. "Oh, you are going to get married and have children just like your mommy," she said.

I was fascinated by costumes and uniforms during that period. I thought of doctor's, soldier's, judge's costumes and tried to imagine what it would be like to wear them. It was a shock to realize that the only life open to me was one that didn't even have a special outfit. My life was stretched out in front of me with no surprises and no room for improvisation.

It was during my adolescent years in Lebanon that I became fully aware of my condition of exile. I began reading and asking questions. I drilled my family about what life had been like in our homeland and asked why we had left and when we would return. At my school, the director was a knowledgeable woman who invited important Third World personalities such as Nehru to speak. I was very impressed with the eloquence of Nehru's statement and his humanitarian philosophy. Exposure to such personalities and their ways of thinking as well as the entire political scene in Beirut, which at that time was alive with ideologies, parties, and movements—from Arab Nationalism to communism and Baathism—affected me very much. I became active in politics. My mother worried about me. As I came and went to various political gatherings, I often heard her murmuring anxiously to no one in particular, "What am I going to do with a communist daughter?"

With the rise of the PLO's relative power in Lebanon in 1967 I was able for the first time to go to the refugee camps. Before then there was a policy that Palestinians inside and outside the camps were to be kept separate so as not to influence each other. I was shocked by the wretched conditions in the camps. I realized for the first time what it meant to be hopeless and without control over one's destiny—to be in exile. My family and I were forced to leave our home. The choice to go back was taken from us. But the Palestinians in the camp were separated from their human essence. All significant choice was taken from them. The condition of the Palestinians in the camps meant to me that as a people we were all robbed of power to control our destiny.

During these years, along with awareness of exile, I gained a sense of myself as a woman. But not until the war in Lebanon did I articulate the feminist beliefs that were gradually taking shape in my mind. As a Palestinian I placed my political agenda above all else. I believed that so long as we were fighting for our survival, the issue of Palestine must consume all our concern, energy, and attention. Somehow the larger condition rendered all else, especially women's issues, frivolous by comparison. So I internalized my feminist ideas as the situations and incidents I experienced continued to strengthen my feminist beliefs.

I married a Lebanese man when I was twenty. I couldn't afford to go to college. My husband started an office-cleaning business. After a while he wanted to move to a new field, so he turned this business over to me. I had unsettling experiences trying to manage this company. In my work I dealt with banks and other large businesses. Like any young Arab woman working in this atmosphere, I faced recurring instances of sexism. My husband's cousin, whom I had appointed foreman and who knew very little about the business, was asked questions, called, dealt with as if he were the manager. The Arab businessmen simply would not recognize me as the boss. People called on the phone and wanted to talk to the foreman because he was a man. I was a woman; therefore I was nobody, even if I did have the title of manager and even if I did know more about the business than anybody else. I sat with all the answers to the questions that were never asked of me. It took many years of hard work finally to be recognized as the boss. I resented having to prove myself above and beyond efficient handling of my business.

In the refugee camps it was worse for the women. They were completely subservient to the men. Many men went to the Gulf States to work. The responsibility of the family fell on the women. There was very little of the necessities of life to go around. In 1948, UNRWA gave four cents a day per Palestinian man, woman, and child. Four cents meant more then, but still it was nothing. Palestinians were not allowed to use cement or bricks to build. They had to use zinc, which had to be replaced every few years. The dwelling places were drenched in the terrible rains and smoldering hot in the summer months. When the PLO came, they began for the first time to use cement in building. They started to cover the sewage system. The women were protected from the abuses that had taken place earlier. They began to enter the work force in large numbers. Gradually it was accepted that women could work and still be "good" women.

I worked in the camps helping to set up childcare facilities, helping women produce marketable handicrafts, and assisting them in selling their products. I was becoming increasingly aware of the unfairness of my own and other women's condition. But I kept my feelings to myself. I was a woman with a family. I was a business-woman. I was an active participant in the liberation movement. I could not afford to articulate my feminist beliefs and lose my cred-ibility in all these areas. I walked a tightrope trying to live a feminist life while staying within the bounds of "respectability" in the social, financial, and political worlds to which I belonged. Of all these, the family was the strongest deterrent. I had two daughters. I was very conscious that if I transgressed the norm, I would jeopardize the future of my children. I was already guilt-ridden because of the unconventionality of some of the roles I had undertaken. This bur-den, always the woman's, ties one to the status quo. With every new step, I weighed all the alternatives and evaluated the costs to myself and my family.

My family's many journeys in exile were all considered temporary. Our stay in Egypt was to have been a very short one. A few months and we would be back, my parents had thought. Amman was claustrophobic for my father, who was a very outspoken man and a committed Palestinian. If we had stayed, he would have been in trouble. But Lebanon became a place of permanence. I had married, developed relationships, managed a business there, built ties. When the war came I had no intention of leaving. The very idea of another journey into the uncertain and the unknown was repellent. I vowed to stay no matter what happened.

In the early 1970s there were a number of seemingly unrelated but unsettling incidents in Lebanon. No one connected them into a pattern or gave them serious thought. In the spring of 1975 there was an incident in the south of Lebanon where a group of Palestinians coming back from a celebration on a bus were attacked. It was a horrible event, but we all thought it was an isolated incident that would not be repeated. Around this time I decided to travel to London with a friend, taking our children for a vacation. After a couple of weeks my husband called and asked me not to come back. He said that the outbreak of fighting had brought the road from the airport into town under constant fire and it would be unsafe to take the children home just then. As I listened to him on the telephone, my immediate concern was not that Lebanon was in a state of chaos but that I, a Palestinian, was being told again to stay out of a country that was for the moment my home. I decided that I would go back no matter what. My friend stayed in London, but I returned.

It was dangerous living in Lebanon. There was constant fighting, the government had lost control, and the rule of law, once a pride of the Lebanese, seemed to have vanished. But I decided I would not leave. I thought to myself, "I am a Palestinian and I have suffered from being dislocated and plucked up by the roots too often. I have suffered in this way. My parents have suffered the same. Lebanon is my children's home. I am not going to let them live in exile." I waited for things to settle down, but the situation worsened daily. My children went to school each day leaving me to wonder whether they would be back. There was a complete breakdown of law and order.

There were bombs everywhere. Kidnapping was a daily occurrence. There was a great deal of conflict between the values I taught the children at home and what they experienced in the world outside.

People were foul-mouthing, killing each other, stealing. Religion had become a cause of rancor and hostility. I had taught my children general concepts about Christianity. But they came home with questions. Are we better or worse than the Muslims? Why are we different?

The chaos, anger, and vindictiveness came home to me one day when a small battle broke out over capturing the Holiday Inn Hotel close to our house. It was a tall building and every faction wanted it in order to gain control over the area. There was considerable sniper fire and many were killed randomly. A wave of vindictiveness swept the neighborhood. Everyone was mobilized to capture and stop the snipers. They finally succeeded. But by then it wasn't enough that they had killed them. They straddled one of the bodies on the hood of a car, each leg tied to a tire with a rope. They drove through the streets exhibiting the body. I was completely opposed to the sniper's politics and abhorred the random murder of innocent bystanders. I had wanted them defeated. But now the captors were calling us all to come to the street to gloat over the mutilated body. That was the moment I decided I could no longer expose my children to this atmosphere. Like it or not, I had to leave Beirut.

The Palestinians were willingly or unwillingly involved in what was happening in Beirut as they were in most of what happened in the Middle East. They were fast becoming a target of vindictiveness in Lebanon. We decided to go to London, thinking that we would come back when things quieted down. As in our other journeys in exile, there was to be no return.

In London, being on tourist visa, I was not allowed to work. I could not bring myself to settle down. I lived in limbo, waiting to go back. I had time to think. I thought of my role as a woman and what I wanted my life to mean. I considered the political role I wanted to play. I reviewed my involvement in Palestinian politics and tried to evaluate its meaning. I came to the conclusion that it was nothing substantial, that I had made no real difference. I learned that issues that mattered to me were not merely political, external to myself. I learned that my personal life, my individual consciousness, and how I experienced my moments and what I made of them, were what mattered to me. It was a time of dealing with the reality of exile and coming to terms with the practicalities of my own and my family's future. I came to the conclusion that in order to build a life for my children I must come to the United States. On an earlier trip I had disliked the lifestyle. But in 1981 it seemed the only place for a woman in exile. There one could build a new life and develop a sense of security for her children. I came to the United States with a one-way ticket, determined to stay and like it. I settled in Virginia, near Washington, D.C., and discovered that liking my new home was a lot easier than I had imagined.

During the first few years I was cautious in my political activities and in making public statements. I felt vulnerable as a Palestinian and an exile. I was constantly aware that I was here by the grace of the system and not from any native right to the land. I felt that if I said something or made myself conspicuous, I might be deported. During my early years in exile there had been recurring incidents of violence against Palestinians. Every few years there were incidents where Palestinians were attacked and killed. The conditions differed, but the end result was the same. These attacks had created a gnawing feeling inside me that I was not wanted, that I didn't belong. No matter what country I was in and how I tried to organize my life and work, there was always the sensation that I was there by someone's permission and that the permission could always be withdrawn. I created a life, I made an existence, but I was constantly imperiled and threatened.

In 1987 I became an American citizen. Once I got my American passport, I felt liberated from my fear of being sent away. I felt I had a claim on the country. I took my right to the First Amendment and the Bill of Rights very seriously. I felt protected. I began to lose the sense of helplessness and precariousness characteristic of life in exile.

I joined Arab-American organizations. I began articulating my feminism. I felt free in this area as I had never felt before. I could be what I wanted to be, say what I wanted to say, without fear, without endangering my children, my reputation, or the honor of my family and without all the guilt that presses down upon a woman and a mother in my own culture. My feminism flowered—that's exactly how I feel—like a large, healthy plant which is given water and air and sun until it blooms. I began to feel unencumbered. I had a voice with which to express my thoughts and feelings. My mind filled with stories I wanted to tell, I needed to tell. I began writing.

For my husband, it was much more difficult. Being a man and a Lebanese meant that he would suffer a harrowing experience. A Palestinian has learned to expect uprootedness. A Palestinian is always in danger, never belongs anywhere, does not have a sense of permanence. The Lebanese could not begin to imagine such a state. Being a man, he had a more vested interest in the status quo and gained less in the transition.

I have come now to consider myself an American of Arab origin. I have reconciled myself to living here as a citizen. My husband is an Arab living in America. There is a great difference. An Arab living in the United States cannot let go of all those cultural characteristics, good and bad, that bind him to his original heritage. Many Arab men cannot let go of the past. It results in constant tension and conflict. You cannot live in a totally alien culture and bring up children and conduct a life on the basis of cultural traditions of a distant land. You cannot grow roots. The children cannot have a healthy life. You suffer as an individual. That is why I have insisted in bringing up my children as Arab Americans. They are fully integrated into American culture, but they have their ethnic Arab roots to enrich their lives. They are not Arabs lessened by distance from their home, but Americans enriched by their dual heritage. I keep their traditional culture alive for them through food, music, and art—not by reasoning but through my own love for that culture.

I was able to lead the family into this adjustment because I am a strong woman. I had to fight my husband every step of the way. He wanted to hold on to the past. I knew it would not be healthy and constructive to do that. I had to struggle with him and with my mother and many others of the older generation. It drained me. At times I felt I couldn't continue and gave in. I felt I had to carry a heavy burden, dragging the whole family forward into the new way of life. My husband didn't want to move along. So I let him be. Being in the United States, I could afford to go on with my activities without waiting for permission. In the Arab world it would not have been possible. I did what I felt was right for me and I don't feel that in the process I have compromised my children or my integrity as a Palestinian woman.

My husband stays within his Arab social circle. I move in both worlds. I find much that is positive in each culture and try to build a world based on the best of the two. I miss the support system in my home and the security of old age there. Old age is natural there. Each family takes care of its elders. Here the prospect of being isolated in an institution frightens me. As I am enjoying the pleasures of individualism and independence, I begin to think of the price I may have to pay in later years. I am beginning to think of the alternate structures such as insurance and retirement plans. But these will only supplement the financial and material means of survival in old age. The spiritual cannot be bought on an installment plan.

But even though I want to be away from the adverse and limiting parts of my culture, I am aware that I really don't belong here. I am different. I understand Americans, I have friends among them, they are responsive to me, yet I am different and will always remain so. Whenever there is an upheaval in the Middle East, I feel especially uncomfortable. In 1982, when the Israelis invaded southern Lebanon and the Sabra and Chatila massacres took place, I didn't want to be here. When the intifada started, I wanted to be there. These are times when I feel most alienated from my American friends. I feel they cannot understand what the Palestinian people are going through. I feel I don't belong here. When the Gulf war started and the FBI's investigation of Arab Americans began, I felt paranoid. I began suspecting every American I met. I kept thinking of everyone as a member of the FBI or the CIA. The telephone became a tool of my paranoia. The most innocent question by a friend sounded suspect. The television and the newspapers were all against me. In moments like this I feel I want to become small and melt away so that no one knows I am here. But on the whole connections with the people here have been wonderful and enriching. Contact with feminists is comforting. They always seem to connect and to understand.

Sometimes I feel more uncomfortable with Arabs. I feel I have moved on and away from them intellectually. Yet I don't feel comfortable enough to take the comfort for granted with Americans. I don't belong to either culture fully. During bad times, I am an alien in both, during good days I am a native in both. Exile is a no-man's land, where one belongs fully nowhere.

Language remains a perpetual obstacle in the way of communication within both cultures. It is not the words in each language or their translations that cause difficulty for me. It is the intonation and the shades of meaning they imply. For an Arab, if you say, "Please come into my house," the words imply a real wish to have the person enter and partake of the hospitality. Refusal is value-laden and hurtful. An American saying "Come in" is making a casual offer. You have the choice of accepting or not without implying any meaning beyond what the actual words offer. The layers of meaning and the emotions attached to each layer are a part of the system of communication among Arabs whether they are speaking Arabic or English. Americans speak in black and white. Language is more a means of exchanging facts. I have lived with Americans so long now that I have become too black and white for the Arabs. I have lost the grey in my language and bring out emotions and meanings I have no intention of arousing.

The cultural conflicts are strong within the Arab families in America. Women are helping support the family financially. They are trying to adjust to the new environment. Their husbands, being Arab men, are not doing much to help around the house. The strain shows on the Arab women. Families are being affected by the stress. Arab men consider everything American as a threat to their masculinity. They spend much of their energy preoccupied with safeguarding the "honor" of their womenfolk. They are petrified that their wives and daughters, influenced by this society, will involve themselves in sexual relationships with American men. They are more attached to their culture and religion than they were before. They hang on to their traditions fiercely. Yet they accept the ways of this culture in their dealings with American women. They cannot apply the same standards to Arab women. When the son goes out with an American woman, it is cause for boasting and pride. But let the daughter indicate that an American man has invited her to a school function or dinner, and a drama unfolds. The girls cannot deal with this so they are forced to lie.

Recently, a man I know who belongs to a respected family found out that his daughter has a relationship with an American boy. He took the girl to the basement of their house, placed her on a cross, and belted her all night while the mother stood by in silence. The girl had not eloped with the boy, she had not slept with him. She had talked to him on the telephone and seen him a few times. Under these circumstances, being "American" becomes a terrible attribute. A woman like me poses a definite threat to Arab men. For them I represent a challenge to the status quo. Women have mixed feelings. There is envy, but there is also fear. They discuss with me the abstract political issues, but not their sons and daughters and family relations. Through my involvement with Arab-American organizations I have learned that in order to function effectively, I have to maintain rapport with the community. So I hold my peace on controversial family issues and stick to politics.

Sometimes when I think how much need there is in Palestine for technology and skills, I feel guilty that I am here, withholding myself from my people. But I have reconciled these feelings by working with Arab-American groups. I have also established a circle of American friends who know our cause and sympathize. There is comfort in knowing that I can influence in a small way the thinking of the outside world about my people, helping others see us in a better light. In the final analysis, however, I did not choose to be here. If I had had a choice, I probably would not be here. Since I don't have that option, I'm going to do what I can to contribute and to be happy.

As a first-generation American, I know that I am the bridge— that my children will not feel the conflicts and ambivalence I have felt. Someone must pay the price. I console myself with the thought that I am escaping the claustrophobic part of my own culture. I applaud my life here for its privacy, for the control that I exercise over my choices, and for owning my time. In my part of the world, any relative or friend can impose his presence on one's life at any moment. The events of other people's life influence the way one lives her day.

Often I wonder whether being Arab American is something I have passed on to my children as extra baggage in their lives, something not really their own. I ask myself whether that will expand their horizons or limit their chances and choices in this society. Will this quality become more and more fluid as time goes by and they become increasingly integrated into this society? Part of me wishes for them to retain their heritage. Another part wants them to become ordinary Americans, as comfortable and natural in this society as fish in water. There is a sadness in that each choice involves a loss.

In the past two years I have begun to work for Palestine in a new context. I belong to a group of Palestinian-American women who have joined a group of Jewish-American women to work for peace in Palestine. We try to establish dialogue and to understand the things that have made us fear and mistrust each other all through the years of animosity. We work to identify the many things we share. The experience has been wonderful for me because I am relating to the group as a woman and as a Palestinian. I long for peace. I am worried that this most recent effort, like others before, will fall apart and that once again we will be sold down the river. I am also anxious about the future if we do succeed. I am acutely aware of the problems we face as a nation trying to start building institutions from scratch, building relationships, and trying to undo the harm of years of violence, uncertainty, and hate. There is so much vindictiveness, and much of it is internalized. As an Arab people we Palestinians do not express much that we feel. It is all pent up within us.

I think now there is an understanding that the Palestinians and Israelis must recognize each other's existence and their mutual right to be in that land. Palestinians cannot be parceled off to some other country. They must have their own homeland. Israelis must feel secure in their own home. This goal cannot be achieved unless each side feels it cannot have a total victory, that the optimum solution means compromise and a less-than-perfect formula for either side.

As I review my life in exile, I feel proud that I have retained my Palestinian identity while developing and articulating a feminist identity. I am proud that I can relate to others from that premise. I am proud that I write and I am proud of what I have done with my children. On a personal level, I have accepted myself and I am happy with myself. When I decided not to allow my life to be controlled by my husband, by my mother, by the traditional codes; when I learned to say, "I don't care"; when I learned to answer my own inner spiritual needs and to stand up and refuse to be intimidated by the codes; when I stopped caring whether my mother was shocked that I was contemplating divorce—then I began to be happy.

I have made the choice to stay married. I live in the house with my husband. My children understand that we don't have much of a life together. But they prefer that I have remained with him under the same roof. It is selfish of them, but young people are selfish. I think that if my husband had been able to change and grow with the times, perhaps things would have been different between us. But one cannot have control over other people's choices, and often it is impossible to comprehend why someone decides to take one course of action or another. In the end one is answerable only for one's own choices.

The pain of exile is palpable and long-lasting. But there are pleasures also. The greatest joy is the potential to break through the structures, rules, regulations, written and unwritten, that bind a woman and take away her real voice and her true identity. Breaking out of those structures is painful, but the pain can be the signal for a rebirth. I grew as a human being during exile. I felt an expansiveness inside of me. It was something I had always yearned for but could not achieve.

I would like to go to Palestine if it is ever a country. I would like to offer some of the skills I have acquired to help build Palestine. But on a permanent basis I would choose to live here and work with the Palestinians who will remain. I will try to help heal the wounds. But if there is a Palestine some day and I choose to stay here, I won't be an exile anymore. Lack of choice is what exile is all about.

# GE YANG

# A Woman in a Borrowed Country

Another year in exile,
Happily I move to a new home
Near the cemetery
My smile penetrates the tears,
I borrow this foreign place
And make it my country.

*She reminded me of a ruffled sparrow, small and gaunt and fragile. She moved with quick steps. She walked up the red plastic-covered stairs ahead of me, her long black skirt sweeping the stairs as she moved. She talked and laughed in a muffled, musical voice. Xiao, her interpreter, laughed and made reverential sounds in Chinese. Soon we were seated at a card table with the tape recorder between us. Ge Yang was jovial, energetic, her face wrinkled but luminous. When she laughed she showed missing teeth. In some other face this would have been unattractive. In Ge Yang this, as all else, was simply comfortable. I was excited by the prospect of listening to this woman's story. She began by saying, "I am a writer, I know what you want," silencing my question easily, making me feel my needs were being anticipated and satisfied.*

*She spoke in measured, studied tones, weaving her narrative as if she were knitting according to some intricate pattern, the lines of which were visible only to her. She did not seem emotionally involved in the tale she was unfolding. She had the air of someone who is performing a necessary and not unpleasant task.*

*Two years elapsed between our first and second meetings. The second time I met Ge at Xiao Qiang's office at the headquarters of Human Rights in China. She wore a grey jacket and black slacks—an outfit that would have passed as ordinary in China, even in the days of the cultural revolution. What made her seem to be more of her present world was an intangible new air of belonging. Her movements were less birdlike and ethereal. She insisted on communicating in English. She hugged me warmly and said, "Two years have passed. I have learned English. Where have you been all this time?"*

*In the past decade I have been very aware that I have missed the process of change in my friends' lives. The revolution in Iran has flung us far apart and I have not witnessed the events that have affected them or the evolving of their personalities in response and in relation to these events. I have regretted very much that I have not shared the moments or seen the changes as they happened. Ge made me feel I have missed yet another series of changes in yet another friend's life.*

*This time she concentrated not only on her own telling but on the interpretation. She interrupted to correct and expand the English rendition when she felt it necessary. She seemed proud of her newly gained skills. She was in control of the situation, careful of the nuances of her narrative.*


I WAS BORN before 1919. That was the year of the liberation of women in China—the year of the May Fourth movement. I was born in Jiang Su Province in the city of Yang Zhou. Yang Zhou is called the city of beautiful women—women so strikingly beautiful that, according to legend, emperors made long journeys there to see them. The city is also known for a rare flower called Chiung, with blossoms as pure and white as jade.

I was born in an unhappy family. My father was a teacher. Just after my birth, my mother heard that my father was keeping a consort. One night when he didn't come home she went searching for him in a boat. It was snowing and the waves of the river beat hard. She came back at dawn, soaking wet and exhausted. She fell ill and died soon after. I was one month old when she died. My sister was three years old.

After my mother's death my father gave up teaching and opened a small bookstore and tried to take care of us. Soon my sister took ill and died. My father gave up trying to care for a family, perhaps gave up caring altogether. He sent me away to live with my uncle and his wife, who had no children. He sent with me a box of books. My uncle's household was not a happy one. They had little money and felt their life to be incomplete without children of their own.

I was about five years old when I first realized what it means to be a woman. All the little boys in my neighborhood went to school but I couldn't. I really wanted to read. Having a box of books as the sum of my wealth spurred my curiosity. I began copying the boys' textbooks, drawing the words the best I could.

Very soon other aspects of being a woman became painfully apparent to me. First I had my ears pierced. Then began the process of the daily binding of my feet. The piercing was a one-time quick pain. But the binding was a never-ending process. In the daytime I kept the ribbons on out of fear, but at night I tore them off. I rolled off the three meters of binding tightly wrapped around my feet. I had been told that I must have "the three-inch golden lotus" feet. But the image was hateful to me. More than the pain involved in the process, I disliked the stillness and smallness evoked by the lotus image. My uncle had a second wife. Since his first wife hadn't given him a son, it was accepted that he would take on a second wife. My uncle's wife was a very strong woman. She worked out a plan whereby she saved face while observing the custom. She allowed my uncle to have their servant girl as the second wife. To the world outside, she was the only wife, yet her husband got what custom allowed him in these circumstances.

The servant girl came from a peasant family. She was twenty-six years old and still unmarried. So we all called her "Great Girl." She and I were very good friends. We shared a room together and talked late into the night. She told me of her misfortunes. Since no man had wanted her, they had always tried to get her into the second-wife position. She came to the city and became a servant in order to be independent. She felt cheated at my uncle's house. She felt she was now both a servant and a second wife. She had no choice really.

She believed if she had only had an education, she wouldn't have to put up with all this. She encouraged me to study, and every night we talked about getting around the rules about women—rules about ears, about feet, about minds, and about bodies. We talked of the necessity of becoming financially independent and the need for education as a way of reaching that goal.

I didn't have books to read. One day I opened the box my father had given me. There were all kinds of books there. The first one I became interested in was a historical novel called *Dream of the Red Chamber* by a famous Chinese writer, Cai Xueqin. Before the appearance of this novel, written and spoken language were different. The writer of this book was one of the first to write in the simple language of the people. This was a long, tragic love story, so women were not allowed to read it. Great Girl and I used to draw the curtains so my uncle and his wife wouldn't see the light and we sat up all night reading the book. Since my uncle's wife was hard of hearing, once we blacked-out the window, we could talk, read, laugh and cry and she would only look at the window and seeing that it was black assume we were safely asleep. Soon, however, Great Girl was forced to do needlework to make extra money for oil, since my uncle's wife, always careful of the family's budget, was becoming suspicious about the amount of oil we used.

In 1927, when I was twelve years old, the Northern Expedition, known as the "Conquering Army" came to our town. It was the revolutionary army fighting the emperor's men. They began teaching the people new ideas. One of these ideas was the equality of men and women. The new atmosphere gave me the courage to fight for the chance to go to school. Finally my family agreed to support me. Great Girl was on my side. My uncle was influenced by the new ideas and agreed with us. My uncle's wife, who was worried about costs to the family, disagreed. But we won.

I was too old to enter first grade, so they gave me a test. Thanks to the box of books my father had sent with me, I did very well on the reading and writing, though not in mathematics. It took me two and a half years of hard work to graduate from primary school. I was qualified to enter a professional high school. My uncle's wife was happier now, hoping that I could finally make some money. But the professional school merged after a year into a regular high school, and my ongoing fight with the family continued as I asked for support to go on with my education. When I was away at school, my friend Great Girl was left alone with my uncle's wife, who constantly abused her. Each time I went home she told me, "When you are away life is like a dark night; when you come home, you bring sunshine." This was not my uncle's feeling, because every time I came home I asked for money and there was always a big fight. Once my uncle's wife burned my box of books. Emperor Qin Shihuang, the first emperor of China, had boasted that when he gained power he had burned the books and killed the intellectuals. I told my uncle's wife, "You have become a tyrant like the first emperor." This was a common phrase in China.

The only school I could go to that was free was the teacher's college. So I went there. By this time I had become outspoken on the right of women to an education and to independence. At the teacher's college I heard about communism. I heard that communism seeks democracy, freedom, rights for all the oppressed people, including women, and an end to the nationalist regime that had become corrupt and distant from the people. I joined a reading club. That was my first communist group activity. During that period communism was outlawed and connection with it drew harsh punishment. Actually, the law allowed for the execution of members of the Communist party. There were stories of young party members who when captured had stood up to their captors and shouted slogans of freedom and sang the Internationale as they were taken to be executed. They were heroes in the eyes of the people.

These days people ask me, "How could you work with that terrible movement?" They don't understand that at that time the movement was against the Nationalist government and for freedom and democracy. As an increasing number of young people faced execution with courage and strength, the prestige of the movement grew in our minds. It had been my experience that the more a government oppresses the people, the more they unite against it; and the more the movement expands until it takes in people who had no wish to be against any system and had no particular ideology. So all the young people began to be drawn to the Communist party. In Nanjing there was a place where political prisoners were taken to be executed. They were placed in a sack and then they were shot and buried. People talked of this place as if it were sacred ground.

Then came the war with Japan. Many young people moved to Yanan, a remote place in Shaangxi province in northwest China, to join the Red Army which had made its capital there. I wanted to go there too, but for the first two years I decided to join the Nationalist forces to fight the Japanese. In 1937, two months after I graduated from high school and started teaching, I joined the Shanghai Youth League to Save the Nation. This was a communist front group that published a paper called *People*. I became the editor of this publication. At this time I had hopes of becoming a writer. I had written a few short stories that had gained some recognition. But with the outbreak of the war those dreams were forgotten.

At this time my organization moved from Shanghai to another city in the south and joined the Nationalist forces trying to hold the frontier. There was a famous battle in Xuzhou. Many young people fought in that battle. They hadn't had any training, but they fought with all their being. The Japanese were angered by the unexpected resistance they met. They surrounded our forces on all sides. It was a horrendous task trying to break through their lines. We finally managed, but with a tremendous loss of life. I walked into the village afterwards. The whole place was on fire. The ground was covered with the bodies of the dead. I wrote my first article describing the terrible scenes in this battle.

After that I wrote a number of articles for various leftist journals. My positions became increasingly radical. Before long I was blacklisted by the Nationalist government, and in 1941 I was forced to escape and join a group called "The New Fourth Army," which was part of the communist army. From that time and for the rest of my life I was mostly an exile—at first in my own home and finally outside my country.

In the Red Army I was a reporter. I traveled to various provinces throughout China. At that time the atmosphere within the Red Army was still egalitarian. There was not much difference between soldiers and officers. There were very few women in the army. I didn't notice the inequality of women then, but now when I look back I see how mistreated they were. Many ended up marrying the officers. Liu Shaoqi, who later became the number two leader of the nation after Mao Tse Tung, married a new woman in every town through which our forces passed. I had decided I would resist falling into the abyss of that sort of marriage, but many women were unable to avoid it. Their life was not easy. Among the limitations placed on women was the pledge to keep out of politics while they were married to officers or leaders.

Immediately after the end of the war with Japan the civil war started. We talked of ending the Nationalist dictatorship and bringing democracy and freedom to China. The young and the intellectuals supported us and the masses followed. Soon we were victorious. I was in Tienanmen Square when the ceremony establishing the People's Republic of China took place. At that moment the huge mass of people were almost as one, crying with common tears of joy. It took several years to take away the harmony and peacefulness that were in the air on that day—the day of young people crying and laughing and dancing full of hope.

Soon the communist leaders moved to the houses in which the emperors had lived. There were guards at the gates. The officers moved into the houses of the Nationalist officers, and every day they moved further away from the people. By the mid-1950s Mao had begun persecuting the intellectuals. He boasted that if the first emperor had killed 460, he executed millions. Under Mao, one wave of persecution was followed by another, suffocating any signs of independent thinking. To him, those who thought and wrote were the most dangerous, and so they were the ones most oppressed by the system. *Intellectual* became a dirty word. In 1956 he announced that anyone who had any criticism should speak out and he would be heard. He said, "Let a hundred flowers bloom," but as soon as the writers wrote or spoke they were labeled "rightist" and "counter-revolutionary."

I was at this time the editor of a journal called the *New Observer*. I wrote about freedom of expression and published many articles on issues related to democracy. I was not surprised therefore to hear that I was declared a "rightist." All my life I had struggled to learn, to get an education. My education made me an intellectual. Intellectuals ask questions. To inquire was to suffer in China. I knew the consequences of my actions. To be branded a rightist in China at that time meant that one ceased to exist as a person. I lost my job, my house, my position in society. I was sent to the country to a labor camp in a village commune. My task was to feed the pigs. There was a lot of hard work involved. The peasants lived under inhuman conditions. The collectives were called "one step forward toward communism," part of the Great Leap Forward, but it was really more like slavery. Politically China was a dictatorship. Economically no free enterprise was permitted; culturally no independent thinking was allowed.

Life was hell. The peasants were suffering. Between 1959 and 1961 there was starvation everywhere. We ate everything—leaves, even the husks of the corn. Once I saw strange meat being sold on the street and asked about it. The peasants told me it was the flesh of human children. I had read in history that such things had been done in the distant past. We have a custom in China where uncles take figurines made of flour when they visit their nephews and nieces. It comes from a legend that says an uncle went to his brother's house and found no one there and proceeded to kill and eat the little nephew. From then on the custom of bringing figurines made of flour dough developed to show the uncle's expiation and good faith. The richer the uncle the bigger the figurines.

I barely survived this period. I grew very weak and thin, so thin that when the doctor wanted to give me an injection, he couldn't find flesh enough to put the needle through. I was literally a bag of bones. I had contracted hepatitis and my liver was ailing.

I had a husband, a well-known artist who had also been declared a rightist, and five children when I was exiled to the commune. I was not allowed to see them throughout the first year. My youngest daughter had been born two months before I was accused. She had never known what life is like in a normal household. The first time she saw me she didn't even know me. On our second visit she had just begun to talk. She couldn't believe I was really her mother. When she visited me during my illness, I walked with her to the clinic. She said, "Mommy, I wish I was a donkey so you could ride me." She didn't know that at one point I even had a car. I had been member of the board of the writers' association and editor of an important journal. No one was immune from a sudden fall from grace. The slightest show of independence would bring the destructive forces of the state upon one's life.

In 1962 I was "pseudoliberated." That means I was cleared of the charge of being a "rightist," but the charge of *having been* a rightist remained. I was not allowed to live in Beijing, but they let me edit what they considered a politically innocuous journal. Soon the Cultural Revolution was announced and after a short while I was again in disgrace. Something I wrote brought the new charges. In 1966 I was demoted to the position of janitor at a general's house. From dawn to dusk I washed bathrooms, scrubbed floors, and did errands and chores around the big house. From time to time I was brought to demonstrations to be held up as an example to the crowds. My faults and sins were enumerated and the crowd shouted and sometimes spat at me.

In 1969 I was told to report for a new assignment. This time I was sent to a camp for hard labor. The camp was on the construction site of a dam on an icy river. We lived in a hut built right on the ice. We had to huddle together for warmth. We woke before dawn and rushed to wash with a cupful of water we were given. Before we finished washing, we hurried to eat and halfway through the meal we were lined up and they called out our names. Then we walked miles to the place of work. As we walked we had to engage in self-criticism, confessing our shortcomings and the sins and mistakes we had committed since childhood. Our work was to haul away the muddy, frozen earth from the dam site. I had to pull the cart full of heavy mud for interminable distances. I was getting weaker and sicker every day. When I was allowed to see a doctor to complain about my liver condition, he asked how old I was. I told him I was fifty. He laughed and said, "You are living on borrowed time, you should have been dead already."

Finally because I couldn't move or be of any use, they sent me to Mongolia. I wanted to go there myself because I had heard there was plenty of meat in Mongolia. I was so weak and thin that I really needed the meat. For the next ten years I lived in Mongolia.

All of this I have lived through, I have experienced. But then Mao died in 1976 and the new rulers said, "Ah, we made a mistake." All of that was simply a mistake! Twenty-two years of my life were a mistake! All of that time I did not live, I did not experience anything of value, I accomplished nothing and I suffered. How can you call that "a mistake"?

They talked about reforms. At that time we thought that was the only hope for China. There was no opposition force and no other parties, so we thought reforming the Communist party was our only hope. I and some others decided to try to help reform the system from within. In 1979 I became once more the editor of the *New Observer*. But the situation did not move smoothly—or in the right direction. The next ten years China basically adhered to the Communist party line, while trying to change to a market economy. It did not work. There is a seesaw kind of process when leaders open up the political breathing space; the people begin to move, they move a bit too fast for the rulers, who fear loss of control, the rulers shut down the system, and again the needs of the economy force another opening, followed by another shutdown. The last great opening and shutdown was the events leading to the massacre at Tienanmen Square. Deng Xiao-Ping simply wants to use capitalist medicine to extend communist life—in effect, to retain his own power. But the many openings have changed the consciousness of the people. The old men are trying to keep power in their lifetime. I am old myself but I am against politics of old men. I think the old politicians in China are stale and rotten. They will disintegrate and the system with them. China is like an egg, fertilized, about to burst forth with new life. The inside is completely changed, but the shell remains unchanged. I think communism will not last much longer. They are celebrating the seventieth anniversary of the Communist party, but actually they are observing its funeral without knowing it.

When I was reinstated at the *New Observer,* I gained back all I had, all my privileges—the house, the office, the car. I used my newly regained office to push for freedom and democracy. In Beijing we established a circle of liberal intellectuals. I published political statements others would not. My magazine became the spearhead of the democracy movement. There was another magazine in Shanghai called the *New Economic Herald.* The two journals collaborated. When Hu Yaobang, the reformist leader of the Communist party, died, the *Herald* and the *Observer* worked together for a memorial ceremony and a special issue. In my journal I talked of the death of communism. One million copies of that issue sold. The *Observer* was the first to be closed after the June Fourth crackdown. In the establishment papers I was named as the "mother of turmoil" and my long history of counterrevolution was described in detail.

I came to the United States in April of 1989, at the height of the democracy movement. Before I left, there was a memorial service for the death of Hu Yaobang, former general secretary of the Communist party. When I came out of the Great Hall of the People following the ceremony, I saw thousands of students shouting slogans of democracy. Between me and the students there was a wall of police. At that moment I composed a poem I later called "This Side and the Other." It is about a land divided by violence.

> On the one side there is the cold mountain
> On the other the warm waves of the ocean.
> On the one side is the body of Hu
> His soul is on the other side.

Three student representatives tried to cross the line to the other side to present their demands to the authorities. The police stopped them. At that moment I realized a new generation was coming to take control of China. I had sometimes been on the side of the old, but my heart was on the side of the young and the new.

I came to the United States to speak at a conference about the May Fourth movement. As I left China I somehow felt that I would not return. I am not sure how I knew, but being an old fighter and survivor who has been through much, I had a feeling I would not return. I came to New York by invitation of a dissident leader to discuss publication of a journal called *China, China*. On the morning of May 19 I received a number of messages from China. They all said, "Don't come back." I was supposed to go back to China on the twentieth. On the evening news I heard martial law was declared in China.

Suddenly I realized that I was no longer a visitor, a tourist. Once again I was in exile, once again I knew nothing about what was to become of me—what lay ahead. I had no place to live and no way to support myself. I had visited a Buddhist Temple in Los Angeles at the beginning of my trip. I decided to stay there until I found a way of handling my life. I stayed at the Buddhist Temple for a hundred days. I followed the upheaval and chaos in China on television. I spent the days thinking about the crisis in my life and in the life of my country. I had never thought I would live in a temple. But it was a good place for me to review my life and come to terms with my destiny. I realized that communism in China, like the Nationalist government before it, had reached a stage where it had alienated the entire population. I concluded that change is inevitable.

It is frightening to be without a home, without a country. But it is also fortunate, because for the first time in my life I can think freely. I have done much thinking about my life's ideal, which was communism. This century has been the century of communism. This hundred years of communism has also included my life span. In historical terms, it is a privilege to have witnessed the life and death of this movement. Sometimes I have thought that my whole life is a waste since its main cause has come to nothing. But I think it is never too late to gain wisdom, to learn. I look back to the day of joy on Tienanmen Square when I witnessed the birth of the People's Republic of China. I recall the day I saw the students rise up against the Republic when I observed the beginning of the process of its death. At the beginning I thought Marxism was good theoretically, but the implementation was faulty. But in time I realized that Marxism is like a religion. Its ideology is incapable of being realized. Marxism is a religion that means to rule. It is like the Christian Church in the Middle Ages that brought the Dark Ages to Europe. Communism brought the darkest age to China. During the reign of the emperors the country was ruled by dictators, but there was economic freedom. Marxism controls all spheres of public life; therefore, it is more oppressive.

I believe I have just begun a new adventure. In a way, these are the best days of my life. I have established a routine for myself. I wake at five o'clock in the morning. I write in my journal. I work on short stories and my autobiography in English. It is hard work learning to be comfortable in the new language and the new culture. But it gives me a sense of starting life all over again. I also write a monthly column for a Chinese language magazine published in Hong Kong. It is entitled "Letter from New York." In my column I write about things which interest me—a book I am reading, a conversation I have had, a current event of significance.

I have lunch at the Senior Center. I like the conversations I have there. I have a feeling of togetherness and I have a chance to practice my English and learn more about America. In the afternoons I go to English classes. My teacher is one of my best friends. She understands me very well in spite of the difficulties with language and our diverse cultural backgrounds and experiences.

After leaving the Center I go for a walk and buy a few things for my dinner. I have never been happier with my life. I carry no heavy burdens any more. I used to feel a heavyness that I helped the

Communist party. Now I have come to terms with myself. I think I have suffered so much that I have paid for all that. I helped this evil cause, but I paid in suffering and I am free of it all now. I feel no guilt. I am at peace with my past. I neither want anything nor struggle for anything. My efforts at learning are not a struggle, they are a joy.

Now my life is wonderful—much better than all my days in China. I have the four freedoms—to think, to go where I wish, to write what I want, and to read what I like. These are most precious to me. I am familiar with physical hardship, and my life now is luxurious compared to what I have experienced in the past. Of course I feel the pressure of not having money and not knowing what will happen tomorrow. But I can write freely and I have much to say.

It is not very often that I miss my country. I have cut my ties with China. I have nothing that connects me except my daughter. She called me from Beijing last week to tell me that once again I have been purged from the party. I laughed. I was surprized at my own reaction. Instead of anger and anxiety, I responded to the absurdity of the situation. I have disengaged myself from China today. Distancing myself from the public scene there has released me from tension and from want and fear.

I miss my family and friends. I feel sad for those who are in prison. But to me the important thing is that China will change. Even though I am old, I have so many things to do. Compared to many who live in China, I have the freedom to express and explore my ideas, and it is my duty to myself and to them to do that. As to the future, I never think of it. It is a habit from my past life. I can die anywhere, any time. I have a poem I wrote last year:

Another year in exile,
Happily I move to a new home,
Near the cemetery
My smile penetrates the tears,
I borrow this foreign place
And make it my country.

Each night as I lay myself down in my borrowed country I think of my birthplace and what might become of it. I worry about China. This system has changed my people. They have lost their initiative and energy. They have lost their will to transform their country. They have become lazy. After forty years my people have lost their capacity to survive on their own. They have given themselves up to the government. A society will move when its people wish it to. Communism has robbed the people of the will to change. My own case is a good example. If I were to live in China I would have a house, a job, a car, and no material worries. But I live here, with very little. I do my own chores and I feel useful. In China the government has robbed the people of this attitude.

America is not heaven. There is a lot wrong with it. But when I saw during the Gulf War people demonstrating against the government's policy, it made me tolerant of the shortcomings. Something like that could never have happened in China. When China was fighting Vietnam, people were arrested for thinking against the war. This society has tolerance for many different types of people so each individual can grow according to an inner model of goodness and humanity. In China the government creates a model of the good citizen and everyone is expected to fit the mold.

I see my life as a path toward death. I have no fear of my destination. If I walk straight and strong on that path, I will be satisfied that I have fulfilled my duty. I live alone, I cook Chinese food, I think what I wish, I write what I will, I talk to my new friends, I write to those who are still at home. The traditions of my native land are inside my head and I take pleasure in my life in my borrowed country.

# AZAR SALAMAT

# Of Chance and Choice

*It is not easy to arrange a time to record my friend Azar's narrative. She is selling an apartment, buying a town house, working on next year's budget for her project, and busying herself with the care and feeding of her children. But when we get together after our long day's work and have dinner with the children and go to her bedroom to sit on the floor with the tape recorder between us and get over the initial awkwardness of recounting a life story for me, much of which I have heard before and parts of which I have participated in, we begin in earnest. We are not convinced of the seriousness of our effort until her daughter Leila brings us a tray with teapot and cups and her son Ali follows with a plateful of cookies. It is going to be "our story," they say. We believe in the project when they begin to.*

*Azar is a mixture of strength and vulnerability, vehemence and softness, world weariness and innocence. She has gone through extremes of suffering and loss, she has survived. It is a wonder that she contains so much energetic joy in life. Yet she partakes of the luxury of whining from time to time. She doesn't take her role as a tragic heroine very seriously.*

*I remember sitting at my dining room table convulsed with grief that she was in hiding with her little daughter somewhere in Tehran and that chances were they would be caught. I had a photograph of* the fat little girl with brown hair and twinkling blue eyes and two small front teeth showing in a laugh of pleasant surprise. I couldn't erase this picture from my mind or the thought of what they would do to her were they to capture her with her mother. After days and nights of coded messages on the phone and interrupted calls and second-hand rumors, she was finally smuggled out and flown to Washington. Pan American had had a change in terminal and my husband had gone to check the gate and had run into them. Leila's first contact with the United States was the sight of a huge stuffed pink panther. She told my husband she didn't have a pink panther, and so they walked toward us, Leila carrying with some difficulty the ugly stuffed animal a foot taller than herself.

That night she began telling me the story which she was to tell me again after eight years. Having belonged to the opposite side of the ideological battle, I was so full of anger, disbelief, affection, and many other conflicting emotions that I had not listened to the actual story the first time. I had been preoccupied with the paradox of a ten-year-old girl's leaving a feudal Iranian household to grow into a Marxist adolescent in Berkeley, California.

The passage of time has softened everything, making events seem hazy like a photograph taken through a filtered lens. Azar is no longer a Marxist. She no longer has a husband in prison, whose love connected her like a thread to a dark spot on the opposite side of the earth, staking a claim on every cell of her body. And I am no longer torn between resentment and care for the man who changed my friend's life along with his own and brought her to the edge of destruction—a man she loved with the recklessness of a life lived in recognition and acceptance of death.

This year for the first time she forgot the anniversary of his death. But he will be a constant presence in her life because to her own ties and memories are added Leila's remembrances of her father and Ali's efforts to collect every story, sign, and image that helps him imagine the father he never saw.

We are all wiser now. We are all less likely to put our faith in large, violent movements that promise us utopias. We have come to believe in the tea tray the children have brought and the importance of stories told and understood.

I WAS BORN in the city of Kerman to a landed family. As a child I was sometimes pampered and often ignored. Our household was a large one. My uncle lived next door and there was much coming and going between the cousins and relatives and the household servants. The only person who was consistently served and seen to was my father. The others, especially the children, were focused upon only when they were sick in bed. The rest of the time they had more or less to fend for themselves.

Meals were elaborate affairs to which much care and attention were given. But the schedule did not correspond to the body clock of small children. Lunch was at 2:00 P.M., and dinner at 10:00. Long white cloths were spread on the lush carpets. Huge round trays were carried from the kitchen in the opposite side of the front yard, up the stairs to the dining room. Numerous dishes of saffron rice, meat and vegetable stews, fresh herbs and cheese and bread were placed in the middle of the *sofreh,* the large rectangular white cloth spread across the room. A host of people sat around and ate in industrious silence. Conversation was generally discouraged. Children were not allowed to eat with the elders until they were of school age. My brother and I ate our dinner at 7:00 P.M. in our room. I was slow and unfocused during meals. My brother was deft at swiping choice morsels off my plate. I didn't care much, but nanny became furious, often chasing him around the room after each such attempt.

My father was a distant figure with whom there was little contact and no conversation. My mother moved about in beautiful robes, smelling of powder and perfume, a bundle of keys to various storage trunks and closets tinkling in her pocket. She hugged and kissed me at least once a day and went about the business of running the household and seeing to my father's needs. We did not see much of either of our parents until we were in school.

I remember little else of my childhood except that one day mother was not there any more, and soon after I was in Tehran living in a two-room apartment with my grandmother. Life changed drastically after my parents were separated and my mother left for the United States. My grandmother earned her living as a dressmaker. The living room of the apartment was filled with sewing machines, yards of fabric, and other paraphernalia of tailoring. Our bedroom was used as a dressing room where the fittings took place. My schoolbooks were often mislaid under piles of material. More often than not I had hysteric fits in the mornings searching frantically for my homework before leaving for school.

When I returned in the afternoons, I sat in the corner with a cup of tea and bread or a cookie and watched and listened to my grandmother's customers discussing their lives, their husbands, and the affairs of the neighborhood. They sat around the room, leaning against the wall with their veils falling about them on the floor, drinking tea and laughing. I played with buttons and pieces of lace and was sometimes made much of by the women.

My mother arranged for me to go to her in 1958. I was ten. My adolescence was spent in Monterey, California, during a period of political and cultural change in the United States. I was untouched by the various currents, which began at Berkeley and quickly carried over to the small, artistic community of Monterey, only two hours away. I played the piano, listened to classical music, read victorian novels, and felt out of place. During my high school years I struggled to fit into the social scene of my peer group and failed. I was never quite thin enough, my hair never straight enough, my outlook never close enough to the prevailing standards, and the standards, even when they stressed nonconformity, were strictly observed.

In 1968 my father sent me a ticket to go to Iran for the summer. The trip to Iran crystallized my emotions and focused my need to belong. I had left Iran when I was ten and was returning ten years later. I had lost contact with my family, spoke Persian awkwardly, did not recognize the city's structure and spaces. But I felt a sense of belonging as if I had always lived there. The emotional attachment grew into feelings of nationalism that affected my life in the years to come. I was somehow made whole by the realization that this was home and what happened here mattered to me.

On my return from Iran I enrolled at Berkeley. For the first time in my life I was entirely on my own. The Northern California Chapter of the Iranian Student Association was located in the city of Berkeley. The association was a traditional student network, organizing Iranian students to participate in various social activities, including *Noruz* (the Persian New Year) and other festivities. But by the midsixties, it was transformed into a primarily political organization.

During the first phase, many groups and shapes of thinking were represented within the organization. The atmosphere was open and lenient. There were the Nationalists and Muslims as well as groups belonging to various lines within the left, from the followers of Che Guevara to the disciples of Mao Tse Tung, working closely together in unity.

The first day I walked into the university cafeteria, some two dozen Iranian students were sitting around a long table laughing and talking in Persian. They accepted me among them without hesitation, my being Persian the only passport needed. It was like a club. If one needed a job, an apartment, a paper for a class there was always someone to help. It was a natural bonding of foreign people who shared a language and culture. I plunged into the life of the community with great zest. All my friends, activities, plans came from within this close-knit network.

What drew me to the Association at the beginning was more the comraderie than the political cause. The passion for the cause came much later for me. But by then the organization had lost its spirit of tolerance, and I had left mine somewhere behind as well. It seems that passion and tolerance, like water and oil, don't mix.

In the summer of 1970 I was elected secretary for international relations. Having lived in the United States since childhood, I had a better command of English than the others and I could make speeches, write articles, and hold press conferences. We worked tirelessly, sometimes going days with little sleep. I learned a great deal during this period. I gained self confidence and a certain boldness, strength and stamina. I don't think I could have handled my later trials as a survivor without my experience first as a Berkeley radical, later as a political activist.

I met Hormoz, my future husband, during my last year at Berkeley in 1970. That summer, we worked closely together and soon had established a relationship of comradeship, love, and respect, but five years passed before we decided to marry. For many years marriage and even relationships were thought bourgeois in the Association.

At the beginning the Association had been basically a healthy gathering of students who gave each other support and emotional sustenance. But gradually the professional revolutionaries pushed everyone toward radicalism, using the theoretical framework of the far left. The gatherings became more and more regimented. The activities and norms of social conduct and the parameters of politically correct thinking were carefully mapped out. Membership in the group brought with it a lifestyle with a strict and Spartan code of conduct, requiring considerable discipline and self-sacrifice. A large number of women were members of the organization, but they were involved in operational activities and not in theoretical work. They soon became militant, vocal, independent people, but never the analytical backbone of any of the groups.

The Association of Iranian Students had some sixty or seventy branches at various universities. It concentrated entirely on lobbying the American opinion makers—the media, the professors at the universities, the liberal intellectual community. Gradually we learned to use more extreme methods of drawing attention to our activities. Once a group of us chained ourselves to the Statue of Liberty. Another time we held a continuous, forty-eight-hour vigil outside the Iranian consulate in Chicago during the severest winter in years. Often we organized long marches between cities. Gradually the media came to believe in the harshness of conditions in Iran, for how else could this kind of sustained and dedicated protest be explained? But the extent of our exposure depended a great deal on the workings of the pressure groups inside the U.S. government. There were those who were for and those who were against the regime in Iran, and the attention we received on any given issue or event seemed to us to depend also on the inner workings of these groups.

The Iranian revolution took us by surprise. Although we had been consumed by the thought of the revolution, we did not believe that it would happen, at least not while we were still young enough to participate in it. When it did happen, the beginning and the end came in such rapid succession that all we could do was watch and predict and comment, much like political pundits commenting on events. The last year before the February uprising in Iran, the Association's activities basically revolved around keeping up with events in Iran and reporting them to the students abroad. But most of all our time was spent preparing students to go back to join the revolution. As students left for Iran, others, overtaken by the revolutionary atmosphere, took their place. Four thousand students gathered in the Oakland Auditorium for the last congress of the Association. A few months after that congress, the organization was disbanded, overtaken by events.

After the congress, I left for Europe. Hormoz stayed behind to oversee the disbanding of the Association. Along with the euphoria of the impending victory of the revolution, I was already harboring deep doubts about my place in the movement and in the revolutionary organization I belonged to. During the late 1970s the divisions in the left had deepened because of the growing influence of revolutionary groups inside Iran and the confusion permeating the international Marxist movement. The failure of the Cultural Revolution had become apparent, and Mao Tse Tung's line of Marxism had ended in defeat with the arrest of the Gang of Four. The shah's leadership position in OPEC and China's support of his role presented us with a dilemma. It seemed to me that we had lost, both ideologically and politically. Others held similar views. Many left the movement to return to Iran to work and lead normal lives. We claimed that they had become passive, afraid, bourgeois. I didn't want to seem passive, so I tried to convince myself that our actions still made sense.

In February 1979, about a week after the revolution, I went to Iran—my first trip back in ten years and my second since I left Iran at age ten. All borders, including the airports, were closed during the first days of the revolution. A group of us were stranded in Germany. So we did what we knew best. We protested, and it worked. Khomeini sent a plane for us. On the flight back, we were jubilant, singing revolutionary songs and celebrating. But as soon as the plane touched down in Iran, our divisions and differences became apparent. The Muslim students left the plane chanting "Long live the Islamic revolution." We walked out shouting "Long live freedom and liberty."

The Revolutionary Guards controlled the airport, which was closed to commercial air traffic. It was clear from the beginning that they favored the Muslim students, joining them in chanting Islamic slogans. The lines of friendship and animosity were drawn as soon as we left the plane. When we disembarked, many of my friends who had been away for many years knelt down and kissed the ground while all around them bearded youth with machine guns, shouted a cacaphony of slogans. Within four years from that day, all but one of my friends who came with me on that plane were dead.

Now that I was in Tehran I had to go somewhere. In that atmosphere of chaos and excitement I hadn't even thought of where I would live. I didn't want to go to my family or my husband's. I went with my cousin Asieh to her in-laws' house. In that unreal atmosphere it didn't seem out of place to go to the home of someone you had never seen before and sort of settle in. I stayed there for a month. I didn't contact my father or my husband's parents. The revolution took priority over all ties and relationships. There were demonstrations every day. I tried to go to as many as possible. Within days I found a job teaching English, but soon found that going to work interfered with participating in the flurry of activities following the revolution.

This was an exciting time in Tehran. At every street corner someone was speaking from a soapbox. All groups were involved in feverish activity. There was complete freedom coming from chaos and absence of civic control. New newspapers appeared every day expressing every sort of viewpoint. People were caught up in the momentum. Everyone was hopeful and everything seemed possible. I felt exhilarated, swimming in the sea of popular emotion and hope and loving every moment of it. Hormoz had arrived and we had begun for the first time to have an almost normal married life together.

The political situation became gradually more harsh as the months passed. The Islamic elements began to solidify their power and eliminate their opponents by carefully identifying and arresting members of each organized group, breaking one or more of them under torture and making them reveal names and locations of others and then picking up everyone in one fell swoop. Executions became a daily occurrence. The press came under strict control. Khomeini—who had gone to the religious city of Qom, leaving the government in the hands of a secular but conservative government—returned to Tehran and took control of the day-to-day affairs of the country. Persecution of women began in earnest. After a momentary retreat in the face of the first demonstrations by women against the dress code and the nullification of the Family Protection Law, the government began to clamp down on all such protest with savage force. Women demonstrators were beaten, imprisoned, and tortured. The revolution was turning monstrous and grotesque.

Politically the leftist groups were losing their grasp. Many began to realize how badly they had misinterpreted the conditions in Iran and how removed they were from the working classes. One day during the early days of the revolution we were at a large demonstration of factory workers. At the end of the demonstration, a few of us

stayed behind to talk to the workers about the importance of continuing the revolution until we had achieved a true democracy. They
listened politely, but as we turned to leave, one of them called to us,
waving his hand. "Bye bye," he said in English grinning with amusement. Nothing seemed to express more clearly the foreignness of our
contingent to those workers whom we had thought our natural allies.

In the meantime the government's relentless suppression of all
opposition made it impossible for us to interact or to begin to build a
base. Almost every group was touched by the repression; many had
been completely rounded up and destroyed. Of those remaining,
some disbanded of their own accord; many of their members left the
country. Political differences that had begun in the two years before
the revolution became more profound after the revolution, further
splintering our group.

Only the ones who allowed themselves no doubts, no second
thoughts, remained. These were our best recruits. They were carrying
out the strictest directives of the leadership. They remained loyal and
faithful to the group and to the ideology.

By this time I had lost my faith in Marxism. I could no longer
support our political positions. It was easier for me to shift, to
distance myself. But for Hormoz it was very difficult. I could feel that
he was no longer a believer but a prisoner of the mindset he had
helped to create. He was one of the leaders who had helped radicalize
the group. He had motivated others to become "revolutionaries,"
unbending, unafraid, and unchanging. And now he had to stand up
to the young radicals and face their contempt. He knew they would
interpret the change in him as loss of courage, as choosing of the
personal above the cause. They would consider him a cop-out. He
had taught them to think this way, and so he wavered and waited, not
willing to save himself alone, not able to save the others, his mind in
terrible turmoil.

Within the narrow circle of our family and friends, however, we
lived a charmed existence. I was involved in establishing a language
school. Finding Hormoz with little to do except rediscover his family
and his aptitude for crafts and carpentry, I relished every moment of
my newfound domestic tranquility. Our daughter Leila was now an
energetic two year old. I was pregnant with my second child. We read
and talked and listened to music and watched the latest American

films on video, which, strangely enough, were regularly smuggled into Iran. We took very little security precaution for a group fast becoming one of the priority targets for the regime. Some evenings when there was no video to watch we would get together with a group of friends and each act out a whole film for the others. We laughed mindlessly at someone's depiction of *Manhattan;* we were excited and frightened by a rendering of *Psycho.*

I was very happy with my life, but also constantly afraid. At the end of each day I would breathe easier and say to myself, "Another day and no disaster." At the beginning of each day the thought crossed my mind that this may be the last day of peace and safety.

Then one faction of our organization, noting the growing opposition to the regime and the armed struggle of the *Mujahedin* that led to President Bani Sadr's ouster and exile, decided that the time was ripe for overt opposition. They developed a scenario that called for a small group of armed guerrillas to take over a northern town and hold it long enough for waves of resistance to form, leading to a national uprising. The town of Amol by the Caspian was chosen for this extraordinary plan. It took months of discussion among the members to come to a final decision to adopt this plan of action. During this period many, among them Hormoz and I, declared their opposition to the plan. But we were met with disdain from the radical faction. Hormoz was called a coward and an opportunist by the very people who once circled around to hear him speak. The cacophony of name-calling made Hormoz more reluctant to reach a decision about his political future. I am not sure whether he resigned from the leadership or was put aside, but he no longer held a leadership position. He was still not ready to quit.

By January the team was ready. They had moved weapons, tents, and food supplies to the forests near Amol; they had lived and trained there for more than six months without being detected.

The attack took place on January 25, 1982. Some one hundred members of the Union of Communists attacked the headquarters of the police and the guards in Amol and continued to fight for fifteen hours. Then reinforcements came for the guards. Many members of the group were killed and many others captured. The leaders had planned for the attack, but not for retreat. They could not afford to contemplate potential defeat.

There was no news of the event in the media. We heard about what had happened by word of mouth, through some who managed to survive and get back to Tehran. What we should have done at this point was to declare a state of emergency and disband the union. We had people in prison under torture. It was obvious that at any moment someone would break and reveal our names and whereabouts. Those who had been against the plan, including Hormoz, felt that leaving the group now would be abandoning their friends during a time of crisis. So we continued our lives as before. Like a sparrow confronting a cobra, we were paralyzed.

As time passed, our fears were numbed. We celebrated *Noruz*, the spring festival, marking the beginning of the Persian New Year. We went about the business of life with perhaps a bit more gusto and energy than usual, but with no conscious recognition of impending disaster. We watched the mullahs on television, we laughed at their vulgarity, their crassness and stupidity. But even though we were looking at them from the vantage point of our Western upbringing, which made them appear even more ludicrous, we thought of them as ours to deal with, our problem. This feeling of belonging to a society, identifying with it in spite of its faults, is something I have never felt before or after this period. I have never again been a participant in the life of a nation.

I did not discuss Hormoz's relationship with the organization with him. I had made my decision to resign from the organization freely, without pressure and wanted him to do the same. I wanted him to leave the country with me willingly and without guilt. I wanted him to come to terms with his pride. One Friday morning we were having breakfast and Leila was playing on the floor next to us. We had just heard of the Revolutionary Guards breaking into yet another house and slaughtering a whole family including the children. I said to Hormoz, "Have you thought of what will happen to her if we are taken in?" He said nothing and we prepared to go to his sister's house in Karaj for our pleasant weekly outing.

One day, about six months after the Amol attack, he finally asked me to contact a relative whose brother had been smuggled out of Iran. He wanted to know how he had gotten out and who his contacts were. That day I was supposed to meet him at lunchtime at his mother's house. He was going to a meeting, one of few that he attended from time to time after the Amol incident. They were getting ready to organize a council meeting to decide on the fate of the organization. As I was leaving to go to my class, I saw him at the window with his back to me. He looked still and somehow vulnerable. There was only a sheet of glass between him and the dangers outside. I felt a dull pain in the pit of my stomach. I hugged him from behind, kissed the back of his neck, and said good-bye.

At noon as I walked to his mother's house, I went over all the things I had to tell him. My day was never complete until I had recounted everything for him. That day more students had registered for the language school I was planning to set up. Our plans seemed about to be realized. I sensed that he was getting close to making his decision. It was a hot summer day and I was heavy with my seven-month pregnancy. But I felt light and happy, walking briskly, smiling at my own shadow.

We waited lunch for him but he didn't come. At three o'clock, Fatemeh, Hormoz's younger sister and I took his parents to the bus station. They were going to the Shrine of Imam Reza in Meshed. We came back and still no news of him. I began to worry. He always called if he was going to be late. He knew how anxious I would be. I thought perhaps his meeting had taken too long, and seeing that he might miss the finals of the World Cup soccer games he had stopped by a friend's house nearby to watch it. We went with Fatemeh to buy summer uniforms, which by then had become mandatory for women. We came back and still no news. The game was long since over. By six o'clock I decided to go back to our apartment thinking there might be news of him there. Fatemeh said she would water the plants at her parents' and join me soon. It was not like him to be safe and not to call.

The apartment was a mess. I thought to myself I ought to be picking up and cleaning the place, but I couldn't move. I sat on the floor and stared at the carpet and waited. Leila was humming to herself as she put her doll to sleep near me. At eight o'clock, I decided something was definitely wrong. Fatemeh had said, "Go home and I will follow." It had been two hours and she had not come. I took Leila's hand, threw a chador over my head and walked to the nearest telephone booth. I dialed Hormoz's parents home. The phone rang and rang and there was no answer. As I was about to hang up

Fatemeh picked up. She was breathing hard. Before I could ask any questions, she said, "Oh, everything is okay, there is no problem. The brothers are here. You go on to your mother's. There is no problem, I'll talk to you later," and she hang up. I remember holding the phone and thinking, "It's all over." I clutched the phone and said, "I love you Hormoz, and I will never see you again, good-bye, my love, I will never see you again."

I felt calm. I felt my face was made of stone. I put the receiver down, turned around and walked out of the booth. No tears came. I kept murmuring, "You are my world and they will kill you and I will never see you again." I walked back to the apartment and thought, "The house is so messy, I wish I had time to clean it." Then I thought, "What should I take?" "Documents, I have to get all the documents." I mumbled to myself. I went through the drawers, grabbing whatever documents I thought might be of use—passports, birth certificates, Hormoz's green card, my college transcripts. I put them and a few clothes for Leila in a plastic bag. I clutched Leila's hand and pulled her with me out of the house.

I walked around Vanak square with my plastic bag full of documents, dragging the child, almost lifting her off her feet. She looked up at me smiling, thinking I was playing a game. It was *Ramadan,* the Muslim month of fasting. The streets were filled with people taking a summer stroll after *eftar,* the breaking of the fast. "What shall I do? Where shall I go?" I thought. Our apartment was on Vanak Square, a very busy part of Northern Tehran. The main road going through the square passed straight up to Evin, the political prison, so there were always Revolutionary Guard patrol cars passing through Vanak. I knew they would be looking for me. I had to get out of the area quickly.

Hormoz's cousin lived nearby, so I decided to walk to her apartment. I reached the apartment as she and her husband were leaving. I told them what had happened and asked them if they would go to my in-laws' to find more information. They took me to her mother's and left for Hormoz's parents apartment. The mother was visibly frightened to have me there. It was very dangerous to harbor a fugitive. But she didn't say anything, gave me tea, and tried to comfort me.

At midnight, the cousin came back with Fatemeh. It was amazing that they had not taken her. She described what had happened. After

I left, the door bell rang. She had asked through the intercom who it was. Hormoz had asked her to open the door, saying, "The brothers are with me." She had laughed thinking he is joking. But when she opened the door, she saw him coming up the stairs with his hands tied behind his back and two bearded men with machine guns following him.

They had searched the house. It was Ramadan and long past the time of *eftar*. Fatemeh had offered the guards food and water but they had refused. Hormoz had asked for water. Since his hands were tied, she had to help him drink. He whispered to her to tell me to go to my mother in America and to warn the others. Then the woman living upstairs had heard the commotion and had come down. And then the cousins I had sent came in pretending they had come to pay a visit. For a strange hour, they had all sat around the room, silently, while the guards waited for me to arrive. We kept extra clothing and a crib for Leila at her grandparents', where she often stayed. So the guards believed we actually lived there. When I didn't show up at eleven they left with Hormoz.

That night Fatemeh and I stayed up all night. We didn't talk. I lay wide awake in the July heat and stared at my pregnant belly. It took all my energy to keep out the thought that Hormoz was being tortured. We had been told that severest torture takes place during the first three days when prisoners are in a state of shock from the arrest. I knew that if I didn't block out the image of Hormoz being tortured I would not be able to hold myself together. So I didn't talk for fear I would lose the concentration I needed to control my thoughts.

The next days we planned how we would warn the others and I tried to find a place to stay. Wherever I stayed a problem came up. In one place the guards took over the house across the street. In another, they kept getting suspicious phone calls. One family's daughter herself was in hiding. I went through the list of friends who were not targets themselves very quickly. Finally I thought of a family friend who had a secluded garden in Evin, a suburb of Tehran, where Evin prison was also located. I sent word that I needed a place to stay and she answered that I would be welcome.

It was strange to be in that beautiful garden with its ancient oak trees and the stream passing through the peaceful landscape. The garden was a wall away from the Evin prison compound, where

Hormoz and my friends were being held. Fewer than a thousand feet separated us. Every morning at dawn the loud speaker in the prison yard blared out the morning call to prayer, followed by the lectures and organized chants of the prisoners. The sound shook the house. Every morning at dawn I walked to the wall at the bottom of the garden to listen to the chants of the prisoners. I thought if I listened carefully I would be able to distinguish Hormoz's voice among all the others'. I thought if I concentrated enough he would feel my presence nearby. I refused to think of torture. I refused to think that Hormoz would probably not be among those prisoners.

I wanted to stay in Tehran, at least until my baby was born and Hormoz's fate became clear. But each day, it became more evident that I could not. There was nowhere safe for me to hide for long. If I were to leave, I had to do so as soon as possible, before I became too big to travel. We contacted the same smugglers that had smuggled my friend's brother out of Iran. They assured us that it was a short passage across the Turkish border; it would take no more than twelve hours, and we would go by jeep. About a month after Hormoz's arrest, we completed our arrangements to leave Iran. My brother-in-law Hassan, his sister Fatemeh, his wife Simin, their baby Mina, Leila and I set out on the journey.

We met the smugglers in Tabriz. Thinking our journey a short car ride across the border, we had brought suitcases. The leader of the smugglers was a tall, rugged Kurd with a handlebar moustache. He took us to his house, where we were told we had to spend the night. He wanted our passports, for safekeeping, he assured us. But we didn't trust him knowing how valuable passports were in the black market. We refused, and to make sure they wouldn't steal them from us during the night, we tied the passports under my pregnant belly. We were told that we could travel only after dusk. So the next day we had to kill time until sundown. We went to a park outside the city and spread our things as though we and the smugglers were a family out on a picnic. With a small child and a baby, the scene looked credible.

At dusk we all packed into a car, thinking that we were on our way. But after a short distance, the smugglers stopped the car and told us to get out. They told us that we had to run across a plowed field to meet the guides who were going to take us across. It was then that we learned that our journey was to be on horseback. We ran for forty minutes before reaching the other smugglers; Hassan carried Leila, Simin carried her baby, and Fatemeh and I carried what we had kept of our belongings. We rode two on a horse—a smuggler in front and one of us behind him holding on to his waist. Leila sat in front of one of the smugglers. Simin carried the baby. We put our belongings in gunny sacks, which we draped behind the saddle. Because I sat behind the rider, I was forced to stretch my legs across the top of the gunny sacks, which left my belly touching the rump of the horse. Every step the horse took brought pressure on my belly. I soon lost all feeling in my legs which were sticking out over the gunny sacks.

We rode all night. The terrain became more rugged as we passed the Kurdish mountains. Some passages were no wider than two feet, where the horses had to set one hoof in front of the other, moving precariously at the edge of a precipice. I kept asking them to stop to let me stretch my legs, but they wouldn't. At dawn I told them that if they didn't stop I would throw myself down. Finally they stopped. I couldn't move my legs to get off. Two smugglers had to lift me off the horse and set me down. Fatemeh and Simin rubbed my legs until I could move them again.

Soon after, we reached a village where we were to spend the day. We could only travel at night, so we started at dusk and stopped at dawn. We spent the day in a dark, smoke-filled stable, where the only light was a hole in the ceiling. The stable was home not only to the animals but also to the family that owned them. So in reality the family had put us up in their home. We couldn't complain. We fell exhausted on the filthy mattresses that lined the wall of the stable.

The next evening, I insisted on a horse of my own, which after much quarreling, I got. As we reached a mountain top through the narrow path that snaked upward at the edge of a cliff, I thought of the nearness of death. A slip and one could easily roll down into the valley. I put my faith in the horse. It was a strange feeling to have no control over one's life. The smugglers could do anything they wanted with us. We moved in that twilight area at the edge of the law. No country wanted us. No country was responsible for us. We had no protectors. They could turn us over to the police on either side of the border.

Throughout all this, Leila was no trouble. She kept quiet almost instinctively. But the baby was only five months old and at times cranky. We were passing numerous checkpoints and had to keep her quiet. Simin, in desperation, gave her valium to make her sleep. She was holding the baby in one arm and holding on to the smuggler in front of her with the other. At one point she felt her arm getting numb and she was afraid she would let the baby slip out of it. I used my scarf to tie the baby to her arm for the rest of the journey.

Finally we were told we were entering Turkey. It was painful to look back at the Iranian landscape, knowing I might never return to it, knowing also that I was leaving my husband behind.

At every step the smugglers had wanted more money. Each time we had refused, reminding them that we had already paid them handsomely. When we reached the Turkish side, the smugglers changed, and with them their tactics for getting money. We were still only at the halfway point and needed them to get us to Van, the nearest safe village. The new smugglers, however, seemed more like roadway bandits, threatening and sinister. They stole what little of our belongings we still had, and at one point they abandoned us at the roadside, along flat, desert terrain that seemed to stretch forever. Their plan was to frighten us to submission so that they could get what money we had. We, on the other hand, not fully realizing the danger we were in, refused to be threatened. The distance from the Turkish border to Van, a few hours' car ride under normal circumstances, became the most dangerous part of our journey.

Without food, drink, or shade, the baby and Leila soon faced dehydration. In desperation, Simin, an Azarbaijani Turk who spoke Azari Turkish, and I set out to find help. We flagged down a passing van. The driver and his passenger told us they were heading to a nearby village on government business. On their way back, if we still had not found help, they would try to help us. Apparently one of the smugglers had seen us talking to the occupants of the van. A few hours later they returned, afraid that they would be caught for smuggling illegal aliens into Turkey. From this point, however, they made us walk. They told us that to avoid the checkpoints, we had to get off the roads. We had to walk at rapid pace in the dark through overgrown paths and across numerous hills. Leila, a heavy child, had to be carried. Fatemeh and Hassan took turns carrying her. Once, when I was carrying the baby, Simin fell flat on her face from exhaustion, asleep before she had hit the ground. I kept slapping her face to keep her awake. We walked for hours. Once I slipped on a rocky hillside and rolled on my belly all the way down. In the middle of the night, after we had passed our last checkpoint, the smugglers who had lost hope of getting more money, abandoned us again. We were still hours from Van.

Confident that we were now far away from checkpoints, we decided to head for the highway. But we didn't know where it was or which way was Van. We took our chances and headed toward the sound of trucks passing. At six o'clock in the morning, we finally reached the outskirts of Van. We must have looked a sorry sight. Our clothes were torn and dirty; we could barely walk, and out of habit formed of our recent trek through the mountains, we walked single file, one behind the other, like the remnants of a ragtag army.

We found rooms in a small, shabby hotel. I sat on the iron bed in the empty room. I lowered my head on the pillow, closed my eyes and fell asleep. Suddenly I woke up feeling I had stopped breathing. I tried to open the door, but it was locked from the outside. Simin, thinking I was asleep, had locked the door behind her when she had gone downstairs. I became hysterical. I banged on the door, shouting for someone to let me out. People must have heard and fetched Simin. That moment was the closest I came to breaking down. It marked the beginning of my life in exile.

I arrived in the United States on August 30, 1982. I spent the first months at my mother's apartment in Monterey, California. I busied myself with furious activity. I wrote letters, I made phone calls to Iran. I tried to get all the necessary cards—social security, driver's license, library card. I found a childcare center for Leila and began attending word-processing classes at the local high school. I tried not to disrupt my mother's life too much.

When I arrived in Monterey, many of my friends had already returned to the United States, some across one of Iran's borders, as I had, some, legally. But I was more fortunate than most of them. Having been raised in the States, I felt comfortable with its ways. I spoke the language and knew how to get about. Most important, I had family here—my mother, my sister and her husband, and my brother. Each one helped me in a special way. My brother helped get me out of Turkey, my mother gave me shelter and love as only a mother can, my sister gave me emotional strength and set standards that pushed me forward, even when I didn't think I could go any further.

My son Ali was born on September 25. By that time, the government had announced the arrest of the Amol group and families were given permission to visit the prisoners. Hormoz had learned that I had arrived safely in the United States and that we had a son. The weeks that had passed had dulled my sense of the impending doom. Slowly I gained hope. First the prisoners had been allowed visitors, who reported that Hormoz and his comrades were well. Then I began hoping that they would not be tried for a while and in the meantime the regime would fall. Finally, I hoped that Hormoz's jailors would be bribed. We were led to believe that if money were paid to the right people, they would see to it that the prisoners were somehow smuggled out of prison and eventually out of the country. It was wishful thinking of course. Reason told me not to expect anything. But reason had nothing to do with the state of my mind. I busied myself with raising money to bribe the jailors.

The trial took place six months after the arrest of the Amol group. It was a circus. The officials had packed a large hall with relatives of the guards who had fought or been killed in Amol. The walls of the hall were draped with slogans against the defendants, who were seated on a stage facing the rowdy crowd that shouted insults at them and demanded their execution. They were not allowed a lawyer. The judge was the notorious mullah that had earned the title of "hanging judge." The charges were the same for everyone: *mofsed-e-fel-arz* (corrupt of the earth), *mohareb-e-ba-khoda* (fighting against God), and, worst of all, cooperation with the Great Satan, the United States.

The group all used the same defense. They confessed that they were communists and that they had worked against the Islamic Republic. They went on to say that their actions were wrong and had undermined the revolution. Their trial took three weeks and they were all condemned to death.

Even after the sentence was announced I continued to hope. My mother kept Leila with her and sent me and Ali to my sister in Washington. She couldn't bear to be with me if the news of the execution were to come. On January 24, the day before the anniversary of the Amol uprising, my sister and I went to Clyde's in Georgetown for lunch. We knew that following their own weird psychological blueprint, the government would most likely show its clout by executing the perpetrators on the anniversary of the uprising. We passed the hours and even minutes as if we were listening to a countdown. People were eating and watching the Superbowl on television. The whole place was feverish with excitement. I felt so alien. The world with which my life was interwoven and the world in which I found myself were far apart.

The morning of the twenty-fifth arrived. This was the day I had assumed the execution would take place. The day came and passed and no news reached us. The next day, my sister went to work. I was feeding Ali. The phone rang. My brother-in-law answered. The conversation seemed clipped and short. He left. Half an hour later, I heard my sister coming up the stairs. Tears were streaming down her face. I thought something had happened to one of her friends. I thought my mother had been in an accident. I thought of everything except Hormoz. I asked, "Why are you crying?" She looked at me a moment. I realized she was crying for me. I tried to get up. I noticed Ali's bottle had slipped out of his mouth. I reached for the bottle and slipped it back in his mouth. This was the first of many moments when the needs of the baby in his self-contained obliviousness dragged me away from my reality. Even my most spontaneous reaction to grief became studied and slowed to take account of his immediate requirements.

The baby was taken away. I was given a tranquilizer. I had depended so much on Hormoz's presence. The days became real only when I had recounted every detail of my experiences to him each evening. But part of the experience of losing him involved carrying alone the burden of raising and supporting the children, a burden that would not allow me my time of mourning.

In the next months I moved to Berkeley, an area I knew well from my days at the university. Every street and every corner held a memory, not only with Hormoz, but with many of my friends who had been killed with him. I asked a friend who had a print shop to give me a job. I worked with him for nine months, during which time I learned about printing. I didn't know it at the time, but the experience would help me enter the field of publishing when I moved to Washington, D.C., in the fall of 1984. I had many friends in Berkeley, but most of them were battle-scarred like me, having lost family members, friends, and belongings. They were going through their own period of adjustment, their own state of shock and mourning. No one had time for others.

I lugged the baby to a childcare center. I took Leila to a nursery school, and then I went to work. Just getting them dressed and their supplies packed for the day took two hours each morning. It took another two hours to get them back home in the evenings.

In a year my mother retired and we moved to Washington, D.C. I found a job as an editor. Slowly, I learned the necessary skills to move up in my field. I had to care for my children, learn a profession, and earn enough money to support my family. Not only had I lost my husband but also my closest friends and colleagues. One night when I was going through my album with Leila, I realized that almost every one she asked about had been killed.

Leila and Ali ask often about their father. I don't know if I have ever given them satisfactory answers. I only know that I had to give them the details in stages. A few weeks ago, Ali, who just turned eleven, wrote a poem that ended with these lines:

My dad is gone,
For reasons I don't know.
All I know is that it had to do with war
What would this world be like without war?
A world with peace? I don't know.
All I know is that there would be one more in the family.

Eleven years have passed. During this time, I have learned and grown and found a new identity for myself. I have found great faith in my own capacity to transcend almost any hardship and to survive. I have seen my women friends become the pillars that hold up the other members of their families, lending support to their husbands' search for a new identity while restructuring their own. I have had the loneliness of making all of life's decisions on my own. The experience has hardened me. But it has also made me self-reliant. I have grown as a person. I have searched within myself for every ounce of initiative, every resource, every strength in order to empower myself not only to survive but to become whole for my children. I am proud of what I have been able to accomplish. My children are attending good schools and are cheerful, friendly, and optimistic people. I have a successful career. I am not bitter about the past. I think of my years of political struggle not from the vantage point of the tragedy that ended them but from that of the idealism and comraderie which marked our goals and our relationships.

I have come to appreciate the United States in ways I never knew before. The fact that in a few years I was able to own a home, establish myself in a profession, raise two healthy, happy children has proved to me that the American myth has a certain reality. But I have yet to feel completely at home here. Even though I understand the different political personalities and relate to their positions much more easily, I have yet to see them on television and feel the way I did when I heard the mullahs present their absurdities. But I also feel distant from Iran. I no longer feel the texture of the society. I have retained my ethnic identity and nowhere do I realize it more than in my children's clear identification of themselves as Iranian Americans. But I can no longer feel actively involved in what goes on there. My plans for the future do not include the Persian landscape.

# ALICIA PARTNOY

# They Cut Off My Voice,
# So I Grew Two Voices

They cut off my voice
So I grew two voices
into different tongues
my songs I pour
They cut off my voice so I grew two voices
in two different tongues
my songs I pour
They took away my sun
Two brand new suns
like resplendent drums I am playing
Today I am playing

*Alicia was sitting on the steps to her small row house in the Adams Morgan neighborhood in Washington. She was talking in Spanish to a neighbor who held a typewritten manuscript in his hand. I was a few minutes early. She looked fragile and a bit tired. A friend arrived with a storybook baby girl with big blue eyes and golden ringlets. Alicia conversed with the friend for a few minutes then walked her to the door and called upstairs to her husband, who was to take care of the baby while we talked. There was some commotion as the husband cooked and fed the baby in the kitchen. The baby ran in to sit on her mother's lap, obviously envious of her mother's attention to me, yet wanting to be allowed to remain, calling me "tia," auntie. Alicia looked as if she were convalescing from her painful past, surrounded by warmth and safety. There was a sparkle in her eye, even later when tears welled up in them. She smiled through the tears as happens when time stands between the emotion and the recollection. I thought to myself, "She will be safe now. If she damages herself, it will be because of her own intensity and her habit of giving. But that kind of damage is like a branch broken off of a healthy tree—it will grow back stronger and greener than before."*

I WAS BORN in Argentina, in a city in the south called Bahia Blanca. My father was a university professor and an accountant. In Argentina you can't live on a professor's salary alone. My mother is a painter. When I was a child, she used to take me to the shanty towns at the edge of the city to paint the houses and the people. That's how I was exposed to lives other than those I experienced in my own pampered world. I come from a Jewish family. My grandparents, like many other Jews, had come from Eastern Europe to Argentina. We had the largest Jewish population in the Americas next to the United States. Life as a Jew in my country didn't present any particular problems for me. At times I was asked silly questions about customs and traditions, but I encountered no overt anti-Semitism. My family were well integrated into the life of the country. We were very liberal and open toward other religions.

I started to write poetry when I was nine years old, and continued throughout my high school years. I wanted to study literature and become a high school teacher. I entered the university in 1973. That was the year we had the first free election of my lifetime in my country. There was great excitement among the young people. Everything seemed possible and change appeared inevitable. My friends were full of excitement about their political activities and soon I too was drawn into their circle.

My first years at the university coincided with a very special moment in my country's history. The Peronist party, after many years of having been banned from participating in elections, had come into power. I joined the Peronist Youth Movement. It was a broad movement encompassing left, center, and right. The youth were generally inclined toward the left and tended to work for liberalization and toward nationalistic solutions to the country's problems. Since I was a good student, they elected me student representative. They thought I would have leverage with the professors. I married while I was still at the university and soon had a baby daughter.

In 1976 the military seized power through a coup. They banned political parties, they banned the constitution, and they placed the media under strict censorship. They instigated a new phenomenon to deal with their enemies. They began to "disappear" people. They would kidnap a person from his home or place of work, take him away, torture him, sometimes kill him and always deny that they knew of his whereabouts. Bodies were never returned. Argentina has a population of 30 million. During the military's rule some 30,000 people were "disappeared." This is in addition to those who were imprisoned.

I decided to become involved in opposition politics. It was a very dangerous time for opponents of the system. I think having the baby motivated me to take this step. I knew what was in store for me, but I couldn't accept the alternative of doing nothing and allowing my daughter to grow up in such a repressive society.

I established stronger connections with the young Peronist movement. We couldn't do much actually because of the high level of repression and the strict controls. We organized three-minute demonstrations. At night, when the streets were deserted, we painted the walls and wrote slogans. I gathered information on human rights violations. When I was arrested I was gathering information about a woman who had been tortured in a concentration camp and who had managed to survive and escape. I was printing that information in a very makeshift way. We had a kind of gel that formed a mold. We placed the paper on this mold a page at a time to make a copy. Then we let the paper dry. I had this material in my home. They had already arrested some of my friends, and one of them had revealed my name under torture.

On January 12, 1977, at noon they came for me in two military trucks. My daughter who was one and a half was with me in the house. They knocked loudly at the door. I stood for a moment in a panic. Then I started to walk toward the front door. My daughter followed me through the passageway. Then I heard pounding on the door and shouts of "Army, open the door!" I hugged my child goodbye and ran to the backyard. I turned and saw my daughter at the window for a moment just before I jumped over the wall. The soldiers broke the door down and followed me. They caught me on the other side of the wall. For the next five months I had no idea what had happened to my daughter. I had become one of the "disappeared."

They took me to the army headquarters in my home town. From

there I was taken to the concentration camp they called the "Little School." They blindfolded me and tied my hands behind my back. They forced me to lie face down on a mattress. They beat me and forced me to remain silent. They didn't torture me with electricity because the doctor was not present, and they thought women are weaker than men and they didn't want any of us to die. They had taken my husband from work the same day. He later described to me how he was tortured with an electric prod. Another woman who was pregnant when she was arrested told me as they drove her to the Little School they tortured her by applying the electric prod to her abdomen. She later gave birth to a boy in the concentration camp. Since I was the only woman there at the time, I asked to be allowed to help her, but they didn't let me go to her. She was taken away after she had her baby. She is still "disappeared." Several years have passed, so we assume that the "disappeared" are all dead by now. The mothers, however, still press and plead for information about them. They keep repeating, "They took them alive, we want them back alive," refusing to acknowledge the finality of the disappearance.

One of my closest friends was at the Little School with me. Her name was Zulma. She was twenty-two years old. One night they took her and another girl who was sixteen years old, saying they were going to give them hormone injections to regularize their periods. We had all stopped having periods—it's a kind of wartime syndrome women develop. But instead of hormones they gave them anesthetics. They took them to a house in town and shot them while they were asleep. They strewed leaflets around them, then called in the reporters to see for themselves that there had been a confrontation with the army. It was quite an elaborate scene. They had military men inside and outside the house shooting with fake ammunition. The military were trying to justify their harsh acts by staging confrontations to prove there was a dirty war going on.

After three months in this and two months at another detention center, I was taken to a regular jail for women political prisoners. They kept me for two and a half years in the new prison. During the whole period there was no trial, and no formal charges were brought against me. I had not been a leader. I was not a published writer at the time. But the idea was to terrorize the whole population. All political activity was taboo.

My prison cell was nine feet by nine feet and I shared this space with three other women. There was a latrine in the cell. We ate there, we used the latrine, and we slept all in the same room. We weren't allowed to exercise. We weren't allowed to sing. We had no news from the outside world. But the conditions were a great improvement over the Little School. We were not blindfolded. Our family could visit, and we could see them through a glass wall. We could talk to them through a microphone.

We made our families memorize newspaper headlines. We made a sort of newspaper by writing on a piece of paper which we wrapped in plastic and hid in our mouths and passed on to each other. Any activity that was geared to gathering news or analyzing the political situation was forbidden. Since we were political prisoners, analysis of the news outside was directly related to finding what was likely to happen to us. Three hours a day we were allowed in a common area outside the cell. We whispered to each other what news we had and disbanded when we saw a guard appear.

We were very supportive of each other in prison. I think that is how we retained our sanity. We communicated with each other about our experiences. We discussed our personal lives. Talking about our problems helped us face them. It was a kind of therapy.

In 1979 the government began a new policy whereby political prisoners could choose between staying in jail or being exiled abroad. This occurred during President Jimmy Carter's human rights campaign. I chose to live abroad. First I tried to go to Spain. Spain, however, couldn't lobby strongly enough for prisoners, and I was not able to receive permission to go there. I applied to come to the United States. The Organization of American States had sent a mission to Argentina to monitor human rights abuses. It was a coincidence that I had applied at that time. I was lucky to be granted political asylum immediately. I could work as soon as I arrived and begin rebuilding my life. The refugee program I came under was sponsored by a group of churches in the state of Washington.

They took me directly to the plane from prison. The other prisoners said to me when I left what I had often said to others who were leaving: "Drink, dance, make love, and have fun." But I couldn't stop thinking of those who were left behind. At the airport I was handed over my daughter, whom I hadn't seen for three years. Flying was a strange experience. I had flown once before when they had taken me from one jail to another. I had been blindfolded and made to sit on the floor of the plane. This was a different experience. I was flying with this child who was my daughter, whom I didn't know, and all these suitcases my mother had sent with me, the contents of which were a mystery. The child kept asking me, "Are you sure you know how to take care of me?" Kids can be so cruel. I *didn't* know how to take care of her, but I kept reassuring her. "Yes, of course I know how to take care of you." It was unreal, like living in a cloud. I wasn't aware of what was going on around me.

When we landed, journalists and cameras were waiting, and my husband, who had come two months before, was there to meet me. I had thought I knew English but I was shocked to realize I couldn't express many of my thoughts. The first thing I said when I got out was, "The others, there are many others." I asked, "What will happen to them?" They asked me if I had been raped and were almost disappointed that I hadn't been. I felt a tinge of regret that I wasn't raped. It seemed as if a human sacrifice was necessary to gain the concentration of the media.

There was a group of refugees from Argentina in Seattle. We all had the support of the churches and of Amnesty International. They helped with medical and psychological checkups. More important, they provided a forum for us to speak. They arranged a number of speaking tours for me to talk about my experiences. I discovered the healing effect of talking about what I had gone through. I talked to anyone who would listen, at conferences, to audiences, to the bus driver, the cashier at the supermarket. I talked and talked, telling everybody my story. In a sense this is what I have been doing since I went into exile. I have been talking about what happened to me in the framework of what happened to the whole country, to the whole continent. That's the way to make people understand.

Americans don't seem to relate to collective experiences and collective tragedies. They have to relate to you as an individual to be able to sympathize. Once that happens they understand the rest. We come from Third World countries where collective experience weighs more heavily on the individual than in the "developed world." There is the tendency in the United States to try to understand massive repression by paralleling it to Nazi Germany and the holocaust. Since I am a Jew, people are tempted to parallel my experience with that experience. People here are always looking for easy ways to understand. They move through schemes and transplant reality, looking for similarities. Many people from the holocaust seem to have experienced survivor's guilt. I don't believe that every survivor experiences it. I am aware that I am not guilty for what happened. I know I did all I could to change things. If I was defeated, it was not because I was passive or because I lacked courage or because I didn't try. There was little room to fight back, but it could be done. Guilt does not fit into this picture.

So in telling my story I have been using my life, my voice, my body as a bridge so that the other, larger experience may be understood. This process has forced me to put myself in a context, and through that, not to focus exclusively on my own pain, on my own confusion and conflict. I learned in prison that focusing on your own conflict makes you lose the sense of what the conflict is all about.

After a while I began seeking a wider audience. I wrote poems and short stories. Publication of my work allowed me to travel and talk about my experiences to a new audience. Then I began to think it unfair to have my work available in English while the work of many others who have had similar experiences remains unknown. So I began collecting the works which were later published in *You Can't Drown the Fire.*

I had not initially thought of myself as a feminist. But as I told my story and communicated with other women in the process of collecting their work, I began to see the common thread that connected us. I realized that what I have learned from women and about women has enriched my life in a special way. I was also motivated by a wish to break the stereotypes about women in exile. We were sometimes called "innocent," which meant not guilty of being involved in politics. We were seen as mothers or daughters or wives of political activists who were targeted and our predicament defined as an extension of theirs. Or we are seen as the opposite, women who are very outspoken and aggressive. Sometimes we are seen as illiterate peasants who come here seeking better material conditions or highly educated intellectuals who don't have a sense of the realities of our people's condition. I wanted very much to address these issues, to explore the many dimensions of the lives of women in exile.

The first years of exile I spent in action, constantly moving and doing. I had no time for reflection. I didn't give myself the chance to think. First I had the problems of earning a living in a new country. I had to get used to caring for a child I hadn't seen for a number of years. I had to get used to a new society and a new language.

I started to work a month after I arrived. I began working in a bilingual child care center. Almost immediately I joined a committee for solidarity with Argentina. I became press secretary because of my language skills. I immediately made contact with the press and started networking with other organizations with similar interests. I became involved with Amnesty. I was in an emotional spin. My marriage fell apart. I started a new relationship. But I kept myself so busy I didn't really realize the extent of the turmoil I was experiencing. I lived out of a suitcase, like most exiles, with one foot here and the other in my country. My life was all action and very little reflection. I didn't want to give myself time to suffer or to mourn.

At the end of 1983, elections were held in Argentina and in 1984 a new government came into power. I flew back with my daughter. It is difficult to express my feelings on my return. I was aware that my fellow passengers, Argentineans who lived in the United States, were alien to my experiences. When we landed they were playing a tango on the loudspeaker at the airport. That's our national music. I thought it sounded like the soundtrack for a movie. I felt like crying when I first saw the earth of Argentina. I wanted to kneel and kiss the ground, but then I thought no, it was dirty, and also nobody around me would understand. My daughter would think me crazy.

The hardest thing on my return was the realization that so many people who were close to me were dead. I had known of the deaths before. My brother had committed suicide three years before. My grandparents had died when I first went into exile. But distance provides protection. You don't begin to process the event until you return. With my friends who had disappeared, there was the pain of not having a body, a grave, to mark their passing, a place to go to mourn them.

This was a time of excitement in Argentina. There was much hope. There was an abundance of art and poetry. I continued my work for human rights in the country and on my return to the United States. When I went back again, disillusion set in. I had changed. I looked at my homeland from the outside, as an alien. The country's economic problems were overwhelming. The trials of the generals who had commanded and ordered such things as my ordeals at the Little School ended with their release. I was frustrated to see that after all we had endured, justice was not served. I felt a great rage.

On my return to the United States I had a stronger feeling of alienation. I now knew that I was no longer really an exile. I had lost the sense of home I had felt in Argentina in my childhood and early youth. Yet I did not feel at home in the United States. The frustration and disappointment I felt at the thwarted legal process in Argentina welled up in me. I have just recently overcome an early discovered cancer. Although I am not sure my illness is related to these events, I think it is at least symbolic of the rage I feel. The effects of exile stay with you all your life. They are like things hidden in a closet. They suddenly jump out at you, like jack-in-the-box toys.

Seven years after my first arrival in the United States and when I no longer had to stay, I finally landed in this country. I became distant from the news of Argentina. The names in the media became unfamiliar to me. Then I bought my first book and started a library. That was a strong indication to me that I was building a home. I bought this house. I had a baby. I got my Master's degree.

I have thought of going back to Argentina to live. But my husband and daughter clearly prefer living here. To be honest, I don't have the strength to start a new life and a new career. And Argentina often seems to me a country with no way out. The economic problems appear unsurmountable. I know I am neither an Argentine nor an American. I am between two worlds. When I go back and look at my people through the distance one gains in exile, I feel an outsider to my own culture as I am in this culture. Yet it is not all negative. I sometimes feel I have gained a new window on the world. I have said it in my poem, "When they cut off my voice, I grew a second voice." I feel that I have another language now to express myself in and to relate to a new world. So in a sense I belong to both places.

Recently I went to Palestine with a group of North American women. The trip helped me by allowing me to focus on the changes I had undergone. As we were leaving for the occupied territories, I said to myself, "All these North American women will suffer, seeing the Palestinians' plight, but I am used to that, I know how to relate to it." And then we saw the mothers of the people who were killed. They were wearing white scarves. In Argentina, it is a tradition that the mothers of the "disappeared" march in front of the government offices wearing white scarves. And the stories were so similar. Only the language was different. We went to the refugee camps and I heard women who had been imprisoned and tortured. We were across the street from what they call the Russian Compound, where the tortures took place. We were in the demonstration that was suppressed, and we were shot at by soldiers. The land and the language were different, but the experiences were the same. We went to a hospital and we heard the stories of children who had been beaten. Their bones were broken. We saw a two-year-old girl who had been burned because a soldier knocked a pot of boiling water on her when he couldn't find her mother. I saw all those things and for the first time I knew how the people felt who were not victims themselves but had been witnesses and denounced victimization. When we heard that the people who had talked to us in the hospital had subsequently been taken out and beaten—people who were already hurt badly enough to be hospital-ized—my North American friends felt guilty, thinking that if we hadn't talked to them they wouldn't have been hurt again. But I who had experienced both conditions told them that there was no guilt in that. Those who had talked had made a deliberate choice—they wanted their stories heard and told.

It took me a while to be able to write about this experience. But when I did, I had finally transformed my life. I had changed from victim to witness. I felt empowered to work for change in my life and in the life of others.

FLORENCE SIMFUKWE

# I Was Never Homesick at Home

*Florence had given me precise directions to her town house in Silver Spring. When I arrived, she walked out to meet me in a long, colorful cotton dress with a happy, flowered design. She seemed to need little protection against the cool winds of autumn. I felt I had overbundled myself in a heavy sweater and wool slacks. We sat at her dining room table. She apologized about some inexactness she perceived in her home, explaining that at the moment she was working at a second job in addition to her nursing duties. We both smiled to acknowledge our conditioning that made us concerned about such things even under the kinds of pressures Florence was experiencing as a single parent living in exile, working a double shift, and volunteering as a human rights activist. She said she would brew Malawi tea for me. We chatted as she prepared the tea in the kitchen. I stood at the door joining the two rooms and watched her move about deftly, fixing a tea tray.*

*Florence is a full-bodied woman with smooth skin, the color of dark caramel, and a pleasant, throaty laugh. Hearing her burst into that laugh one would never guess the struggles and traumas she has undergone as a survivor of political repression, as the sole provider in an alien land for three young boys, and as counselor and "chief" for an extended family.*

*She is unassuming and pragmatic. There is a matter-of-factness that reflects itself in the way she sees her role as care giver in her work as a nurse and in her life within the family. In her company one senses that one is dealing with a capable person who will be where she is needed and will do what needs to be done.*

I WAS BORN in the Nkhata Bay district in the northern part of Malawi, South East Africa. That's where I spent most of my childhood. I was brought up by my grandmother. It is customary in Malawi that girls and boys after the age of nine or ten not sleep in the same house as their parents. The girls sleep in one house and boys in another. Since our village was small and there were not so many girls of our tribe, we stayed in my grandmother's house.

Our village was situated in a fertile valley. At the edge of the village a stretch of wetlands allowed us to grow vegetables all year,— onions, cabbages, tomatoes, beans, sugar cane. Behind our house, about a hundred yards from the building, a small stream ran from beneath the mountain with cool, clear water. There was another, larger river on the other side of the village. The former was for drinking water, the larger one for bathing and washing.

I can still close my eyes and relive a typical day of my childhood at my grandmother's. There were five of us staying in the house. We woke up early. We each helped with hauling water from the well and fetching firewood from nearby. Grandmother would pound sugar cane and sweeten our tea. In the dry season she picked sweet fruits and made a porridge for us. We always had tea because my grandmother, an active woman, worked very hard and grew sugar cane, nuts, made flour from maize and beans. She sold these products in the market in Mzuzu, a town some fifteen miles from our village, and with the money bought what we needed and paid for our school tuition. When there was water at home, we washed at home; when there wasn't, we stopped at the stream to wash on our way to school. Each day when it was time for the evening meal, everyone brought food to the gathering place outdoors. The men sat on one side, women on another, and they all ate together. The women placed the rice and the chicken or vegetables on separate trays, one for the men, one for the women. They called the children to come and carry the trays outside. We all shared the food from the trays, using our fingers, carefully and delicately, as we had been taught by our elders. Afterwards, the children brought water for the men to wash their hands.

My grandfather had gone to northern Rhodesia to work, and for many years he moved back and forth between the two countries. He married again in northern Rhodesia. In fact, he had many wives. He was Christian, but when religion interfered with his marital plans, he put aside religion. My grandmother, however, was a staunch Presbyterian and made sure I knew the values of her church. She would tell us stories of her life. She would tell us how her family didn't want her to marry my grandfather because he was too short and came from another tribe. But he persisted, working very hard to prove that he could successfully support a family. Finally they agreed to her marriage. Then she would tell us about the ceremony and the celebrations.

Grandmother couldn't read or write but she insisted that we all go to school and receive a full education. My education in values and customs came from her. But my initiation into the rites of womanhood came, as was the custom, from her daughter, my father's sister. Aunts have the duty of telling their nieces about the facts of life and about sex and marriage. The negative teachings—what a girl shouldn't do, such as intimate play with boys—came early, even before the start of the menses. But the positive part, about how to engage in sexual relations, traditionally came the night before the wedding. Some advice seemed strange to me even then. I was told, for example, that if I put salt in the food I was cooking when I was having my period, it would cause the men to retain fluid and blow up. But some rules sounded good to me, such as the one which required a woman who has just given birth to refrain from cooking for a week. If someone hadn't thought of that taboo, the poor pregnant woman would have no rest after labor.

I remember my childhood as a very happy time. There was a wonderful togetherness in the family and community. If there was a wedding or a death or a sickness, all the relatives came to help. All chipped in with the expenses as well as the work. No one had to be told what to do. In ordinary times women would come home from the field and prepare meals, while men sat around talking to each other, boasting about their feats. After dinner everyone told stories.

Men, women, and children all participated in the storytelling. It was meant to teach the children wisdom. Some of the stories were about animals. Sometimes they told of a young girl who married a handsome man for his looks and later found that beauty was skin deep and another, less good-looking, man would have been more loyal and understanding and a better partner. I liked to tell my story about a girl who was mistreated by her stepmother and then her fairy guardian came and gave her a magic ring. At night she put on the ring, rubbed it, and whispered her wishes, making the village a wonderful, happy, rich place and herself a beautiful princess. I used to tell this story picturing myself as the little princess.

At Christmas we celebrated for two whole weeks. We bought new clothes. We went to church on Christmas Eve, and prepared a feast of good food. Our delicacy was chicken. Special occasions required chicken. At night we played the drums and had traditional dances. After Christmas we participated in a custom called Christmas Box. The children took a box and knocked at each door and said, "Christmas Box." People came to the door and gave things—sometimes food or nuts, sometimes clothes. It was a time of giving and generosity and the children loved the ritual.

Along with the belief in Christianity, other, older rituals were observed. In the old days, there used to be a ritual for rain. There was a large tree under which men, women, and children would pray, sing, and chant until rain came. But now, I hear, they pray and the rain will not come. Their faith must not be strong any more.

I went to the mission school for the first few years and later to the Catholic school, where I was quite miserable. The nuns and priests were harsh with us. Our teachers were old, white men with beards and long black robes. They seemed strange and frightening to me. But soon I became indoctrinated and seriously considered becoming a nun.

In 1959 the British government declared a state of emergency in Malawi. Young students were taken up in the wave of political unrest that swept over the country as people fought for independence. I became active in the demonstrations and marches. We shouted slogans and threw rocks with great enthusiasm. Eventually they expelled us and closed the school. I went home fearing that my father would be upset with me, but he was very pleased and applauded my activism. The British were interested in instituting the Federation of Rhodesia and Nyasaland. But we wanted independence for Malawi. My father, Orton C. E. Chirwa, and my stepmother, Vera, were actively involved in the independence movement. They were soon arrested and sent to prison in Rhodesia. When they came back in 1960, my father founded the Malawi Congress Party, which is ruling Malawi to this day.

These were truly exciting days. Our house was always filled with crowds of people. There was a constant bustle of activity as they worked on speeches and documents and organized protests. The gatherings took place at night and in secrecy because the right of assembly was suspended due to the state of emergency. Most of the people I saw in our house were arrested at one time or another. It seemed almost normal that they would be there one day and in prison the next. When Dr. Banda, one of the prominent political figures, was arrested, the leaders of the group who worked with my father all fought for his release.

After Banda was released, there was a great convention of the Malawi Congress Party during which my father helped elect Banda to the presidency of the party. During 1960 and 1961 my father worked on the draft of the Malawi constitution and traveled often to England to negotiate with the British. In 1962 the British gave Malawi self-government and my father was appointed minister of justice. He received the honor of Queen's Council in recognition of his distinguished work in the field of law. In July 1964 Malawi gained independence. Banda became president. But once he reached power, all the wonderful promises were forgotten, and he began to work against the group who had helped him gain power. My father's life was threatened twice. Finally he was forced to live in exile in Tanzania.

Agents of the government took over our house and leveled it. They destroyed the house and bulldozed the trees—mangos, papayas, pineapples. They forced my grandmother, my grandfather, all of my sisters and brothers to leave the country. While the rest of the family were in exile in Tanzania, my father sent me to England to study, and in 1969 I received a degree in nursing. In England I met a Malawi man who was working with the Malawi High Commission in London, married him, and lived with him in England for two years.

Because he was married to me, he could not go home. Friends in Malawi told us that if we were to return, our lives would be in danger. In 1971 my husband and I came to the United States with our three small children. We had no home of our own and no job. Soon we realized that we had no way of keeping our children with us. We asked my sister to come and take the boys home with her. For the next three years, we lived apart from them. We found jobs and worked hard, but kept nothing for ourselves. We slept on the bare floor and saved most of what little we earned for the children.

Being away from our children proved unbearable. We talked about them all the time, and finally we convinced each other that we should go home. My husband told me, "Your father was the famous activist. You were only a child when you were demonstrating. They can't have anything against you." So we paid our hard-earned dollars to Air Malawi for tickets home. Before the trip I had been frightened of what might come. I had recurrent dreams of running from sinister figures bearing machetes. But once on the plane, the thought of seeing my boys and my country again caused such excitement and euphoria that I forgot the fear. Our arrival was uneventful. We were happy and excited to be home and when no one stopped us at the airport, we began to hope that we would be safe in our country. There was nothing left of the village that was our home, so we took a bus north to my family. We arrived at night. We didn't want to wake the children. We were too exhausted and nervous to sleep. We sat up all night talking to friends and relatives, peeking in at the sleeping children every hour, waiting for daylight to wake them. We guessed how each would react when they saw us and smiled, imagining the expression on each of their faces. But at dawn the police arrived in trucks and Landrovers. Uniformed and plain clothes men and women surrounded the house. They stormed in, ransacked every-thing and arrested us. The children were awakened by the sounds of the invaders rather than by our call. They didn't know how to feel—happy to see us or sad that we were being dragged away from them. We asked to take the boys with us, but the police refused. Before we had a chance to hold our children in our arms, we were separated from them once again.

At the police station they interrogated us ceaselessly. They asked me what my father was doing. They suspected me of planning some mission on his behalf. I kept saying, "I am a married woman. I haven't seen my father for years. I come from America to be with my children. You are here in Africa. You must know what he is doing better than I do." But they did not want to believe me.

For a week they refused to feed us. We were allowed to drink the water they supplied. For bread, we had to go out with a guard and purchase it ourselves. My husband was not a well man. His kidneys were infected. He became dehydrated. They didn't allow him to take his medication. We were made to sleep on the bare, damp floor. They took all our clothes, our shoes, our watches, everything. The weather was very cold. The beating and the psychological harassment took their toll. He became very ill.

After a week they moved us to the south and renewed the questioning. They told us we had been under surveillance in Britain and in the United States. They threatened to kill us. Some interrogators were interested in the possible political ramification of our coming home. Others were envious of our life abroad. They said, "How can you manage to live in America? How come we can't go there? There must be a plan or support from some quarters." I told them, "It's not very difficult, if you are willing to work hard. Save yourself the price of a ticket and get on a plane and you will be there in no time."

At last we were released. We took a bus to the north to our children. We packed a few things for them and took the next plane back to the United States. My husband had become so fragile and vulnerable that he no longer had the strength to survive. He fell ill with hepatitis and died a few months later. I was so angry that there was little room left in my heart for sorrow.

Suddenly I was faced with the responsibility of raising three small boys. I took two jobs. Between the work and the PTA meetings and other chores and errands, there was little time to spend with the children. Sometimes when I came home, they would already be sleeping. Sometimes I had only a few hours of sleep before running to the next job. I only had time to ask, "Kids, are you all right?" and fix them their food and make sure they had clothes and books. And all the time I tried to think of survival and not to think of how sad and lonely I felt and how I missed my home.

In 1981 my father, stepmother, and brother went to Zambia to visit my sister, who lived some fifty kilometers from the Zambian-

Malawi border. They had planned to spend Christmas there with my sister. But the special branch police kidnapped them from Zambia and took them back to Malawi. When my sister, hearing the news on Malawi radio, called to inform me, my first reaction was fear for my father's life, then helplessness and frustration. Life went on around me as if nothing had happened. I was living in a free country, yet I was connected to another land where the rules of conduct were entirely different and I had no way of affecting the situation. Malawi was far away. I was powerless and my parents were in prison with no access to the outside world. There was no recourse to any political or legal entity.

For days I paced up and down in my room, anxious and miserable. Suddenly it came to me that I need not live according to the rules imposed by the government of Malawi. I was living under new and different circumstances, and I could use the resources at my disposal to help my cause. I spoke with a friend who advised me to contact Amnesty International. People at Amnesty were sympathetic. They adoped my father's case and initiated a campaign to draw attention to it. I became involved in the process. We wrote letters, held demonstrations in front of the Malawi embassy, and organized meetings. I was interviewed by various newspapers and television and radio programs. My picture was on the front page of the *Washington Post*. I wrote to the State Department and went there to present my case to whoever would listen. I called often to follow up. The response through the years that followed depended on the policies of the particular administration. Generally, because of the superpower rivalry then in progress, Banda's government was considered friendly by the United States. He was anticommunist and pro-Israel, and that was enough to bring him sympathy from certain segments of the American government. Various human rights groups, however, joined the campaign. International attention was drawn to my father's case. But none of this had much effect on his actual condition, except perhaps to delay his murder.

In 1982 the Malawi government sentenced him to death after a trial in which he was not allowed to produce witnesses, and the outcome of which was predetermined. In 1984 they commuted the sentence to life imprisonment. He was kept in solitary confinement, not allowed to have visitors or to talk to anyone or to receive mail.

They never gave him the letters his family and friends sent to him. They kept telling him: "Nobody cares for you. Even your family has forgotten. Why do you persist?" They never gave him the cards we sent for his birthday or Christmas. Throughout all the years, they kept his legs and arms tied at all times. Sometimes they woke him in the middle of the night and poured cold water over him.

I worked constantly on his behalf, spending much time to keep informed of events in Malawi and news relevant to his condition. But, gradually, I learned to extend my sympathy and care to other victims of cruelty and violence. I became interested in other people who were undergoing similar oppression. I was no longer obsessed with my father as my father but as an individual whose human rights were being violated—a political leader whose voice was stilled. I began by taking his message of justice and democracy for all to different audiences. Initially I was nervous and unsure as a public speaker. But in time I learned to concentrate on the message, not the messenger or the listener. I focused on the ideas that by now had become my own, and I was no longer nervous. My work evolved from bringing my father's thoughts to audiences into expressing my own personal beliefs.

Finally, under international pressure, Banda was forced to announce a referendum to determine whether the people preferred the one-party or a multiparty system of government. He announced his plans on Sunday, and on Monday night they killed my father. They said he died of natural causes, but we learned later that they had injected him with insulin which is impossible to detect in an autopsy. They couldn't allow him to go free during the referendum, and the increasing international pressure made it impossible to keep him in jail any longer. He was seventy-three years old when he was killed.

A friend called from London with the news of his death. It is terrible when a loved one, especially one whose condition has been a constant preoccupation for so long, is gone and you are in a foreign land, far away. At home, relatives would have surrounded me. There would be support and sympathy from those who knew him, had memories of him, and cared personally about his fate. There would be consolation in their nearness and concern. There would be signs and symbols of the meaning his life and death held for others. There would be comfort in shared ways of grieving. But here in America I was separate and alone. The few friends who came to console me did not know him. Once again I was frustrated by the helplessness of my position and the inability to go home to bury my father. Once again I decided to make an effort to change things.

I explored every channel available to get permission to go to Malawi for my father's funeral. I contacted the Red Cross, the British government, the Canadian government and every human rights organization I knew in order to get help and to obtain permission for myself and his other exiled children to go home. I wanted to mobilize many groups and sources of power in order to make it difficult for the government to harm any of us during our stay in Malawi.

Our arrival this time was much more eventful than the last. There was considerable attention paid to our movements, but we had to fight every step of the way for our right to bury our father in the manner that was befitting his years of struggle. We wanted to bury him in his own home village according to our traditions. The government officials objected, cloaking their fear of the impact of the procession through the countryside in words of appreciation for his position and his lifelong work. They told us he should be buried in the capital. "He was a hero. He was our first minister of justice. He was the first barrister, the first attorney general." It was ironic that they gave us these speeches while all the time they were looking for ways to send us away. We insisted that this was not negotiable. We would bury our father in his home village. For me this was a fight for political rights of an activist, rather than a matter of family pride.

On the journey home thousands of people waited at each stop. At every gathering people gave rousing political speeches, using the occasion as a forum to air their grievances and their hopes. They were emboldened by the example of my father and the assurance that those who struggle for human rights win in many ways, among them, the example they set for those who will follow in their footsteps.

I was happy to see supporters of the multiparty system win in the referendum. The people showed by their vote that they knew that in the past two decades the country had regressed and that they were in fact worse off than they had been twenty years earlier. They showed that they were fed up with being poor, powerless, and oppressed. They chose democracy.

I returned to the United States after the funeral. It had been a good experience going home. It was genuinely healing to see so many cared for the ideas that my father had worked for and that are now the driving force of my own life. Being in Malawi after so long, I felt strange, yet somehow quite at home. Many people I had known were no longer there and many villages had ceased to exist. Some of the people I knew were afraid to approach us because of our political position and the dangers inherent in being associated with us. Others I saw saddened me because they had changed so much. On one of our stops, an old, white haired man walked up to me, leaning on a stick, and asked, "Do you remember me, Florence?" I had to look hard to discover in this broken old man the shadow of the vibrant, energetic young man I had known as a young girl—a man we called "O.D."

The authorities had not allowed my stepmother to take part in the funeral ceremonies. They were unwilling to let us visit her, but we said we wouldn't leave until we saw her. They were so anxious for us to leave the country that they allowed us to visit her in prison. At first she didn't seem to recognize us. She couldn't believe that her youngest boy, who had been a teenager when she last saw him, had become a mature, thirty-year-old married man. Under pressure from European governments, she was finally released. But now that she is free, she is having a difficult time giving shape to her life. Her husband is dead and her children are away. She has spent so many years in jail that it takes a lot of reorganizing and restructuring of her habits and her personality to survive in the world.

In African politics, if a member of a family takes a public position, everyone in the family becomes involved: mother, father, aunts, uncles, and cousins—they all benefit or suffer. My father's life touched the lives of many others. Some benefited from his struggle, others suffered for his sake. His mother and his aunt suffered. His aunt had a heart attack the day it was announced that he would be executed. His mother died in exile in Tanzania. I went to see my grandmother in 1986. Life was very difficult for her. She didn't speak Swahili and the separation from her home and family was impossible to adjust to at her age. At first she lived with my father, sharing his exile. But when he was arrested, another sorrow was added to her life. She grieved over my father's fate. She kept asking me, "Are you sure your father is alive? Maybe they are lying to us—maybe they have already killed him." But she couldn't bear the thought that her son might already be dead. She would start moving about, taking up some task, or talking of a different subject in order to distract herself. I think she died of grief over his imprisonment. As for me, my father's political activities caused my first exile and inspired me into the second, which became my own choice.

Emotionally, life in America is very difficult. When my husband was alive, whenever I began to worry in the night about some problem, I would say to myself, "Let him worry about it," and I would sleep peacefully, thinking there is someone else to deal with our responsibilities. But when he was gone I had to be mother, father, driver, and teacher of our young children. In addition, I had to support the family. All of this was added to my homesickness—the constant urge to go home. But I began to realize that a place where they will kill you if you go there cannot be called home. Yet America was not home either. I have friends here, but their concept of friendship is different. They will fit you into their schedule when it is convenient, not when you need them. At home, in the village, your problem is everybody's problem.

Those who have not been in exile cannot appreciate the pain of it. Only someone who has been there can understand. It doesn't matter how you get there, whether you cling to the belly of an airplane, are a stowaway in a ship, or walk over mountaintops, once you arrive, the real journey begins. My American friends tend to think that since I am healthy, have a job and a home and well behaved children, I ought to be content. They don't realize that my family and roots are elsewhere, and it hurts to be away. An exile's home needs not have been a castle—it could have been an ice igloo, but it would have the warmth of home and the history that gives meaning to every part. I try to explain that the difference in living at home is that you never feel homesick there, but it is hard to make myself understood. They don't understand how I miss the scenery—the very special green of the countryside and those particular mountains and lakes that are like no other. I miss the freshwater fish from the river near my grandmother's house. Perhaps if I had left by choice and were allowed to return when I wished, it would not be so painful. I don't want to remember that the house and our whole village are gone. When I think of home,

I only remember the way it was in my childhood, not the way I saw it on my return. It comforts me to think that father is buried there now and his spirit will protect the place.

I continue to work in the maternity ward as a nurse, as I have for the past twenty-five years. I work in the birthing rooms, helping bring six or seven babies a night into the world. It is a new and wondrous experience each time. Women have kept the secret of the pain of childbirth for centuries. They react to it in a variety of ways, some showing no sign that they are in pain, some behaving as if they are about to die. But all women participate in keeping the secret. As soon as the baby comes, the mother smiles peacefully and pushes the memory of the pain to a far place in the back of her mind. I have loved my work which has allowed me to be part of all this. But I think I have given my job as much as I have to give and learned all I can learn from it. Now I want to work for human rights. There is so much for me to learn in that field and so much that I can do.

Last year we started a human rights organization called The Malawi Action Committee. I continue my work with Amnesty's Survivors of State Violence project as well as with this organization to help change the conditions in my country. I want to be able to go home to work for my people. They know now that they can speak up, but they don't know how easily that right can be taken away from them. They have yet to establish an indigenous democratic culture within which differences of opinion can exist without causing rifts or antagonisms. I want to help with building civil institutions in Malawi. My goal is to make certain that others are not abused the way my family has been for the last thirty years. My boys have become Americanized. I have tried my best to keep them from being completely absorbed in this society and from losing their ties to their past. Malawi needs them and others like them.

When I compare life in Malawi with life here, I realize that the major difference was that we didn't *question*. Life had many facets—some pleasant, some not, some fair, some not. We didn't challenge the way things were; instead, we learned to adapt to them. In Malawi I considered the division of labor between the sexes as natural. Now I get upset at the way women are treated. When my friends who are married to African men come home from work and immediately set to work to prepare dinner while the husbands lounge around waiting to be fed, I become furious. I have learned in this culture to question and to speak up. Because we didn't challenge the system, our society as a whole suffered. I have also learned here the importance of dedication to the law as embodied in the Constitution. Even the deep-seated racism that exists in this country began to be changed when some appealed to the Constitution and its underlying concept of equality. The respect for law gives one a sense of security, a certainty that there is always recourse. That for me helps to fill the void created by the absence of the communal bonds of home and kin.

I work toward the twenty-first century with the dual consciousness of an exile. In the day I am a nurse and a human rights activist in America. But in the night I dream of my grandmother in Malawi. I see her tall, strong figure busy at some task. She works calmly and peacefully. She looks up and sees me coming toward her and smiles, touching her black and white hair with the back of her hand. I offer her the gifts I have brought from far away. She puts on a red blouse I have offered to her and laughs. I see myself moving with her, going to ceremonies—weddings, funerals—hard to tell which. There is community and togetherness, food and laughter, and the calm that comes from knowing one's rightful place, and the right thing to do in all circumstances. I drift into a still and sad wakefulness.

# SIMA WALI

# I Realized I Was the Enemy

*I arrived at Sima's apartment a little frazzled. I had driven around, in the vicinity of her home, half an hour past our appointed time, unable to find the right building. She smiled warmly and led me in. Her luminous, dark eyes and her quiet demeanor gave a sense of calm that soon eased my tension. She was wearing a beige silk blouse and a skirt in a heavier material of the same color. The room was decorated in very light taupe with salmon accents. Grace was the word that came to mind when I later tried to describe Sima and her home. She brought me tea and sweets that tasted of my own childhood. She put cardamom in our glasses of tea. The smell was very familiar, but the taste, mixed with the tea was a pleasant novelty. Coming from the same cultural background, yet separated by nationality, I came often to experience this reassuring oneness, and the interesting surprize of variation when communicating with Sima.*

*We talked on into the afternoon. The sky outside her large windows grew darker. She turned on the lights. When she spoke of the upheaval, tears came to her eyes. It was the first time for her since exile that she was reliving her past. So much of her story was so close to my own experience that for me hearing her story was an intensely emotional process. When she talked about hearing news of the death of friends and acquaintances, I remembered seeing pictures of the bodies of my friends and colleagues in the newspapers along with reports of their execution. The images looked like the people I had known, yet*

*were strange and unfamiliar. Like her, I found it difficult to believe*
*these things were really happening. Her father waiting for the guards*
*with a small suitcase packed and ready brought to mind so many I*
*knew who had waited in the same way, trying to anticipate the situa-*
*tion and thereby retain some control over their life and their dignity.*

*Since that first interview, we have sat together to talk about her*
*life story many times. We have also worked together on many issues*
*related to Muslim women and to women's human rights. She has*
*impressed me with her calm, rational, and cultured ways of dealing*
*with things and the extraordinary strength that lies behind the un-*
*ruffled quiet of her face.*

*She is a woman with a deep sense of herself and the values that*
*have shaped her life. She is fully engaged in the process of empower-*
*ing herself in new ways not of her childhood and youth, yet she draws*
*up from her past cultural base the moral values and the dignity that*
*make her a potent presence. She wills herself into making the most of*
*the harrowing experience of rootlessness, choosing the best of her*
*past and her present in reinventing her new identity.*

I SPENT MY early childhood in India, where my father headed the
Afghanistan National Bank. I was educated in English. I learned
Persian in the Zoroastrian school in evening classes. During the six
years we spent in India I learned very little about my own country. I
was exposed to Christianity at the Christian school I attended and
through my Irish nanny. I was made aware early in my life that I was a
Muslim, but I learned to be tolerant of other religions.

When we returned to Afghanistan for the first time I began to
learn about my religion. I went to a school where most of the teachers
were women and a number were French. We had very few male
teachers, among them the religious education teacher. What I learned
of Islam in school was very negative. I didn't understand the Quran,
which was written in Arabic. And as a student and a young woman I
was hardly permitted to question or inquire. In the world outside
school, Islam seemed to present an oppressive agenda for a woman. I
noticed that my mother was not allowed to pray in the mosque, and
when we attended a funeral, we had to sit in a separate section or a
different building.

At school I learned for the first time about myself as member of a particular class. I had always viewed my lifestyle as quite ordinary. There was nothing luxurious or outstanding about my family's way of life. But we belonged to an extended family that had ruled Afghanistan for decades. One of my ancestors was Sardar Tilai, who ruled Afghanistan and then conquered Pakistan. He had accumulated so much gold in his conquests that he had been given the title of "Tilai," or "Golden." We joked among ourselves how we regretted that we received his name but not a penny of his gold.

At school I noticed that although I studied hard and behaved well, I was singled out for harsh treatment. It took me a while to understand that this was due to a sort of reverse prejudice—that I was being punished because of my family name and position.

The school I attended was located in a very old building. It had large spacious rooms and beautiful gardens with old Wisteria and Jasmine trees. I can still see the piles of white and purple flowers and smell the sweet fragrance in late May. The eglantine wound its branches around the large trees and then draped down in a profusion of delicate flowers like a gauzy white veil. I also remember well the discipline of those years. We studied thirteen or fourteen subjects, each of which required rote memorization of whole textbooks. Strict adherence to texts was required and discussion and questioning were discouraged.

I had three brothers who were much older than I. Whenever my father was preoccupied with something, they saw to my discipline. What I remember of my high school years is this strictness. It was rough, but it helped shape me in many ways. It helped me to understand male-female relationships in a traditional tribal society and to know where the inequities are and where change must begin. Family is the most important institution in Afghanistan wherein a woman's values—personal, social and political—are formed. I learned to seek the root of our problems in the basic interrelations within this institution.

After I passed my final high school exams I enrolled at the University of Kabul. I was privileged to have a strong English-language background. Since the courses were mostly conducted in English, everything was much easier for me. Sometimes the teachers would give me the lesson plan and let me teach in their place. I was feeling religiously rootless at that time. I had a teacher who was a *Sufi* (mystic), a wonderful person with a good grasp of many subjects. He knew Arabic. I asked him to teach me the Quran. His teachings made me realize how the mullahs had corrupted the ideas of the Quran. He also introduced me to my own literature. I had known the famous English writers, but now I began to read with joy the great poets, Hafiz, Saadi, and Rumi. I gained a sense of pride that this magnificent literature was a part of my heritage.

During my first years at the university, the monarchy in Afghanistan became more lenient politically. Divergent political groups began heated discussions at the university. There were strikes and for a while the university was closed. When it reopened I did not go back again. I had two semesters to finish, but I felt I didn't learn enough to justify my spending time there. I had been working part-time for the Peace Corps and was much impressed with the concepts and implementation of their programs. So I decided to work full time at the Peace Corps headquarters in Kabul.

I was completely apolitical, very naive about issues and problems. My father had resigned his job in the government and deliberately kept away from politics. I had been taught in school, especially in religious classes, to observe limits, to accept authority, and to subdue curiosity. I was truly oppressed by my education. I was terrified to overstep the boundaries set for me as a young person, a student, and a woman.

I found contentment in conformity. I liked my job. I spent time with my family and friends. I lived with my parents. In Afghanistan a woman leaves her father's home only to enter her husband's. I had no responsibilities. I felt secure and happy.

During this period the country's political system seemed stable. There had been a "white" coup in the country when the king was replaced by his cousin. Nothing much changed. There were some attempts at reform. But in fact one member of the tribe had simply replaced another. There was no violence. But the communist coup was something else. It came without warning. There was nothing unusual happening prior to the coup. No demonstrations, no strikes, nothing in the papers, no indication of what was to come.

The night before the coup we had gone to a party. I don't remember what the occasion was, only that it was some sort of celebration. We went to bed late and were awakened by the sounds of war. There were bombs shattering the windows and the noise of rifle fire. For a while there was no official news. We had no idea what was happening. Neighbors ran in from time to time with bits of news and rumor. Some thought a military maneuver was being carried out. But I knew something was terribly wrong. We lived close to the palace so we heard the sounds of fighting. It was very frightening—the constant terrible noise of the shooting and not knowing what was happening. The phone lines were down. The radio was dead. Then tales of horror began pouring in. One visitor told us he had seen arms and legs blown into branches of trees. Another had heard women were being gang-raped. Those who had dared to walk closer to the site of battle told of bodies strewn on streets.

I had a friend who had sat next to me at school from the seventh to the twelfth grade. She was a beautiful person. We had continued our friendship after the school years passed. She had married the president's son. She knew nothing of politics. Now someone counted her name among some fifty who were killed in the palace massacre.

Ever since that day whenever I hear of statistics concerning deaths or atrocities in times of turmoil in various parts of the world, I have to fight a feeling of nausea. I know now what I didn't quite feel before this—that the numbers mean faces and bodies of people known and loved by other people. People who would be missed, whose loss would change the entire course of other people's lives, people whose death would be lived and relived by the survivors for years to come.

We were still not sure who the opponents were. Then the radio began broadcasting. Soon the servants started to leave one by one. Suddenly there came the realization that we were the enemy.

A few months before the coup I had decided to travel to the United States for a few months. I had a Peace Corps friend who had invited me. I thought I would go away for a while, have a chance to think and decide about my future. My father was very angry that I was planning to live alone in a foreign country. He would not help me get the necessary papers. For a while he wouldn't even speak to me for having made this decision on my own and for planning to explore a new world without a male escort from the family.

When the coup happened I had my passport. My family, even my father now encouraged me to leave Afghanistan. My father felt that if

I were to leave, he would have one less female family member to protect. He was burdened with so much and the threats were constant.

Now, when everyone suddenly wanted me to go, I didn't want to leave. I wanted to stay with my family. They were in danger and I wanted to be with them to share their fate. It was a puzzling and frightening time. I am still analyzing some of the events of that period. I felt innocent yet singled out—I was the enemy. I didn't feel animosity and couldn't target the hostile group. Later, when I came to the United States, I studied international relations in order to try to understand what had happened to me, to my family, to my nation.

Soon we were placed under house arrest. I began feeling claustrophobic. The family continued to pressure me to leave. I decided to get my exit permit. First I tried to send the office driver to get it for fear of being identified if I were to go there myself. But the driver came back with the news that he was to bring me in "to answer a few questions." This was in the afternoon. I went there without telling anyone. A few days before, I had sent a telegram to my brother Abdul-Wali in Germany to the effect that if all went well I would join him there soon. I was making preparations secretly for fear word would get out. I wasn't telling even my closest friends. I no longer knew whom to trust. I was also trying to find ways of getting money out. The government allowed only fifty dollars. I bought German marks at the black market. My brother helped me drill the money in the sole of my shoe. I knew that if I got caught I would go to jail and that would be the end of me.

At the Communications Ministry I was answering questions which some young government employee was asking me. Suddenly two soldiers with machine guns burst into the room. They told me to go with them, pressing their machine guns to my ribs. I felt totally helpless. The young man who was questioning me immediately knew I was in serious trouble. He started to vouch for me, using the word *hamshireh*—one who has drunk the same milk, or sister. He was risking his life to protect me. The soldiers took me to a building I didn't recognize, through a long dark passageway into a large, harshly lit, smoke-filled room. All around stood burly men exuding a sense of their newly gained power.

I was wearing a short sleeved blouse. My hair was uncovered. I felt weak and vulnerable. I knew that to these men who had seldom seen a city woman in Western dress, I was immediately outside the category of mother, daughter, sister, wife. I was the other—loose woman, prostitute. If they were to discover I belonged to the ruling family, they would consider it their duty to harm me. They spoke Pashtu and I could only pick up a few words. This too was taboo, not knowing the people's language. Farsi is the language of the elite. Initially there was no physical violence, but clearly it could lead to that. I looked around searching for a woman's face, but there was none.

There was a lot of confusion. I looked as if I belonged to the ruling family, yet this young government worker was claiming I was a relation. Then suddenly he was pushed out of the room and I never saw him again. They asked me many questions. I felt powerless and strange, as if I had been caught trespassing on some other person's property. This land and these people were fast becoming foreign to me. My dress, my culture, my language, my past, my name were all perceived as other, and incomprehensible. My exile began that afternoon in my own country.

The telegram I had sent to my brother, whose name, Abdul Wali, was the same as the king's son-in-law, they thought was a coded message. I was interrogated for several hours. My defense mechanisms worked very well. I had to tell a lot of lies. I was amazed to hear myself make up all these stories. I am usually no good at that. I said that my brother was very ill and I was going to visit him and return. Luckily I had a round trip ticket. Then I heard one of the men tell another, "Oh, let her go, what harm can she do? She is only a woman." It was a miracle, but they let me go. It was only six weeks after the coup and there was still chaos. They didn't know what to do with me. I was visibly shaken and that appeased them and calmed their assertiveness.

I didn't even pack my bags. My brother took me to the airport. He was taking a chance. He was under house arrest and there was a strict curfew in force. The rest of the family couldn't risk coming to see me off. In the car, passing through dark, deserted streets my brother said nothing. My mind was a swarm of images that ricochetted from the distant past to the unfathomable future to the uncertain present.

I knew there was a good chance I would be stopped and searched at the airport. Chances were slim that they would let me through. But once again I was fortunate. I ran into a commercial pilot I knew who was traveling on the same flight. He saw me but gave no sign of recognition. That would have been dangerous for both of us. He saw the guard singling me out to be searched. He began to complain angrily about the plane being late and the likelihood of his missing his connecting flight. He kept raising his voice and soon he was surrounded by anxious attendants. We were all rushed through in the commotion. On the plane he told me that twice the planes he had flown were returned to Kabul because women of the family were identified on board. I did not feel quite safe until we left Afghanistan's air space. Once I passed that point and sighed with relief, I began to realize the implications of my situation—I began to understand that from that moment, the price of being safe was separation from my country and my home.

My brother met me in Frankfurt on my arrival later that night. He had heard very little about what had happened since the coup. I recounted for him the events which had led to my hurried departure. A few hours after I finally went to bed, I woke up with a high fever. My whole body had swollen. My eyes were so puffy that I could hardly see through my eyelids. My skin was red and itched terribly. The next day my brother took me to a doctor who gave me a sedative. Apparently arriving safely had triggered my body to finally react to severe stress.

On the flight to New York I had time to think. I was terrified about the future, deeply grieved about the past, worried about my family's immediate situation. But above all I was fearful of the heavy burden of representing my family—upholding the name, the dignity, and conducting my life in the manner expected of me, retaining the pride and projecting it in a new context. And all the time images rushed through my mind of my friend, my teacher, and my relatives who had died.

I was sitting next to an American businessman. Although I was too frightened to talk, he must have felt my agitation. I had not been able to bring my address book with me. Having names and whereabouts of Americans in my possession would have been interpreted as connection with the CIA. I only brought the number of a friend of my sister's who was married to an American. On our arrival in New

York, the businessman helped me dial my sister's friends in Washington, D.C., and charged the call to his office. I was embarrassed that my first act in the United States involved receiving help I couldn't repay.

I arrived in Washington late at night. My heart was full of fear. I had traveled before, but always in the care of pilots who were friends of the family. I was always met by next-of-kin on arrival. I was delivered like a special delivery package from one end of the journey to the next by one relative or friend to another. This was the first time I was arriving in a strange, big city alone and at night. Since the Kabul curfew, moving in the night had always been clandestine and dangerous. As soon as it got dark I began to feel a mounting anxiety. I was afraid the airport would close and I would be left with nowhere to go. Finally my friends arrived and took me to their home.

The next few days I spent doing nothing. I had somehow lost the sense of time and place. Finally I came to myself and decided I must do something. I didn't want to overstay my welcome.

I called the Peace Corps Office and found the phone number of my former boss, who had been the Peace Corps officer in Afghanistan. He sent friends to pick me up. When he learned that I was not staying with my family, he insisted that I stay with him and his family in a little town in Virginia called Waterford. He was wonderful to me, and soon he and his family became my American family. With his help I filed for political asylum and began searching for a job. The asylum application was not easy to process because I was a pioneer of the Afghan refugees, and the State Department had not yet decided on the status of those who were forced to leave Afghanistan.

The first job I found was in the Secretariat for Women in Development at the New TransCentury Foundation. Eventually I became the communications officer.

The first few weeks I had no news from home. I wrote many letters. Brief ones with coded messages. Phone calls were impossible because all the lines were down. Besides it would have been very dangerous to put a call through from the United States. It would take months for my family to get my letters and I received none from them. The first real news I got was when my brother fled over the border and called me from London. He described how he had heard from a friend in the family that they were coming to pick him up the next day. We all had friends who worked with the opposition but retained their family and tribal loyalties. He put on a tribal outfit and with his wife they took the mountainous route through Kaybar Pass to Pakistan. They paid a lot of money to a smuggler who knew the routes. They fled, riding donkeys, then walking for days and nights. They slept in fields that were being bombed. When they arrived in Pakistan, his friends there couldn't recognize him with his beard and tattered clothing. He called me when he got to London. He was the first family member to arrive after I did.

During the first few months my life was filled with efforts to find a new place in the world. Visa, work permit, a place to live, a job. All of that consumed my time and energy. It also saved me from the anxiety of thinking about the past. I kept myself very busy. I met and married an American with little education and no real profession, a person I thought was furthest removed from my previous life. I had suffered in the past because of my family and connections not because of anything I had done myself. Marrying this man was a complete break with the past. This was a period when I was trying to understand the upheaval in my life—so total, so unexpected. But soon I realized that breaking totally with the past was not the way for me. The marriage ended in a short time.

My parents, surprisingly, had not objected much. By now I had made so many sensible decisions about my own life and had done so much to help other members of the family in overcoming their problems of settling in the United States that they hardly questioned my choices. They thought at that stage in my life, they must trust my judgment.

For a time I lived in a group house. I was facing a very different lifestyle. The loss of status was difficult. I had started going to school in the evening. I was immersed in feelings of guilt and sorrow. I felt guilty that I had survived while my family were in constant danger. I was grieved that I had lost my home and the life I knew. But I had no one with whom I could share my feelings. My companions didn't know where Afghanistan was and cared very little what happened to it. I felt that to be a complete denial of my identity. Here was a country with which my selfhood was closely connected and they didn't even know where it was. This question of identity was the hardest to come to terms with. I went to a store to shop and somebody would ask for my ID. I had never been asked that in all my life. It was as if I were not trusted—as if I had to prove who and what I was.

For a time I had no news of my parents, and I was terrified for them. I kept picturing my father, the way I had seen him during my last days in Afghanistan with his little suitcase containing his toothbrush, pajamas, and extra shirt all packed up, ready to be picked up by the revolutionaries. I began thinking seriously about going back. My colleagues warned me of the dangers of such a move, but I was anxious and depressed. I needed to know what was happening to my parents, and I wanted to share their fate. I was so tense that I jumped at the slightest noise. The sound of a door closing with a bang would set my heart thumping wildly. I felt claustrophobic in any dark place—the movies, the subway, an elevator. I felt my life was a series of meaningless movements along a path around a circle. I could not and did not wish to enter within, and no one wished to, or could, walk out to me. I went through the routines of life like an automaton.

One hot summer day I broke down in the office. I am not the sort of person who shows her emotions. I don't yell and scream a lot. But suddenly I burst out crying uncontrollably. There was a mental health counselor at our office who works with Vietnamese refugees. She talked to me and assured me that I was having a very normal anxiety reaction.

Finally I got word that my parents were safely out of Afghanistan. They had waited until all their sons and daughters were out of the country in order to leave. They had been captured on their first attempt to cross the border. They had spent months in a damp prison cell where they were made to sleep on the floor. They were given little food, and were interrogated constantly. Fortunately an official of the prison who had worked with a cousin of my father's in years past found out that they were being transferred to a maximum security prison in another city. He risked his life to save them on the way to the new compound.

Now my whole family were out of danger. I advanced in my job to become executive director of Refugee Women in Development, an organization I founded. I derived great satisfaction from my work, which was closely related to the condition of women coping with problems such as I had experienced. Their courage, strength, and dignity in the face of extraordinary hardship provided a continuing source of inspiration. I established a very special and respected place for myself among my countrymen and women in exile. They looked to me for advice and counsel. They were proud that I represented them in international forums.

My family also took pride in me. They approved of the decisions I had made about my life, not only concerning work, but also in advancing my education. They felt that I had kept the family image and the name. But I have been very careful not to press the family men or the community in certain areas. I am working right now, for example, on a special project on Afghan women. But in transcending social and political barriers I have to be culturally sensitive to the heightened vulnerability of men who are living in exile. They have lost their status, they are afraid, and their women are faring better than they are. The women are the pillars of support in their community. I draw on my own personal experience and I try not to be threatening to the men. My role has been a humanitarian one. The Afghan community appreciates my visibility within that context because of the way I have handled my interaction with them.

I had married someone outside my nationality, culture, and religion. The marriage did not work. I was divorced. All of this is taboo. Under ordinary circumstances I would never be forgiven. They would fear that a woman who married so far outside her own family and failed would drive other women to press for their rights and encourage them to leave their men. But I hear through the grapevine and through other women that my role is appreciated and trusted by the community in general. I feel responsible to use my good reputation sensitively and effectively to help the position of women.

I avoid all confrontation in the community setting by staying away from discussions of politics. There are subjects raised about which I have information or an opinion. But discussions always become emotional. I have tried to keep the family interaction more social. In other groups I express myself and enter discussions easily, but I feel that within my own community, it is easier to avoid confrontation. In general, I avoid political activity. I don't want to use my position in my organization as an entree. It would alienate the men. Also, because we haven't exercised our political and intellectual opinions in debates in the past, political discussions become emotional exchanges, and reasoned analysis is lost. Voices are raised, fights ensue, and people are hurt. I just don't want to be a part of that sort of exchange.

But a major change is happening in the minds of Afghan women in exile. Women are beginning to think about and question their assigned traditional role. They don't have an outlet to analyze issues intellectually, primarily because they have very little educational background. Women who have been illiterate in their own language are undergoing continual drastic changes. Whereas at the beginning they clustered within their own community, they are now gradually beginning to move out toward the mainstream. So it's all about change. It happens at the social, political, and emotional level. But there is as yet no avenue for it to be appropriately channeled.

Some women hang on to values and relationships at any price and tolerate aggression and violence. "A slap here, a slap there," they rationalize, "isn't worth breaking up the family." But for every one of those who have bought into the male value system, there are many others who are beginning to stand for their rights and to reevaluate their choices.

Sometimes this process takes a wrong turn. The women, feeling frustrated, isolated and terrified in an alien culture and without comfort from their immediate family, turn to fundamentalist religious beliefs. The men have the relief of their own groups and the socializing opportunities within those groups. They hang out together and drink and talk. Women don't have that. They have to work. And then they come home to their second job as wife and mother. Men's socializing means more work for women, who have to cook and clean. Back home they had the support system of household help or extended family. The women are experiencing an internal turmoil for which they have no outlet. They haven't been able to discuss their problems as women in exile. They just don't have the opportunity to come together. The situation often becomes explosive within families. Couples who have been living together in marriage for two decades and more are seeking divorce. It is something totally new, and it is partly due to the process of coming to terms with exile. So the story of change in the lives of exiled Afghan women can be seen as both positive and negative. The young girls face the problem of the lack of an appropriate role model. The mothers' lives are not quite relevant, so they cannot serve as useful role models. The American model is unspecified, complex, varied, and often inappropriate. And then there is the question of relationships with boys. God forbid that an Afghan girl contemplate dating an American boy. She loses forever the chance to marry an Afghan man. But the situation is evolving. Young women are taking some aspects of their own culture and adapting them to certain realities of this society.

As for myself, I am still in the process of sorting out my thoughts and my values. I am constantly defining and redefining myself. I find that the statement "the personal is political" applies in my life. I work with refugee women within an organization I have helped found and shape. It is an emotional experience, because so much that I am dealing with relates to my own personal experiences. But I have learned a great deal about the world through working with these women. Their strength, courage, and leadership capacity has convinced me that a civil society and democratic institutions cannot be imported; that grassroots activists who deal daily with the people on these issues must be fully involved in the process; otherwise ideals will never become reality. I find that the formulas presented in international dialogue often miss the mark when it comes to bringing about change in developing societies. I feel the West can act only as facilitator, providing resources for grassroots efforts in the developing world. They cannot define the problems nor can they propose solutions. We must find our own way through the labyrinth. But I am often alone in my position in gatherings. I am troubled by the stereotypes and misunderstandings about Islam, and I am often the only one in any given gathering to speak out on these topics. I am therefore considered by Western friends and colleagues as much too "Third World," and criticized for failing to define issues in the context of feminism. I believe that fundamentalism is threatening the advancement of women throughout the world. In our part of the world it has become the most volatile subject and the most dangerous to confront. When I speak about fundamentalism, not in terms of religion, but in terms of power relationships and ideology, I am often the only one to voice this position. I am attacked by fundamentalists as agent of Western cultural hegemony. I started from being a victim, built a life and a career, and empowered myself. Now I feel once again that, facing the larger issues, I need to draw on a new reservoir of courage and strength. Once again and within that larger circle, I am the enemy.

I have become disillusioned with some characteristics of this society. The justice system for example is a disappointment. During my divorce, my lawyer explained to me that what is right and what is just are quite irrelevant to the legal system. The winning formula must be sought within the appropriate legal vocabulary. This was disillusioning. The rampant materialism sometimes wearies me. Most of all I miss the texture and permanence of friendships and personal loyalties that are taken quite for granted in our culture. It is these loyalties and friendships that saved my life and the life of each member of my family. For each case of saving a life, someone had to risk his or make a great sacrifice. I don't see that sort of give-and-take in this country. The pace of this society imposes a lack of depth and permanence on people's interactions. Life becomes mechanical. Nothing stays the same for long. Whole neighborhoods are transformed overnight. The pace of life does not match people's needs to form personal relationships and attachments.

I don't feel completely integrated into this society. I am also certain that if the time came and I went back, I would not feel integrated into the indigenous Afghan society. I suppose some of us, the women in exile, become internationalists. It is not easy. It is like being torn between two worlds. But there is the possibility of becoming comfortable in both worlds. We have multiple vantage points from which to view the world. We are less likely to take things for granted. We are more prone to asking ourselves questions about identity, about values, about cultures, about the laws and regulations that govern our coming together and our staying apart. I haven't quite come to terms with all of that yet. I know there is something lacking, but I also know that I want the striving for understanding to become the driving force of my life. I am resigned to knowing that this is a continuing process of assessment and evaluation and change. This is the positive aspect of my life in exile. But the negative stays with me. The knowledge that I can't go home again. That someone has stripped me of that right. That someone has decided to take away my status, my citizenship, my country. The rage stays with me.

At a certain point in my life of exile, I realized that I had the choice to remain frozen in the trauma of exile or to use my personal, professional, and educational background to empower and develop myself and to assist other women in the process. I decided to recognize my feelings, to allow myself to realize what caused them, yet not to immerse myself in my trauma. I decided to take charge of myself, to gather up and focus my energies. The successful struggle to transcend the condition of exile has strongly shaped my life. It defines who I am.

# MARJORIE AGOSIN

# I Invented a Country

Don't conspire with
oblivion,
tear down the silence.
I want to be
the appeared woman
from among the labyrinths
come back, return
name myself.
Call my name.

—Marjorie Agosin

*Marjorie opened the door of her small, pretty house, and the face I saw framed in the doorway was soft with a youthfulness that has little to do with age. Her blue eyes and wavy, golden hair reminded me of colored cutouts of angels we used to collect as children. She smiled warmly and asked me to come in. She introduced me to her friend, a journalist who sat at the kitchen table holding a mug of coffee close to her face. She handed me a cup and asked me to look around and find a comfortable place. I was grateful that she sensed my need to relate to a particular corner of a given physical space. I picked a spot behind the couch in the living room, near the kitchen. I sat on the floor and without a question or a smile at my odd choice she settled herself directly in front of me.*

*She told me her story in soft, hushed tones, pouring the words out with the steady sound of a small, gurgling stream. To Marjorie being a poet is being. She has willed herself into a poetic perception of the world by defining her exile in terms of her language. To her exile means not hearing her language. She has built herself a cocoon of the finest colored threads and rests watchfully inside. Her words sur-*

*round her and protect her from any real or perceived harshness outside.*

I WAS BORN in Santiago, Chile, in 1955. I had a very happy childhood. My parents were intellectuals in Chilean society. I grew up in a free environment where ideas mattered more than money and where differences among people were considered an enriching part of life. We grew up mixing with a diverse group of people and having tremendous respect for the ways of others. My father was a prominent scientist and we traveled a lot because of his work.

My first trip to the United States was in the 1960s when we went to Berkeley. I loved living there so much I didn't want to go back to Chile. When it was time to return, they told me we were going to Disneyworld and suddenly I found myself landing in Santiago Airport. My first contact with the world outside my own country was a wonderful one.

In 1971 my father was offered a position at the University of Georgia in Athens. Chile was undergoing a time of political turmoil. Supporters of Salvador Allende were in constant conflict with others on the right. Before this period my family had been apolitical. My father concerned himself with pure science and thought the university should not be a place for the playing out of political games. He has changed a great deal since then. The times have affected the way he looks at politics.

But in 1971 he was sick of the political tensions in Chile. There were demonstrations at the university. Opposing forces brought their feuds to the classroom. Sometimes he went to his office to find the door locked. There were days when he couldn't enter the university at all because of the demonstrations and the chaos they caused. There was violence on the streets. My father decided to accept the invitation of the University of Georgia.

I didn't want to leave Chile. I had nightmares as we prepared to leave. Every night I dreamed I had lost my satchel with my school notebooks in it. In the dream I looked everywhere for it—on the mountains, in the sea, in far corners. But it was nowhere to be found and I couldn't leave without it. For the first time in my recollection, my parents had arguments. Once my mother was so angry she threw the enormous Santiago phone book at my father. It wasn't that we had to leave in a hurry. But my father had taken ill. He had developed an extreme case of hyperthyroidism because of severe emotional stress.

It was in Georgia in 1973 when we heard that Salvador Allende had been killed. We all felt we no longer had a country. I was sixteen at that time. I remember repeating to myself as I walked to school, "I have no country anymore." It was a powerful feeling. The event brought sad years for my family. There was no formal barrier to our return to Chile. But we felt we would be returning to an occupied country.

My father decided that we should live in the United States until the dictatorship ceased. He felt he couldn't raise his three children in what he considered a nation under occupation. I grew into adulthood feeling I was a woman without a country. The loss of my country brought me a new love for it—stronger and more studied than any I could have experienced outside the condition of exile. In a way, I invented a country. I wanted to recuperate what was lost. I did it through language. That is the reason that even though I left very young and I have always written, I have never written in English. Taking up another language would be a betrayal, a deeper separation from my native country. In times of pain and sadness, writing in my language made me feel safe. Writing was security. The Spanish language gave me my identity.

Exile brought me a sharpened sense of my feelings for my country. I found my identity and a more vivid sense of my life-experiences through words. Being cut off from my past made me more intensely aware of my memories. I recreated the past over and over again. I have many versions of events and scenes, and they are all palpable and detailed. When my uncle died and I couldn't be there to see him, I learned to relive his presence. If I had been in Chile I would never have concentrated with such energy on remembering every detail of his appearance. I would have seen him. There would have been no need for imaginings.

My youth made me feel cheated. I felt the country was taken away from me before I had a chance to experience it from within, before observing it from without would take away from me the feeling of being a native. I was like a tree without roots. I felt unsteady, insecure, easily toppled by any strong wind. I grabbed at everything Chilean to steady myself. I returned often to reestablish my ties with my relations—my uncles, my aunts. I needed to connect with the land. I used to walk around the seashore and I would repeat to myself, "These are my stones, this is my sea, these are my waters." I wanted to appropriate the land for myself.

The United States has been very welcoming. But that in some ways is terrible, because the surface acceptance covers lightly a deeper intolerance for differences, for foreigners. If you dress unusually, have an accent, look at the world in a different way, you are made to feel your otherness. This sense of not fully belonging here moved me toward closer connection with Chile. I am not sure which was the cause and which the effect—whether my strong involvement with Chile kept me from being fully integrated into this society or my lack of attachment here drove me to even closer ties with my home country.

I became more and more involved in Chilean politics. Almost without planning it I became involved in dangerous political activities. I began working for people who had suffered inside the country. I believe that women suffered the most. I began working with the mothers of the "disappeared." I gathered oral testimonies from these women, I did oral life histories, I wrote a book called *Scraps of Life*, describing the work of the women who made pictures from scraps, which depicted their life stories. I always returned to the United States, using this country as a safe haven. From here I talked about the women who were caught in Chile and suffered on their own account and on account of their loved ones.

The dictatorship forced the women into taking an active role in the life of their country. They organized themselves into groups and worked actively for freedom and for human rights. The women were the initiators of this type of organization and they were the ones who sustained the effort. Women from various strata of society worked together. I saw that once the sincerity and commitment to the common cause were established, differences in lifestyle did not cause a breach between women. Emotional necessity drove them into developing an effective and organized political network. I enjoyed working with women.

Since childhood I had always enjoyed the company of women.

My nanny's stories told to us in the kitchen as she pressed the cotton sheets with her heavy coal iron have stayed with me. Women have always been profoundly real in my life. Working with them during exile was a source of strength and stability.

During this period I saw my own role as someone who could build a bridge of understanding and communication, someone who could help bring the cases of these women and their suffering to the consciousness of the Americans. Having language as my main tool, I used it in the service of a cause that has now become my cause.

Exile became a positive thing for me. I wrote profusely. I wanted to let people in the United States know what it is like for those who cannot return to their homes, for those who are stopped at airports, for those who live in terror of their government. I wrote about the emotions of exile, about the grief in not hearing the language, not seeing the landscape. I explained how I long to walk on the streets of my city. I described how I miss not having to spell my name, not being asked where I am from—how I miss not being there.

When I go to Chile, people ask me what I mean to do there. I usually say I am going to do research. But basically what I always want to do is to walk in the streets. Exiles need to put their bodies in the territory. The experience is very physical—to be present in the land.

Since I have started my work with the mothers of the "disappeared" in Argentina, my world has broadened. I have learned to be both more aware of my own country of origin but at the same time more conscious of a sense of the universality of my concerns. Exile has brought me closer to an understanding of the condition of women in Latin America. I have felt their cause to be my cause. By collecting and translating the work of Latin women poets, I have tried to build a bridge of understanding through language. Being in exile, I have grown from feeling I have no country to accepting the whole world as my country.

The years of exile have changed my father. From being an apolitical person he has changed into a radical. Now that the government has changed, my parents have gone back to Chile. Their move is very important to me. I don't know whether I will go there to live, but I know that my life is closely connected to that land and I will live part of my life there. I am not able to go back and live in Chile because of what has happened to me in exile. I have grown another life here. I have married an American. I have given birth to an American child. I teach at an American college. In my mind I am close to Chile. But in practical life I have grown apart. I feel an outsider in both cultures. The idea of Chile is precious to me. The physical space is an obsession with me. But, like the past, it is more tangible at a distance.

As I became more involved in human rights activities and documentation of the cases of the "disappeared," it became dangerous to go home. I began to be afraid to get off the plane. I was uncertain whether they would let me in or, once I was past immigration, whether I would end up in prison. On every trip I felt they would be coming for me this time. I often felt I was being followed. A car that no one knew about was parked in front of the house for long stretches of time. There were threatening phone calls and anonymous letters telling me to leave and never return.

There are many levels of belonging to a country. I belong to Chile mostly through the language, through my poems. I believe in Mizlowz's concept of language as the only homeland. Maybe no one really has a home except one that he invents.

Hearing the sound of the language is necessary to me. No one questions my accent there. I know what to do. Even after living here for so long, I still don't know exactly what to do and what to say. I don't know what is expected of me. I don't know the limits of intimacy. I have felt betrayed by American friends. I think perhaps we don't share the same understanding of the demands and limits of the relationship. Even now, in a very primitive sense, I always feel I belong in Chile. On another and more practical level I wonder about jobs, education for my child, a house, and the feasibility of transferring what I have built here. But in a visceral sense I belong in Chile.

Now that it is possible to return, I am obsessed with the idea of buying a house there. I want to own a piece of the land. Knowing that I have a key that opens the door of a house in Chile will make me feel much more serene about my life here.

My husband loves Chile. Whether he loves the country because of my love for it or not I don't know. He is wiser than to interfere with my feelings for my homeland. He does not know my life of poetry. We relate closely to each other, but there are parts of our lives that are not shared. Now that I have bought a house and have a baby here, I feel more at home in America. But what I miss is the closeness between people. I remember when I was a teenager here, I couldn't understand going to someone's home around dinner time and not being asked to stay. In Chile we would have expected it. In America, it seems there is always a point when you can not stay to share, you must go home.

When I am in the United States, I get letters telling me what's going on in Chile. It was a strange dictatorship. Some books were published, others were banned. Some people were followed, others were not. There was an insane randomness about the orders. Here I got together with other Chileans and we talked endlessly about the situation, about the future, about what is to be done. It was as if we were here physically, but our souls were there. It's strange how I have no loyalties here. I feel no loyalty to the college, but I feel loyalty to the little school I attended as a child in Chile.

There was always great difference of opinion between Chileans. Some felt they must never leave the country, no matter what the circumstances. Leaving, they felt, was a kind of betrayal. Many lived in exile but never felt they had a home in the United States. All they thought of was going back. Some lived in Chile but envied the ones living abroad. Others resented the exiles, thinking them opportunists, using the exile condition to gain recognition for themselves. I feel that if I had lived in Chile I could never have written *Songs of Pain.*

Being in exile is being outside, at the edge. In that sense perhaps all women are in exile perpetually. They are in exile from the political arena, from important jobs. Ironically, the dictatorship made women less of an exile because they were forced to go out of the home and participate. The dictatorship brought out the worst and the best in Chile. Women were the first to go out and object to what was happening to people; they were the first to denounce the disappearances. Emotional necessity brought them courage and the urge to act. They came together and decided to support each other and to fight. They did not fight through the regular avenues chosen by men. These were women from all classes, the upper to the working-class poor. They organized soup kitchens, they formed the Association of the Disappeared, they organized massive protests. The movement which they began out of necessity helped to bring them into the mainstream of political activism. They became less peripheral, less marginal, less exiled. Their decision to take things into their own hands, to fight, was an important step. But more important were the ways in which they fought. These were different from the avenues chosen by men. I worked with these groups in 1978, '79, and '80. I was never a revolutionary or a radical leftist. I was always quite middle class. But the drive to bring women of various classes to work together was made easy because there was no ill-will. There was trust in each other's motives. No one tried to be something other than they were. The lower-class women were also middle class in their aspirations. They wanted a comfortable home, enough food for their children, hot running water, electricity. I learned not to make metaphors out of poverty and out of exile or even out of life in the rural areas. It was important not to aggrandize the country for the eyes of others. For my inner self, yes, but not when dealing with others.

My trips to Chile helped me realize my feminism. Out of my own marginality in exile, I began to understand and communicate with "Women of Smoke," beggars, women in mental hospitals, disappeared women, veiled women. I made poetry out of such horrible things, but the words grew out of complete identification, direct association, and empathy. When I go back, I go back to these women. They were subjects for study in my book *Women of Smoke,* but now they have become my friends. I have become a good poet through these intense relationships. I don't know about my writing, but I am certain of my poetry. When I was asked about my writing in the past, I used to make excuses, but then one day I didn't need to any more. I write when I am in pain, when I am sad—I write to feel safe. Writing brings me closer to the language which is my inner self, my reality, my identity. I think life in exile has sharpened my feeling for and my appreciation of the Spanish language. Things become sharper because one uses one's memory and imagination more. I wasn't there when my uncle died. I think about him being dead. I want to see his face. I try to recreate his face to remember details about him. The need to reconstruct images when you are away comes from distance itself. If I had been in Chile I would never have thought about his face. He would have been there and I would have seen it. The intensity and focus would have been unnecessary.

I cannot go back there to live. I have a husband, a child, a job, a home. I cannot go back any more. But I have this physical longing to have a house there. A house to which I would have the key. I would go there anytime I want and just simply turn the lock and enter. I have a terrible need to own a piece of the land in my home country.

Meanwhile I speak with my husband in English, with my son in Spanish, and keep my many worlds apart. The world I feel happiest in is the one inside my head—the world of the words of poetry. There are things I don't share with anybody, not even my husband. They are mine. Perhaps it is a schizophrenic existence, but in a way I've managed to bring order to chaos. I hold the pieces of my world together with the thread of poetry.

I feel I want to be buried in Chile. It frightens me to think I will grow old in this country. I don't want to think of myself in the future retiring as a professor at Wellesley College with a few people and a few cookies celebrating my passage to old age. Above all, I don't want to be buried here. In our culture there is little distance between the dead and the living. When I go home I visit the gravesite of the dead the same way I visit the living. I know that if I die here, no one will come to my burial and no one will visit my grave.

I have no close friends in this country. I have learned to divide my time and to live my many lives. Like my father I have learned to protect myself. When there is tension in the house or when something in the world outside begins to intrude upon my inner life, I simply say, "I must protect myself." My husband doesn't care because he is a scientist with his own world to which I have no access. But in our twelve years of marriage we have become good friends in meaningful ways. We are a strong couple even though we don't share every aspect of our being. He thinks I love Chile because I had a wonderful childhood there. But he is too intelligent to interfere with my love of Chile. He is very respectful. He appreciates the closeness with my family—something he lacks in his American family. I have not had a close relationship with his, but he has gained the affection of and intimacy in my family.

I dream of my grandparents house. In my dream I still see the steps leading to the closet beneath the kitchen where all the good things to eat were kept. It was magic. In my dreams I see my grandfather waving goodbye to me from the balcony of his house the way I saw him that last time. I knew then looking back at him and waving that I would never see him again. He died four months later. Last week I dreamed I painted my kitchen a bright yellow and it turned into my grandmother's kitchen. Often I dream I am in my childhood home, walking toward a door. I open the door looking for someone, and it's me that I see on the other side. I go looking for someone that I loved and I find myself there—a younger me.

In all this I have learned that women are deeper, stronger than men in their relationships. They are capable of intimacy without too much preparation, too much hedging and insurance. During the period of exile, the women who had never worked, never supported a family, women with little education picked up the pieces of their lives and started building. They were the pillars of the family structure. They held everything together.

As for me I have learned a lot from exile. I have learned to love my country with a passion. I have learned the nooks and crannies of my language and have come to use it to give structure to my inner life. I have also learned to broaden my horizons. The world has become a smaller place. I can feel good anywhere. I have an image of carrying a home on my shoulders by carrying my language with me. I can go to Yugoslavia or Argentina and feel fine because my home is in the imagination.

# TATYANA MAMONOVA

# In the Frame of My Life
# I Saw My Mother's Picture

*I met Tatyana at a book party at Robin Morgan's flat. She is an attractive woman with severe and sturdy good looks, boyish short hair, and a robust pink complexion. She has been profoundly affected by the sudden celebrity she was plunged into when in the preglasnost days she became the first feminist to be exiled from the then Soviet Union. She was whisked from lectures to television talk shows to consciousness-raising meetings—always in the company of luminaries of the Western feminist movement. A slender young woman accompanies her like a shadow—inseparable. It is not as easy to establish rapport in the presence of a third party who does not share the experience of exile. Tatyana was at first ill at ease, often referring me to other interviews, as if she were bored with her own version of her life.*

*As a poet, she felt uncomfortable with her command of the English language. She felt claustrophobic within the confines of her limited vocabulary and felt her stark and shadowless exposition unworthy of the emotions she was trying to convey. But soon she dismissed her worries about her language skills and began to share scenes that still touched her and affected her actions and decisions. We experienced together the frustration of knowing that the mother and the father who vexed us or filled us with fear, pity, or dismay is no longer there; that if they were there, no matter what comforting words they would choose to tell us today, they could no longer tell it to the child who suffered and who has ceased to exist. We shared the sadness of knowing that the countries we had loved and left have disappeared, and what has replaced them will never fill the void the past has left in our hearts.*

I WAS BORN in a small village near Moscow even though my family is from Leningrad. My mother was pregnant with me during World War II. When Leningrad was blockaded by the German army, the Russian government evacuated all pregnant women from the city. I can't recall much about the village where I was born, but my intuitive feminism remembers having been surrounded by women. The men were all gone to war. There weren't many children around when I was little. I remember being the only child of my age in the village. The atmosphere of love and understanding that surrounded the women in my early life has been an important influence on me.

At the end of the war, when I was still almost a baby, we moved back to Leningrad. It was a difficult time in the city in those days. There was a shortage of fuel and food. My memories of my childhood years after the war are of cold and hunger. My mother took the responsibility for me and for my brother, who was born three years later.

My father was a lawyer but I don't recall much justice from him. He tried to raise my brother differently from me. He never stopped reminding me that I was a girl and that my place was in the kitchen with my mother. He did not have such expectations for my brother. My earliest memories are of clashes and arguments over why I should do household chores and not my brother. I asked him why my brother didn't have to wash dishes even though he ate just as I did. My father's answer was always, "Because you are a girl." What does it mean to be a girl, I wondered. Does it mean dirty dishes and hot stoves and taking care of other people's physical needs? If that's what it means I wasn't sure I wanted to be a girl.

My fights with my father strengthened my personality. I was able to find ways to stand up to his arguments. I evolved into a strong feminist even before I had any notion of the meaning of the term. My brother was influenced by me, and he began copying me. He became a feminist later, but he wasn't really on my side during these early "debates" with my father.

My mother was not a revolutionary personality. In later years she feared my oppositional work against the government and didn't support my feminist views. At first, however, I didn't have a formulated ideology. I just wanted to be an artist and a poet. I was naturally drawn to that life.

In the 1960s I began to realize myself as a personality. It was a period of liberation in the Soviet Union. There was a considerable flow of information from the West. For a short period, we were once again allowed to be in touch with our own history. I began to experience a certain freedom and to experiment with various ideas, philosophies, and concepts and to reach inward to my own essential needs and feelings.

My education came from reading many books. I didn't learn much in school. The strict, prisonlike discipline repelled me. There was no warmth in the relationship with the teachers and no room for experimentation and curiosity. My high school years ended at the beginning of the euphoric sixties, and the atmosphere of that period helped shape my personality.

I was sensitive to language and was disturbed by the pornographic references to women in the everyday speech of Russian men. They may have been unaware of the implications of their language, but it deeply offended me. I felt instinctively that a man's way of gaining security and a sense of personal empowerment in a repressive society is to oppress the woman in his life. Women didn't have such an outlet.

The discrepancy between the rhetoric of the state and the actual practice concerning women upset me. I was repulsed by the hypocrisy involved. We were constantly told about the equality of men and women, but I saw this neither at home nor in society. I was quite confused. I wanted to be free to explore the limits of my own personality, to express myself the way I was. But society was pushing me toward a stereotype I couldn't accept, one that my mother willingly embraced. She considered the rules of patriarchal society the only normal standard possible. In another society my mother could have become a much more interesting person. She lost a lot by allowing the state-sanctioned models to mold her life and shape her existence. I didn't want to repeat the same fate. I didn't have a clear idea of the life I wished for myself as a woman, but I knew I didn't want to become my mother. The frame offered by Soviet society for a woman's life was limiting—it allowed only an image such as my mother represented. I looked at my life within that society and in the frame of my life I saw my mother's picture. It was frightening.

I love my mother and I pity her, but more than anything I want to be unlike her. Now that my work has been recognized, she seems to appreciate my positions, but it is the success rather than the ideas that appeal to her.

I don't know how I learned to become an activist feminist. Perhaps reaction to my parents' relationship was instrumental in shaping my thinking. Perhaps living in the village surrounded by all the women had something to do with it. It may be that when my brother was born and I saw the difference in the way my father treated us I became rebellious.

My mother was good at mathematics. She worked a full day outside the home as an accountant and a full day as a housewife caring for all of us. My father spent time with his friends after finishing his day at his prestigious job. He smoked and drank and read his newspaper in peace. He hardly ever took on any chores at home. Sometimes he did his own ironing, but he was embarrassed to admit this to his friends. So we argued and I asked questions about the difference in status and prospects between men and women. He couldn't answer and my questions, and arguments became stronger. Finally he came to respect me.

With my mother I didn't even discuss or argue. She was a victim of patriarchal society. I remember her as being always very busy, caring for the mundane things of life. She never had time to read or go to the theater or do anything for pure pleasure. She spent a lot of time with us. My father was a free agent. He ate out most of the time. He drank a lot and in fact became an alcoholic. He was violent to my brother. It was part of the male tradition to hit a boy. He was also violent to my mother out of an unreasonable jealousy. I am sure he played around with other women. My mother never had the time to consider any other man, but he was irrational in his jealousy. He never hit me, however.

My first important job was with the official media. First I worked with television and then the magazine for youth, called *Aurora*. I worked in the poetry section. It was a prestigious job—one I had dreamed of getting. But when the editors showed reluctance to publish my poetry on the ground that it was too avant garde and "formal," I became disillusioned. They told me the poems don't sound "Soviet." I wasn't writing about red flags or about Lenin. These weren't themes of my poetry. They did, however, publish my translations from French, German, and Polish.

I read a lot of literature coming from the West: philosophy, poetry, novels, but not much feminist theory. Some of the work of the men at that time displayed a feminist sensitivity, but not much written by women was available in the Soviet Union. I read a short article by Karen Horney that had a strong influence on me. Some of Simone de Beauvoir's short stories could be found in bookstores or libraries, but none of her feminist writings. I didn't know she was a feminist. *Feminism* was a strange word. The approved designation was "emancipation of women," a phrase used as a respectable cover for the exploitation of women. To be an emancipated woman was to have the burdens of work outside the home added to the burdens of life under patriarchy. Men continued as before. The model was "wonder woman"—beautiful, impeccable housekeeper, doting mother of many children, and hard worker at the factory. It was an impossible model to emulate, and it held every woman to a standard that made her a born failure.

The official view of sexuality was very puritan: Sex is no good. But at the same time the sexual revolution was in full swing in the Soviet Union, and I was participating in it with great vigor. After the confinement of school, I felt the real world had opened up to me and I wanted to be involved in everything—the sexual revolution was just part of the whole picture.

Meanwhile my work continued. My official position was literary consultant, but when the administrators found I knew many languages, I was given extra work for which I received additional pay. But they continued to refuse to publish my poetry. They said the poetry was good but it didn't fit the official point of view. However, they published certain poems of a very progressive nature which I translated from French or German. Different standards applied to literature coming from abroad. They thought my poetry was affected by the corrupt bourgeois world. But I had no actual contact with this corrupt bourgeois world, so it must have been my own ideas that I expressed in my work. The openness in my poetry was unacceptable to them.

During this period I found a close friend who worked at the magazine with me. We talked at length about our views and our experiences. The exchange of ideas with her helped form my feminist consciousness. We talked about freedom to be the way we are. It was mostly about self-esteem. The way to be, we decided, was to be true to our nature, not to some official recipe.

At one point we tried to organize a women's group. We did some *listovka*, or posters, inviting women to organize. I wrote up notices and left them inside books at the library as a way of communicating with women. Instead of receiving a reaction from women, I received my first call from the KGB. It was 1968. I was young and naive, and all I really wanted was to get a group of women together to discuss our problems. But even though there was a great deal of talk about openness, the KGB controlled every movement. They must have picked up the announcements from all the books.

In the early seventies I became involved in the nonconformist artistic movement. I was spending much of my time painting and writing poetry. I participated in a number of exhibitions with my miniatures, which illustrated my poems. I was the only woman to be included. We organized exhibitions in Moscow, Leningrad, and the Baltic Republics. Soon I realized that sexism was by no means limited to official circles. My colleagues among the nonconformist artists displayed quite a bit of it as well. Their nonconformism did not carry over to their relationship with women. Sexual revolution to them meant what amounted to raping women. So, even though I was quite successful within this group and sold a lot of my art, I decided to leave them.

In 1973 I married an artist who shared my views. In 1975 I gave birth to my son. This event influenced me very much. I had a terrible experience at the maternity clinic, and what I saw there brought home to me the reality of the condition of women in Soviet society.

During the ten days I spent at the clinic I was not allowed to shower. They were afraid I would faint or fall. They couldn't let me go alone and they wouldn't let someone accompany me. They didn't permit my husband to visit me in the maternity ward or to talk to me. My male gynecologist treated me with extraordinary lack of sensitivity. When the baby came he announced with a great deal of joy, "It's a boy." I had always wanted a daughter. I had pictured in detail the daughter I would have. I gave birth to a son and quickly learned to love him. But to be confronted with the doctor's prejudice at the moment of my son's birth was unpleasant. It made me feel as if he were letting me know that I had enhanced my value to society by giving birth to a male child. I saw other women being mistreated there. They accepted it all quietly and meekly, as if it were all quite normal. I realized that even standards by which to determine what is normal were created by men. It was these standards that were at the root of our condition.

When I got out of the hospital I wrote an article about my experience of giving birth at the maternity clinic. This was the beginning of my almanac *Woman and Russia,* my second and more serious attempt at creating an unofficial women's organization. During my travels in the Soviet Union as a journalist, I interviewed many women on issues of importance to them, but I was never able to publish the interviews. The almanac gave me a chance to publish these interviews. I showed my article on the maternity clinic to a number of women. I realized from their reactions that almost all of them had experienced similar conditions, either at the maternity clinic or in some other situation that involved sexist treatment.

The women's eagerness to exchange experiences and to talk about their condition showed me the importance of sharing and discussing mutual problems. But I realized also that women were afraid to be published in an unofficial journal because they knew of the arrests and maltreatment of dissidents. The tyranny and terror of the Stalinist era was fresh in everyone's minds.

It took four years to organize a group of women and to publish *Woman and Russia.* I didn't consider my plans "political" at first, but I soon learned that whatever work we initiated as women in a group was considered political by the system. The system feared women and worried about grassroots efforts to organize them. In 1979 the KGB called me once again, and, very politely, invited me to their office. On December 10, which coincided with International Human

Rights Day and also my birthday, I was interrogated. There was a sinister quality to their politeness when they questioned me. I was frightened and they were aware of my fear. I had agreed to go because I knew that if I didn't, they would search my house and find some pretext to arrest me.

They let me go with the understanding that I would cease my activity on behalf of women. It was implied that if I refused to comply I would be sent to Siberia. I was lucky because by this time I already had a network of women activists and good connections among the diplomatic community and foreign journalists. I informed my Western contacts of what had passed. They invited a press conference and the Western press publicized my case. The faux pas about the date helped in the publicity.

Our feminist meetings took place in my apartment. They were really quite innocent. We talked about giving birth, health clinics, rape, sexual harassment, and the double burden women are forced to carry. We discussed our children and the inefficiency of the childcare system. We wrote down some of our ideas and discussions. I typed five copies of the almanac and gave it to five trusted women friends. They each typed five copies and gave it to five others. That is the way *samizdat* is prepared and distributed, each small circle taking the idea to a little larger circle—like a pebble thrown in a pool of water, creating a widening series of ripples.

I never knew how many and whom to expect in our meetings. Sometimes women came from as far away as Central Asian and Baltic Republics. But by the time I published the second volume of the almanac, the government decided to try a new tactic in order to stop me. They decided to eliminate whatever danger I represented as quietly as possible. First they attempted a campaign of false rumors and propaganda among my neighbors and acquaintances. They were quite successful. Agents of the KGB who were present in every group and neighborhood attacked everything about me, from my integrity as a Soviet citizen to my capacity to mother my child. They tried to build a case for taking away my son from me on the ground that I was an unfit mother.

It was a frightening and suffocating feeling. I felt the atmosphere around me thickening with innuendo and hostility. It was like moving in a dense fog. One felt threatened but couldn't identify the cause or the source. I continued my activity, but I was tense and fearful of what might come.

On the morning of July 20, 1980, I was awakened at 5:00 A.M. Two men from the KGB were at the door. They searched the apartment. They told me to pack. They said I would be leaving for Austria. They searched me and my four-year-old son for jewels and documents. My husband and I were rushed to the airport with our son. We were allowed two suitcases. My home, my belongings, my library, my Soviet passport were taken away from me.

In a few hours we found ourselves in Vienna, dazed and confused by the shock and the suddenness of our leaving our homeland. We were taken to a dirty little hotel with bugs crawling around and pornographic magazines strewn everywhere. I didn't know at that time that my almanac had already been published in book form in France. In a short time the diplomatic contacts I had established in Russia contacted French women leaders and soon they organized a large press conference for me in Vienna. The media around the world picked up my story. The press conference was very successful. The only thing that the journalists were skeptical about was my prediction that the Soviet Union would change radically in five or six years. I am proud that I knew my people and my country well enough to foresee the coming upheaval.

I was taken to a four star hotel where we had the whole floor. It was an incredible change. My husband, who had assisted me in my work for women, had shared my initial panic. We had experienced the terror caused by disruption of our lives and the insecurity of our new and alien surroundings. What will we do? How will we survive? we had asked each other repeatedly, neither of us capable of producing answers. But the Vienna press conference changed my life. I received international publicity and overnight I became a star of feminism.

Before I could form any special plans I was invited to Paris to work with French television. I kept my contacts with Soviet women and continued to publish the almanac. I published a number of issues of *Woman and Russia* in France, England, and Germany. The government's effort to silence me by sending me into exile in the West gave more publicity to the feminist movement in the Soviet Union than any effort I could have made inside the country. The almanac was published as a book in twenty-two countries and in eleven languages, thus attesting to the universality of the problems that women face.

The changes that have taken place in my country in recent years have influenced my life once again. I follow the unfolding of events in Russia with great interest and ponder, especially, their effect on women. Although there is much excitement as Russian women begin to interact freely and choose new areas of activity and interest, it seems once again that changes in political structures and shifts in the composition of the ruling elite do not necessarily and automatically improve the condition of women. Women's status within various societies is determined by the patriarchal structures on which they are based. It is these structures that we must transform throughout the world and in every society, and it is in this struggle that I wish to be involved.

Seeing the need and the opportunity to reconnect my Russian sisters with women from around the world, and noticing the continuing lack of a forum for women to learn about each other's lives, I felt it was time to find a way of dealing with these problems. Two young American feminists with whom I have developed a deep friendship have helped me to better understand this society. Sharing our varied backgrounds and our experience of other societies, we have studied carefully the underlying connection between patriarchy and women's oppression worldwide. In response to our analysis of the condition of women, we decided to found a journal entitled *Woman and Earth* with the goal of providing a forum for global communication and interaction between women. Our growing awareness of the need to pay greater respect to our environment also forms an important part of *Woman and Earth*. I consider this journal to be the sequel to my *samizdat* almanac *Woman and Russia,* for it expands on the initial goal of providing an opportunity for women to exchange ideas. The positive response we have received to *Woman and Earth* indicates that there is great interest in providing women with a global forum.

Realizing the importance of communication in bringing about understanding and cooperation, I have produced a series of television programs in the United States and have sent the videos to be aired in Russia.

Recently I have gotten my green card. Ironically, my Russian passport has been returned to me at a time when I no longer need it desperately. My ideal is to arrange a dual citizenship whereby I can be connected to both countries but totally dependent on neither. I want to work for the cause of women within both societies as a way of dealing with women's rights globally.

Even though my work and my friendships keep me busy and fulfilled, I often miss my city Leningrad, now St. Petersburg. I think it is the most beautiful city in the world. In my dreams the setting of my life is always Leningrad. Often I dream I am flying over the city. It is a wonderfully happy experience. It's usually a sunny day. The sky is storybook blue and there are puffy white clouds and I feel very slender—almost transparent, and light as air. I glide over the city smoothly and silently. There are no people and no conversation in my dreams. It is only when I daydream about going back home that I imagine conversations with people.

I miss the nature in Russia—meadows, rivers, forests. Once at a conference here in the United States I walked out into a meadow. The smell of grass was like Russia. Tears came to my eyes. But then I thought, "It is the earth which is my home. The meadows everywhere on earth smell the same. It is the earth I love."

America has been both good and bad for me. As I grew up in the Soviet Union, I developed a very idealistic image of the West. The cleanliness, the plenty, the freedom could never have been what I had imagined. But what I hadn't expected was the absence of the human element in interactions with people, the coolness and distance in relationships. Worst of all was the realization of the condition of women. It was disappointing to see the double standard of the patriarchal system which encourages the subjugation of women. I had thought of the society here as very progressive. I was shocked to see the defeat of ERA.

I am grateful to America for the discovery of the work of the many wonderful feminist writers. It is a feast for the soul.

My son has conflicting feelings about this country and his own. The media's rendition of Russia is often unflattering, sometimes hostile. At times he feels ashamed of his origins. But deep in his heart he feels attachment and affection for his native land. He speaks many languages because of our travels, but he is still very comfortable with Russian. This is one fortunate aspect of exile—when you leave home, you go elsewhere and there you learn about the language and customs not your own.

Virginia Woolf once said, "As a woman I have no country." Exile has taught me the same lesson. It is the other side of the coin when I say I am a citizen of the world. I feel a citizen of the world in my own country and a citizen of the world in America. The feeling has nothing to do with passports, identity papers, legal documents, permanent addresses. It is a feeling inside that says the bond has been broken. You belong nowhere. Sometimes there is the momentary pleasure of feeling at home in the exchange of a friendly glance, in the taste of a fruit, in the color of a landscape, in the words of a poem. But as life progresses, I wait to feel the unquestioning attachment to a land again. It has yet to happen to me.

# SAMNANG WU

# A Lucky Woman

*I waited for her in the Chinese restaurant near her house. She walked to the table, a tiny woman with big, round, questioning eyes. She moved with caution and glanced at other tables before approaching me. I told her about myself and the reason I had asked to meet her. We talked about the maze of people who had led me one to the other, and finally to her. I did not mention to her that two of her compatriots had expressed their doubts that anyone would be willing to share the painful experiences of the Pol Pot period in Cambodia. I thought the reticence of her compatriots might lead her to question her own sensitivity or the propriety of telling her life story. I felt uneasy withholding this information from her, although I knew that my silence was meant to avoid placing her in an awkward position.*

*After that moment of holding back, I felt withdrawn from our conversation. She finally smiled, her eyes twinkling, and said, "I want to be part of the biography. I must tell you that after you told me about your Iranian origin, I was worried. 'Who is this woman?' I thought. 'I have escaped the deadly events in Cambodia to harm myself with this Iranian who may be a terrorist?' I called Sima Wali at Refugee Women in Development, and she assured me that you are one of us and that I should join the project."*

*I laughed with relief. I knew now that I could share with this woman the reaction of others from her country and it would have no effect on her evaluation of her own narrative or the manner in which she recounted it.*

*She met me next in my office on a Saturday, bringing rice and meat stew she had prepared. I brought Persian cookies and oranges. We talked of our adventures, the telling of which no longer seemed to have a discernible effect on our appetite.*

I WAS BORN in 1952 in Pnom Phen City, the capital of Cambodia. That's where the king and queen lived. I am the middle child in a family of four sisters. There are no sons in our family even though my father would have loved a son. My mother died after giving birth to stillborn twins. She had swollen arms and legs and high blood pressure in the last months of her pregnancy. During labor, she began to hemorrhage. For two weeks she bled heavily. They couldn't stop the bleeding and she died. I was nine years old at the time.

We lived among an extended family in a villagelike suburb of the capital. But even though there were so many kinfolk near us, I missed my mother very much and my life was empty without her. My little sister was five years old. I couldn't explain to her what had happened. She couldn't understand the idea of death.

My childhood had been a happy one. We were surrounded by aunts, uncles, cousins. There must have been one hundred kinfolk living in the neighborhood. In Cambodia it was customary for young people to marry close relations. The first choice of marriage partner was one's first cousin. The marriages between close kin created complicated relationships. Often cousins were also aunts and uncles and a huge network of ties connected members of a family together. My grandparents on my mother's side were affluent. They had a large house and servants. My father came from a farm family who lived in a village outside the city. His rank was much below that of my mother's family. My mother didn't mind, but she resented his lack of education. She had gone to school for a year. She was taken out of school because my grandmother thought if a woman learned to read and write, she would use her skill to write love letters. But my mother was determined to learn. She paid her brother to teach her to read and write. My mother's family took pride in their education.

My mother had refused to marry her first cousin, as required in our culture. She said she had played with him since childhood and he was like a brother to her. So my grandparents were unhappy with her and they chose my father even though he was from a lower class and uneducated.

Our family life was peaceful and pleasant. Each night we gathered together for the evening meal. We spoke of what had passed during the day and we discussed any accomplishments or setbacks we had experienced. Father advised us on our behavior. We gathered around the radio and listened to it together. At bedtime we prayed, and if we had made mistakes during the day, we knelt down on the floor and confessed to our parents, saying, for instance, "I shouted at the cat today," or "I told a lie," or "I got zero in my mathematics class," and asked for forgiveness for our shortcomings.

Every week my grandmother took me to the temple to listen to the monk's sermon. I was five years old and uninterested in the monk's talk. I dozed off regularly. My blissful weekly naps in the temple continued for another two years. Then my grandmother decided that I was old enough to benefit from the talk. She began poking me to wake me up and said it is a sin to ignore the sermon of the monk. She told me about religion, explaining the importance of good acts and truthfulness. "If you lie," she admonished me "you will come back as an ugly girl in the next life, your mouth big and your skin dark as coal." I never lied until the communist regime forced me to lie for my survival.

My mother's uncle was a soothsayer. He drew horoscopes for the royal family. He had old books which looked very strange and complicated with numbers and drawings—books in a language we couldn't read. He gave us advice about the future. We were privileged to get advice and information sought and paid for by the court. My granduncle told us stories. He wore long, white robes and kept his hair tied back at the nape of his neck. When he came to our house, he would sit on the floor, stretch out his legs on the carpet, lean back against the cushions, and talk. Some twenty children would sit around listening, taking turns massaging his legs and feet as he told his tales. He enjoyed the massage and the rapt attention, so he told us one tale after another. Most of his stories had a moral or a point that was intended to help shape our character. He told us many stories about *Kruplaek,* the perfect woman. Each city or village had a special tale about a woman whose behavior was unusually courageous or smart. They used these stories to teach the young how to act. My granduncle knew many stories about the "perfect women" of different areas. I learned from these stories, and in later years recollected the women's choices and decisions to remind myself of the course of action I ought to follow.

We asked for my granduncle's advice in the choice of name for every newborn baby in the family. He decided on the name to suit the destiny of each child. He chose my name, Samnang, which means "lucky." I was a premature baby, and all the wise women and the elders were sure that I wouldn't last. My mother mourned me at my birth. My granduncle consulted his books and charts and predicted that I would survive and grow up to become a very strong woman and represent my family in pride. He chose the name for me to reflect that belief. My mother, who set great store by his word, stopped crying when he told her his prediction. In later years, I came to share my mother's conviction about my granduncle's words, even though some of my family members with a European education did not. But whether they believed or not, they all had to keep quiet and assent. One doesn't challenge an elder member of the family. Often my grandparents told me things that didn't sound right to me. I talked to my father about this, telling him what I thought. My father agreed with me and told me I could believe what I like. But, of course, he told me not to contradict the old people to their face.

After my mother's death, my father increased his efforts to succeed in his work. He designed delicate and beautiful jewels in the old style. Gradually his jewelry business became successful. Soon he decided to remarry. His new wife was young and pretty. My grandparents were worried that the second wife would mistreat us. One day my grandmother came to our house and asked my father to let her take me and my sister to live with her. My father said, "My two daughters are like my two eyes. No one can take them away from me."

I was a good student at school. My mother's catch phrase, "an illiterate person is blind," stayed with me. I studied hard and my teachers gave good reports to her. She was proud of me. When I finished high school, I started working at the Red Cross office, distributing food and clothing to the refugees from the villages who had fled the Viet Cong. We brought food and clothing with us to be distributed in the temple. I felt good about working with children who were so much in need of help, those who were hungry or needed cover for the nights.

One day while working at the temple, I met a man. He looked shriveled up and aged from exhaustion and lack of nourishment. He told me he came to the city when the Viet Cong took his village and was staying at the temple while attending law school. Although the weather was balmy, he shivered with cold. I gave him a blanket I had brought to distribute. He took the blanket, brought it to his nose and said, "Hmm, that smells good." I told him it was my own blanket. His hand was icy. I was curious about him. He looked too old to be going to school. I couldn't ask his age directly so I said, "I am twenty one." He said "I am twenty four." I liked the way he talked—very gentle.

The temple was near our house. I often thought of going to see him. But it was not proper for me to visit a stranger alone. One day I decided to go there without telling my father. The medicine and food had made such a difference in him. He looked like the young man that he was. We talked about his plans to go back to school now that he was well. I told him if he needed help to buy books, I would be glad to assist. In my culture there was no allowance for the kind of feeling I had for this young man. I could not acknowledge, even to myself, that I was attracted to him. But I kept surprising myself by showing up at the temple at every chance. One day I went to the temple to see him. He was sitting with a group of friends. The boys smiled and snickered and exchanged knowing glances. It became very difficult to go to the temple alone.

I knew he needed to go to the library to study because he couldn't afford to buy books for law school. So I went to the library, half hoping to see him, half afraid that I would. I told my friend who came with me that I intended to help a young man with his studies. She laughed, saying, "Yes, it makes sense that a pretty high school girl suddenly feels a need to help a handsome law student study." That remark upset me. I thought of going home, but decided to move to another part of the library. The young man came and sat next to me. I began to worry that my friend would notice our relationship and word would get back to my family. I was distant and silent. He was depressed by my attitude. "Is it my poor clothes and lack of money that makes you be cold and distant?" he asked. I said, "You are very wrong. I don't think that way."

We kept meeting each other at the library. This was a time of war and young men were being drafted into the army. He asked me how I felt about the military services. I said, "I respect the military who are defending our country, besides, I love a man in a pilot's uniform." He said, "How about the man in the uniform?" I said, "I love both the man and the uniform."

A couple of months later he came to my house with my aunt, who had discovered that the young man was a distant cousin of ours. He was wearing a pilot's uniform. After he left that night, I sat next to my father on the floor. I told him I had known the young man before. I told him I knew him through the Red Cross work at the temple. I added that I had seen him at the library. "How many people were there when you met?" He asked. "The whole library, father." I skipped a few details of our relationship, and he didn't press me. He said that the young man asked for my hand in marriage. I was overjoyed. I was so happy that my aunt had found the necessary family links and could vouch for him.

My father reminded me that an inquisitive and lively girl like me is not easy for a man to handle. He told me to think for a while before answering. He asked me to get to know the man. He arranged for us to go out together but my aunt came with us everywhere.

I had asked for tutoring in mathematics, and my father decided to ask my suitor to teach me. During the first sessions, seven or eight members of the family sat in the room to chaperon. They didn't keep silent and tried to participate vigorously in the teaching process. I complained to my father that I found it impossible to concentrate while they sat with me. "The teacher finds it difficult with so many participants, some of whom don't even know how to read and write," I said. My father agreed that I work with him alone.

I tried very hard to learn as fast as I could. It wasn't easy to concentrate. He insisted on sitting close to me while he showed me the drawings or read with me. Sometimes he would ask, "Can the teacher hold the student's hand?" I was very nervous about our relationship. I wanted to see him, but I was afraid of our times alone together. In spite of his flirtatious attitude, he was strict with me when it came to my studies. When I didn't do my homework right, he chided me, telling me how lucky I was to have a kind family, enough food, many books and how unfortunate it would be to get bad grades in spite of all this. So I worked hard and improved my mathematics.

We were married on January 25, 1975. Three months later, on April 17, the communists took over Cambodia. My husband and I lived together only three months. We had a long courtship and a very short married life. During the first weeks he was sent away to a military base. He went on flying missions regularly. The phone lines were cut by the Viet Cong. We could only communicate through writing. He wrote me twice a day and sent his letters through the military pouch. He kept pleading with me to join him. Finally he wrote to my father and asked him to let me go to him. At this time my mother's cousin's husband, who was a colonel, was transferred from the city to the town where my husband was stationed. He offered to provide us with a room in his house on the base. My father hesitated about allowing me to go. He asked if I trusted this young man I had just married. I said, "If you believe in my intelligence as you have always said you do, trust me." So I went to live with my mother's cousin and her husband the colonel.

For a short while my husband and I enjoyed a few hours of happiness each day. He left for his missions in the morning and I spent the time reading, walking, practicing my English. As the afternoon wore off, I began to feel anxious. By late afternoon I could do nothing but sit outside the house, waiting for him to arrive. I ate only when he came, so by then I was starved. When I think of those afternoons, I remember the ache in my empty stomach and the choking in my breath for fear that he might be dead somewhere in some field.

Before the communists came, many military left in helicopters. I asked my husband to leave also. He said he couldn't leave me. Besides, he said he wanted to die in his own country on his own land. He told me that if something happened to him, I should go to America. A few days before the communists came, my uncle and his wife went to Pnom Phen.

The communists rushed into the city bringing fear and death. I had never seen communists before. They all wore black clothes and the "kramar" scarf and held guns. They burst into the house, stomping through the rooms, kicking doors open, banging stuff off tables, knocking books from the shelves, sticking the barrels of their guns into the servant's chests. I ran into the kitchen. I was feeling nauseous before they came. I didn't know then that I was pregnant. I squeezed myself into a corner, trying to fill as small a space as possible. One of the men came to the kitchen and pulled me out of the corner I was hiding in. He shouted at me, showering my face with spittle, "Tell me who you are before I kill you?"

Everything my grandmother had told me about the aftermath of lying and the ugliness to be endured in the next life completely left my mind. I said, "Please don't hurt me, I'm just a servant." He said, "Good, comrade, we belong to the same class." And he pointed his gun toward the door. I started to leave, but thought to take something with me from my uncle's room—some money, some jewels, something. But when they saw me move toward his room, they asked, "Why are you going there?" One man moved toward me and said, "There is one of the officer's nieces living here also, do you know her?" I said, "She went to Pnom Penh with her husband." Then I started toward my uncle's room again. "What do you want," they asked. "Some money," I said. "In this country you will not need money any more comrade," they said.

One of the men shot open the safe in the bedroom. Another who had already yanked the phone out of the wall, started talking into the receiver. It was strange they hadn't seen a telephone before. A woman started to eat the soap in the bathroom, thinking it was chocolate. They were from the mountains, they knew very little about life in the city.

They shoved me out of the room. As I stumbled toward the door, one of them kicked me out of the house and into the street. I was without a penny, without a plan, without an idea of what to do, literally left with the clothes on my back. As I walked about I heard a loud speaker announcing that those who wished to join their husbands in the military must catch the train that was leaving in an hour from the station in the city. I ran in the direction of the station but soon felt tired and nauseous. I walked with difficulty and had to stop often to catch my breath. I arrived at the station just as the train was leaving. I was desperate and heartbroken that I had missed the chance to go to my husband in the mountains.

Three days later, I saw a woman on the street in torn clothes, near death. She told me what had happened to the passengers on that train. She said the communists had machine-gunned all the servicemen in that camp and abandoned the women and children without food and water in the hundred-degree heat. Almost all had died, including her children. There must have been many camps and many scenes like those she described, because for years people found human bones as they walked on farmland or in the forests of Cambodia.

Every day brought new horrors. Sometimes I was able to include myself among the downtrodden the communists were claiming as their own. Some days I was included in the targeted group. But on the whole chaos prevailed. Armies of young men, hate drilled into them until they lived and breathed it, death-trivialized until they saw no import in it, walked about, hostile, hateful, violent and ignorant, taking pleasure in ordering people about arbitrarily, killing with little provocation. One day they decided to herd passersby together on the street, ordering groups of people in various directions and destinations, the purpose of the activity unexplained. A friend who walked with me along with her parents was ordered in one direction and her parents in another. She tried to follow the old people. No one knew what each order would lead to. Each person lost sight of might be lost for ever. She panicked and tried to follow her parents. A teenaged boy shot her in the back, then shot her cat. I felt nothing, not even surprise at the scene I was witnessing—my friend, fallen down on her face, a narrow stream of blood snaking away from her body and her dead cat spread out next to her.

A mother ran after her child in fear, someone aimed slowly at the running child and shot her and then shot the mother in the foot. The woman fell down whimpering, trying to reach out to her child's body, which lay a few feet away from her. The man aimed at her arm, reaching toward the child, but stopped when someone called to him from the other side of the street.

I moved away slowly and walked, not knowing whether at any moment I would feel a shot hit my body. Nothing happened. I don't know how long I walked. It began to rain. I was outside the village. I sat under a tree, leaning against the trunk. I was conscious only of the rain dripping down my neck and the churning in my stomach. I felt a pricking sensation on my legs and looked down to see two large leeches attached to each leg. I wondered to myself whether this was death or the process of dying.

I was awakened from my stupor at dawn. In the half-light I could make out dark-clad shapes assembled near me. They were people from the village being taken to God knows where by one adolescent Viet Cong with a gun. He shoved and pushed and ordered them and they followed quietly and meekly. He ordered me to join the group and follow him. They told me we were walking toward a village a few miles away where we would be given food and utensils. In a while, witnessing the way the boy hit one or the other of the group with the butt of his rifle or kicked or slapped another, I asked the fellow next to me why we were taking this. We were fifty and he was just a boy. He said this kid had been seen opening a man's belly and dragging out his liver and eating it raw. The communists were creating an unbeatable mythology by acting out scenes of terror and random savagery.

I tried to ask the young man where we were going. I was sick and hungry and walked with difficulty. He wouldn't answer me. They told me to call him comrade. I called out to him, "Comrade," but he aimed the gun at me and told me to shut up. Finally we reached the village and were told to go into the huts and take what we needed. I went into a deserted hut and found a pot and some rice and prepared something to eat. The people in this village had been driven into the next to do more or less what we were doing in theirs. There was no explanation for these moves.

Here I found a relative. A third cousin of my mother's. She urged me to go with her and her husband to the mountains, to a labor camp for lower-rank servicemen and their families. By that time I knew I was pregnant. The people at the camp told me not to let the communists know that my husband was in the air force. They also urged me to hide my pregnancy. They said communists tie up a pregnant woman, open her belly, take out the baby, cook the fetus in wine and eat it to gain strength. My cousin told me to leave right away. I told her I wanted to wait a little to save some rice for the journey. I didn't know the way. But they felt guilty about having brought me there and pressured me to leave. I left one night by the road behind the camp. I walked the whole night and at dawn found myself back at the labor camp again. I discovered that having lost my bearings leaving through the back road, I had walked a circle around the camp.

The next day I decided to walk out through the main gate. My cousin told me to keep an eye on the sun, moving toward the west—that would be the left. I had found a fish cage a few days before. So at dawn I took the cage and walked out of the main gate. The guard yelled at me to stop and asked where I was going. I told him, remembering to call him comrade, that I was going to fish. He didn't stop me. He must have been a new recruit because he was not mean and he smiled at me. I almost said, "Buddha bless you," but stopped myself in time.

I walked for miles. I had no idea where I was going. In the evening I reached a clearing in the woods. I heard people singing. I had dyed my clothes black so I would resemble the conquerors. When I approached, I saw that it was a communist camp. In the new system one needed a letter of permission to leave one village for another. I had written a letter of permission for myself prior to my departure. I presented this to the commander. He took the letter, hesitating, then held it upside down, pretending to read. Apparently he was illiterate. He nodded his head and said, "Fine," not wanting to ask for assistance. Then he asked me whether I was going to Kam Pong Seima village. Not wanting to reveal my ignorance of the area, I said quickly, "Yes, that's exactly where I am going." As I walked away, I heard him shout, "You will remember my name pretty woman. I am Tol." I cared little about his name, and much about being able to get away from him, but he was right—I still remember his name.

The next village turned out to be a village where my father used to live and where he still owned some land. The communist leader there was a man who had worked my father's land in the past. He was what we called "snake with two heads." Such people worked with the government in the daytime and joined the communists at night. The villagers had made a practice of paying the guerrillas to stay away from their community. After the takeover, communists in that area established a more peaceful relationship with the village people. They made people work hard, but they let them stay in their own homes. I found a distant cousin in that village and stayed with her. The communist leader sent his wife to tell me that if I kept quiet, he would leave me alone and not reveal my identity. The wife respected my father and mother and wanted to pay back her debt to them in this way. But she emphasized if I made a wrong move or revealed my identity, her husband would have to kill me to save himself.

I was given the task of washing dishes in the communal kitchen. I threw up all day as I worked. The cook and I talked constantly about various poisons we could put in the communists' food. She and I both knew we could not do it, but it comforted us to talk about it. When I thought of what I had seen them do to others and what they may have already done to my husband and my father, I felt only rage and hate. They were making us be more and more like them as time passed.

I had a difficult pregnancy. I felt weak and ill most of the time. I walked more slowly than most and got exhausted more quickly. I was always hungry. Having to lie about my identity put an added strain on my daily life. I was once asked by one of the guards what time it was and I said, "How can I tell time? I can't read." "Good," he said with approval. I felt disgust at his admiration of ignorance. One day as we carried water along a mountain pass, I fell down and broke the vessel I was carrying. The boss raised her stick to hit me. The woman next to me yelled, "Please don't hit her, don't you see she's pregnant!" I was surprised that she stopped and didn't punish me for my mistake. I pulled myself up and wiped the dirt from my hands. The thought crossed my mind to throw myself off the cliff. But just then my baby moved and I knew that more than anything I wanted to live to see my child. I put aside the thought of dying.

One day I felt a pain in my lower back. I asked an old woman who had become a friend to coin me for it. She dipped the coin in coconut oil and pushed it hard against my skin a number of times as tradition required. The pain got a little better. In the afternoon I felt tired and kept needing to urinate. I asked her to coin me again. She told me she would come to me after work at six. When she came and coined me again and my back pain didn't improve, she knew I was in labor. She sent for the midwife in the next village. The midwife hearing that it was a first child and there was not much pain yet, took her time coming to me. When the man came back and saw that my pain had escalated, he rushed back on the bicycle to bring the midwife to my side.

People in the village had brought in a lot of fish that day and were busy drying their catch. When word got around that I was in labor, they left their work and rushed to me. They boiled water and brought clean cloth. Some started a fire under the bench on which I had to lie after childbirth to keep my skin soft and to gain strength.

The monk had given me his robes to wrap my baby in. Monks left their old robes hanging on trees, and villagers took a piece of it to wear, believing it would bring them long life. I was sad that I had no clothes for my baby, but grateful to have the robes of the kind monk. I dyed the yellow robe black—the color of the invaders, to protect the baby. The village people prepared a large pot of boiling water in which they placed bamboo leaves, preparing the potion I had to drink for many days after childbirth. As the villagers rushed about with the preparations and before the midwife's arrival, the baby came.

I hadn't had enough to eat during my pregnancy, but there had been a lot of oranges in the village where I was staying and, knowing they were good for the baby, some days I ate as many as twenty oranges. Hard work and exercise must have helped also. I was in labor for only an hour.

After the baby came and was wrapped in the black cloth, I was placed on the wooden bench under which they lighted the fire. I was lucky to have had the baby in December, when the weather was cool. Nevertheless, the heat and smoke from the fire under the bed were suffocating. I was glad I had no family with me to keep the fire going for a week as required. Because I was a lone woman, after three days the master of medicine and the midwife came and they carried out the ceremony to end the fire.

My baby daughter was my mother, my father, my husband, my home. I still call her mom or dad or by her dead father's name sometimes. People tell me just let her be. But she has meant so much to me. After I gave birth I became interested in life again. I started to talk to friends and neighbors. Before then, I was always silent. Perhaps that was lucky too, because in those days the less one talked, the safer one was. But after the baby came I felt a need to communicate with others.

I lived with the communists for five years. In 1975, when the bombings began and we heard the explosions in the distance, people began to whisper to each other about changes to come. One villager had a radio and we huddled together to listen to Voice of America at night. We were made to go to propaganda meetings every night, but after the meetings, we gathered to listen to the news on the radio. Some kept watch while others took turns listening. I got to listen more than others because I could understand the English-language programs. Sometimes there was no electricity. People would take turns to peddle a bicycle to get electricity to make the radio work. We were hungry for news of the outside world and what they may do to help us. We listened to the radio and discussed ways to escape.

One night two of our friends escaped. The communists came and questioned me. I told them I knew nothing about the escape. One night I heard a motorcycle stop at my door. A motorcycle stopping at your door in the night meant you would surely be taken to die. But Buddha helped me or someone up there helped me or it was the luck my great uncle had predicted for me—they only took me to a labor camp, which was at a sugar plantation.

The new camp was much easier for me. They did nothing to me. I ate sugar cane all day as I worked. They only told me to clean the weeds from around the cane and not to discuss capitalism. There was also plenty of sweet potatoes in the field. At first I ate the sweet potatoes raw to avoid being detected. I got very sick. So I began to smuggle the potatoes to the cook, and she boiled them for me. So in this place, instead of being further punished, I got fat. There was more lecturing here than in the previous place. I was so tired always that during lectures I fell asleep. I didn't do very well on assignments.

While I worked in the field my baby was taken care of in the commune by an older woman. They had a strict communist indoctrination program even for the very small children. That's how when the children get to be ten or twelve years old, they can kill people like fish.

I prayed to Buddha to take me and my daughter away from that place. I didn't want my child to grow up to think and act like the communists. The bombs were getting closer and louder every day. My daughter got sick. She had a high fever. I took her to the hospital. There was more food there because they wanted everyone to get well quickly and get back to work—except for the very sick whom they left to die. The hospital was very dirty. I couldn't let my daughter take any of the medicine. I couldn't even allow her to lie down on the mattress. I leaned against the wall and had her lie down on my stomach to protect her from the dirt and the lice. The whole night I stayed up holding her and listening to the sound of the explosions in the distance and the moaning and crying of the patients in the next room. The next day I got permission to leave the hospital. My daughter's fever had gone down and I was anxious to make plans and search for ways to escape.

We were five miles from Battambang city. As I walked toward the village, I saw groups of communists walking away from the city. People knew that someone had taken the city and thought they were running away. They kept taunting them and laughing at them. I was very careful and didn't express any emotion. I stopped in front of the temple and kneeled and prayed. I asked Buddha to help me get away. Many communists were marching out of the city pretending that it was an assignment rather than an evacuation. They asked me where I was going and I said I'm taking back my daughter Meta from the hospital. I tried to be nice to them, even though they had made me suffer for all these years. I was lucky to be careful because they came back the next day and killed some of the people who had mocked them the day before. This was a time of fluctuation in the fortunes of the various groups, and a woman with a child named Meta, "loving kindness," has to be careful not to buy herself more danger than assigned to her by her destiny.

The sound of the big guns and the bombing shook the village every night. I nearly lost my mind with terror. I had a plan for escape. I had found a map on which I had drawn a route for myself to the border. I took Meta and started walking. There were many families on the road. They were carrying their belongings on cows. But I had only my two hands and my two feet and the baby. I could carry very little rice with me and nothing else. There was a five-hundred-mile walk to the border. I went to a temple to pray for an idea on how to get there. I found a friend who was the sister-in-law of the governor of Pnom Penh City. She and her husband had lost all their children. Her parents lived in a city about a hundred miles from the border. I started immediately to revise my plans and draw a new route on the old map. I asked my friends to come and live with me in the abandoned apartment house where I was staying. The whole lower part under the house was available. It was open all around, but the weather was warm and it was better than sleeping in the open.

I decided to tell fortunes to earn myself a living. Before long I had plenty of rice. I had a pack of cards that I used in my new profession, but more than the cards I used hunches that came to me about each person. People came and asked me whether they should take a journey, and I would tell them what they should do. Soon the Viet Cong soldiers came to have their fortunes told. I could not refuse them without compromising my safety, and I hated to have anything to do with them.

My luck came to my aid again. I ran into an acquaintance who worked for the electrical company and had a truck. He agreed to take me and my friends to Mongkolborey. It was a difficult journey. There were about fifty people crowded together in the back of the truck. Meta was hot and exhausted. Soon she started having convulsions.

Finally we arrived at the house of my friends' parents. They welcomed us but apologized for not being able to provide food. They had six children and very little to share. Here I became a farmer again to help the people with whom I was living. I got enough for us to eat by selling vegetables and working in the farm.

I was constantly looking for ways of getting to the border. Finally a group that was leaving for the border agreed to let us walk with them. But the night they were leaving, Meta got the measles. Her temperature was very high. She looked red as a beet. I was terrified. I went to the neighbor's house and told them I had a small gold chain I could give them if they could get me some penicillin for my child. They got me the medicine and Meta got better. But I missed the group that was leaving for the border.

This again was a time of good luck for me. The whole group with whom we were to leave were killed. They were pioneers walking through the land mines that the Thailand border patrol had installed in order to keep the refugees from coming across. There was an uproar in the United States and the rest of the world, and eventually help came. But that night, Meta's illness saved our lives.

Many of those in the first groups died while trying to cross the border. Some went through the river and were killed by alligators. Some were attacked by wild animals in the mountains. Some who walked in the valley between the two mountain peaks were shot by the Thailand border patrol. Some who didn't have guides to help them maneuver through, walked over land mines and were blown to pieces. The international press began to write about the situation.

The American media focused on the plight of the refugees. The queen of Thailand became involved, and the Red Cross began to send help. All this took a while to have an effect in Mongkolborey.

Meanwhile I was making plans again. I drew a track on the map, marking the road one could take around the base of the mountain. I dyed my clothes dark green so that they would work as camouflage. I practiced rolling on the ground in case the Thai soldiers started shooting as I walked through the ravine.

One day a number of Vietnamese military men came to me and asked me to work for them. They said they were interested in changing their image among the Cambodians. They asked me to translate for them to help get their message across. The thought of working with these people disgusted me, but I was terrified of refusing them. I decided I must do something quickly. Now that these people had found me and singled me out as a liaison, I would be in constant danger.

My friends decided to go with me to the border. We agreed that we could wait no longer. We would hold each other's hands and take whatever chances we had to take. I carried Meta on my shoulder. I was quite weak from lack of proper food. My friend carried Meta and her husband carried me on his shoulders from time to time to give me a chance to rest. We came to a place some three miles from the Vietnamese border. The group knew that if we passed this distance and survived we could count on living, if not we would be dead. Those who had no children separated from us. Meta and I went with a pregnant woman who had morning sickness. Like us, she had trouble keeping up with the rest. At the last moment my friends decided they couldn't leave without me. They went with us. We walked in the bamboo forest among the thick vegetation. There was shooting, and twice rockets hit trees near us and exploded with a terrifying sound. I was less able to run than the others because I was always famished. But they stayed with me and endangered themselves to keep me company. I cooked small amounts of rice, feeding most of it to Meta and drinking the water in which it was boiled. My friends told me, "You must feed yourself. If you die, the baby will not survive either." But I couldn't bring myself to eat any of the small portion we had.

We ran into a group of young men on bicycles. One of them

recognized me. I had taught him English in the old days in order to earn enough to help pay my tuition at school. This group operated on both sides of the border, bringing foodstuffs and other material back and forth. They had food and offered me some noodles and meat. They also gave me vitamin-C tablets they had brought from Thailand. This helped my strength considerably. I asked them to take my daughter to the border on their bicycle. But they said you must do it yourself. You have the strength and you will make it. So we left on our journey toward the camp at the border. We arrived at dusk.

There were already some ten thousand Cambodians gathered at the camp, guarded by Thai soldiers. Many of the refugees had places to stay and whole families gathered together. I was frightened because as soon as I arrived, I began to hear tales of rape and violence against the young women. I learned that many military were staying at the camp. I walked around looking for a familiar face. Soon I saw a family I knew. I asked if I could stay with them in their tent. They told me that they hardly had room for their own members, but I was welcome to sleep outside. I didn't have mosquito netting, and I knew I would get malaria. There was nothing for me to do but accept their offer.

Soon a group of military personnel decided to form the Cambodian Red Cross. They asked me to join them. They wanted me to write a letter in French and one in English to the International Red Cross to explain our predicament and to ask for help. We looked all over the camp to find pieces of paper on which to write the letters. We sent the letter through a courier—one of the young men who traded between camps—and waited impatiently for a response.

Meanwhile the fighting between the National Front for Liberation and the Khmer Rouge continued. The Vietnamese fired rockets to discourage the Cambodians from attempting to leave the country. I slept in the dark open space and listened to the sounds of fighting and closed my eyes, expecting to be hit by a rocket at any moment.

I had struggled hard to get to this camp, but now that I was here it seemed my troubles had only begun. There were ten thousand refugees in a camp with a capacity for two thousand. I couldn't receive rice because I was not registered, and I did not have a book of rations. There were not enough rations to take care of everyone. One morning I woke up shivering. I was running a high fever and felt nauseous.

I knew I had malaria. Meta's body felt warm in my arms and she looked sleepy and unwell. All around people were digging holes in the ground to shelter themselves from the expected rocket attack. I didn't have the energy to dig. All day I sat holding Meta and watching the feverish activity and wondering whether we would survive the attack. The rocket attack that night was fierce and ear-shattering.

The next day, just as I was thinking I could not go through another night like the one I had just passed, I saw a Red Cross vehicle driving toward me. The loud speaker announced they were looking for someone who spoke French or English to act as interpreter at the Thailand border camp. I whispered to myself, "Samnang, you lucky woman," as I raised my hand. They spoke with me and seemed glad to find someone who could help. A doctor came up to me and gave me his shirt. My clothes were so tattered I was almost naked.

They took me with them to the border camp. In the car they asked me what I wanted to eat. "Everything," I said. I had missed food so much. We had a feast of cold canned soup and cookies. Meta's eyes shone with pleasure.

There was one doctor and three nurses at that camp. They had ten thousand patients in need of care. Within a few hours a long line formed and we worked ten hours a day trying to see as many patients as possible. Here too I had no shelter. Soon an acquaintance of mine who had gold jewelry with which to pay smugglers left for the Thai border, giving me her tent. At last I had some protection and privacy.

The work was exhausting and I was too weak and depressed to take care of myself. One day a Swiss member of the Red Cross team gave me a sarong and a bottle of shampoo and asked me to wash my hair. I took a shower, cleaned my hair, and wore the dress. This caused a new set of problems. I became the object of dangerous and unwelcome attention. The Thai soldiers began taking notice of me. The older man who had organized the camp and on whom I looked as a father asked through an intermediary whether I would like to be one of his wives.

I told the French doctors I was in danger. The Thai soldiers had raped many women in the camp, sometimes murdering their victims. One of the military men who had become my friend told me he had heard the Thai soldiers talking about me. He said he and his friends were ready to defend me. They had no weapons and I didn't want to endanger their lives.

The French team became increasingly aware of the dangers I faced. But the guards would not allow them to transport me across the border. They had discussed the problem among themselves and decided to smuggle me across to the camp in Thailand as a patient. They asked me to lie down in the back of the vehicle, positioning the I.V. as if it were attached to my arm. One of them held Meta on his lap and they drove me across the border to the other side.

When I arrived in Khao-i-dang camp, there were only a hundred people there. I had managed the most dangerous and important part of my journey—crossing the border into Thailand. My plans had finally worked out. I had escaped immediate danger. But I had also left my own torn and battered land, perhaps forever.

My most vivid memory of arriving in Thailand was a piece of cake I was offered by the doctors. I stared at it until they reassured me that once I finished that piece I would get another.

In the new camp they gave me bamboo to build myself a shelter. I didn't even begin to try. I knew I was a capable woman, but building a bamboo hut was not a skill I had or wished to acquire. Once again I slept with Meta lying on my stomach under the sky.

In a few days they offered me a job, interpreting for the French doctors at the outpatient clinic. The French doctors asked for a list of my personal needs. My first list was a long one. I needed everything. Shampoo, toothpaste, toothbrush, underwear. They gave me all the things I needed. For the first time in years I had enough food for myself and Meta.

A flood of refugees began pouring in from the Cambodian side. I was happy to see my compatriots escaping. Some had been starved for so long that they began to eat uncontrollably. Their stomachs were unused to so much food. I saw one refugee die of overeating. The doctors began monitoring the eating procedures, to ensure that the new arrivals were initiated into the gradual intake of solid food. Some had to be fed intravenously for a while, then put on a liquid diet, and finally given solid food.

After a while, one of the American doctors gave me a blue plastic tent. It was too hot to use during the day. But at night it saved me from the pouring rain and afforded some sort of shelter.

Meta loved riding in cars and the healthcare people took her with them on their rounds in camp. She spent a good part of the day riding around the camp in the car. A French couple who had left their little daughter at home and volunteered to work for the Red Cross at the refugee camp became fond of Meta who was the same age as their own child. They were very good to her, carrying her around on their shoulders.

My life was much better in the camp. Now that I and my daughter were out of danger and my immediate needs were taken care of, I had a chance to think about my situation. I heard that my husband and my father were dead. No one knew anything about my sister. Most people in the camp seemed to have found some of their kin. I missed my husband and my family even more seeing the other families together. I had no assurance of my future and what would become of me. I became very depressed. I stopped washing and changing my clothes. I lost my appetite. I used to go every afternoon to the mountainside nearby and I cried to myself and thought of ending my life.

I decided I must try to go to America. I wrote to my uncle who had been in the diplomatic service and stationed in France. I received no answer. I tried to find another sponsor but with no success. Some of my co-workers at the clinic coached me, trying to help me find someone who would marry me and take me to America. They kept looking at the staff member's fingers to see who was without a wedding ring. We laughed about these unsuccessful plots. I began getting desperate and still had no news from my uncle. One day someone showed me a directory with names of Cambodians who lived in the United States. In that book I found the name of a relative who lived in California. I wrote to him asking whether he had any news of my uncle. In a few weeks I received a letter from him informing me that my uncle was in California. A few days later I received a letter from my uncle. I was so happy I danced around the camp, waving the letter in the air. The Red Cross people were very happy for me. We had a big celebration.

The Thai people kept threatening to return us to Cambodia. Even if it were not a real threat, the unease it brought to me was very real. In a while the sponsorship letter from my uncle arrived. Since I was married to a military man, they expedited my case. In the next few months I went through all the paperwork necessary for obtaining permission to travel to the United States. A month after I received the papers from my uncle I had another attack of malaria. They took me to the hospital. The fourth day of my stay I begun to feel better and my fever was reduced. They sent me a priest to comfort me. In Cambodia a monk comes to the bedside of a patient only when he is dying. I thought even if I seem to feel better, I must be dying. I spent the morning writing notes to all my friends saying good-bye and asking them to take care of Meta and send her to America to my uncle. In the afternoon the priest came again. I asked him how much time I had before dying. "Who says you are dying?" he asked. I understood then that this was another cultural misunderstanding.

I took the son of a friend as my adopted son. She came to the camp and left the boy with me to go back and bring her other children. When the time came for me to be examined for permission to enter the United States I told them I had two children.

Finally they gave me an appointment to be interviewed for permission to go to the United States. I was very nervous waiting for my turn. The woman who was before me had nine children, she had been married twice. Her case took very long. It was getting close to 2:00 P.M. when my malaria attacks usually happened. I was terrified that I may have one in front of the official United States representatives. But the doctor who had come with me to help, gave me some medicine and calmed me. There were three officials at three tables. One had to stop at each table and answer similar questions. They wanted to make sure there was no false information offered them. If the answers to the three officials were in agreement, one received permission. The doctor helped by telling the officials that I was a useful member of the medical team at the camp.

I passed the medical examination. My uncle had given every reassurance of support in order to expedite the process. He had given too many assurances, because when I came to the United States I found it a little difficult to receive the assistance I needed.

We were taken to a camp to wait a few days for a flight to the United States. This was the worst place I had stayed in. There was no place to sleep. I ended up sleeping on the ground in the open next to a garbage can. It had been dark when I arrived so I couldn't see my surroundings. When I woke up at dawn I saw the can swarming with worms. I was sick with fear and revulsion. It was such a dirty and poor place that I began to think going to the United States is not worth such a terrible stay. Knowing that in a few days I would leave the region added to my misery. I had wanted to go to the United States, but leaving my home, my kin, and all that I had known in my life was very difficult. It was especially hard to leave without definite knowledge of the fate of my father, my husband, and my sister. But I was strengthened in my resolve whenever I looked at Meta and thought of her future.

We left Cambodia after a long and sleepless night at the airfield. We lay down on the ground, trying to ward off the ferocious mosquitoes. The next day I left for the United States. It was September 15, 1980. We arrived in San Francisco a day later. Because of the time difference, it was still September 15. The miserable day on the plane was one I had lost with no regret. In San Francisco they gave us a clean room with nice sheets. The little boy and Meta were so happy to have landed and to be in a lovely, clean room. They had told us that Americans will steam us clean on arrival. But they did nothing of the sort. They were very kind to us. I asked to call my uncle in Philadelphia, but they said I would be flying to him the next day and there was no need to call.

We were met by my uncle and his family the next day at the airport in Philadelphia. I thought he looked well, but he hardly recognized me. He hadn't seen me in years, and five years of life under a communist government had reduced me to a shriveled up bag of bones. I looked twice my actual age.

Philadelphia was a big, modern city. But having come from years of life in the jungle, any American town would have amazed my senses. My uncle's family lived in a house in Rockville, Maryland. He had come to Philadelphia to study psychology at the university. He asked me about the family back home. He soon realized how difficult it was for me to remember my recent experiences. I didn't cry. I couldn't cry. But he understood the pain in my dry eyes.

I saw my uncle going to the university and began to daydream about studying to be a doctor or a nurse. I had worked in hospitals and clinics in recent months and didn't find it difficult to imagine myself studying in the field. Later, when I found how expensive going to the university was I learned to modify my expectations.

Life in my uncle's one-room apartment was not easy. I was happy to have found a relative and pleased that my children and I were safe. But seeing him laugh and play with his children when they visited and watching his neighbor walking to McDonald's with his family made me very sad. My uncle decided that we would be happier in his home in Rockville. His house was large and we had more room to move about. Meta and the boy could play in the yard. My uncle's family didn't know anything about the life I had led and my suffering. They wanted to help me, but they didn't know how to go about it. I tried to explain to them, but it was like talking to a wall. They did not understand. My experiences were beyond anything they could believe or imagine.

I went to the county government office to apply for public assistance. The offices were crowded. I sat all day without any explanation or any indication of what I was waiting for and how long it might take. Finally it was decided that I was eligible for food stamps and financial help. I was assigned a counselor. But by the time the process began, I had already found a job. I saw the announcement at the social service office. They needed a Cambodian translator for the chest clinic. At first I was worried about my qualifications—not only the technical know-how but my lack of familiarity with courtesies and manners here. My counselor encouraged me, saying if you've worked in the camp hospital with elementary equipment, you are sure to do well in the properly equipped hospital here. As for the customs and manners of interaction, you will catch on soon enough.

I was told that I needed a suit to go to the interview. I had become familiar with the neighborhood church through my daughter's school. They had donations of clothes which they kept in a large cardboard box. I looked through the box and was lucky to find the two matching pieces of a pink suit. I only weighed 90 pounds and the suit was too large for me. The pair of shoes I found were too large also. My feet slipped out of them when I walked. But I was happy enough to have found something appropriate. I spent half of the night trying to alter the suit to fit better. I was a city woman and knew how it should look. It was a snowy day in March when I went to the county government office in my pink suit and oversized shoes. I was two hours early for the interview. I wanted to make sure I had plenty of time in case I get lost.

Two weeks later I received a letter telling me I had gotten the job. I found myself a basement room and moved out of my uncle's home. The church people who came to visit us told me it is not right to live in the damp, cold, windowless basement room I had rented. It was especially harmful for the children. They found me an apartment. I had thought that my salary would cover the rent. But I hadn't known about the various taxes that are deducted from the paycheck. Once again the church volunteers helped me by paying part of the rent.

At first I was shy and uncertain at work. But gradually as I saw how I was helping people, my confidence grew. I became very involved with the refugees who seemed often helpless and alone. I gave them my home phone number and they called me at all hours of the night to help solve their emergencies. If they needed an ambulance, a doctor, the fire department, they called me and I translated for them or made calls. The hospitals called me to translate and thanked me for making myself available at times when they had no access to anyone else.

I became so exhausted and weak with the work during the day and the calls for assistance at night that I ended up in the hospital again with another bout of malaria. This time they gave me medicine through I.V. and in twenty days malaria was completely washed out of my body. During this period, the couple from the church who had become like my mother and father took care of Meta for me. They told me that I must be good to myself and to allow some time for rest. So I became tougher on the refugees, telling them they must learn English and fend for themselves as I had done. In the end it was better for all of us. They were forced to become more independent, and I found some time to myself.

I still had no news of my father and my husband. I was convinced by now that they were dead. I was very young to live alone with my two children. But I had no time to meet anyone socially. I used to take the children to a babysitter who took care of them before school started. One snowy morning I was on my way to the babysitter with the children. I had very little experience walking in the snow. I slipped and fell, rolling down the hillside. I yelled to Meta in Cambodian asking if she were all right. I had landed in front of the steps of the apartment where every morning I had passed a Chinese man who sat quietly, following us with his eyes. He rushed to help me, speaking to me in Cambodian. I learned then that he was half-Chinese, half-Cambodian. We talked for a long time, standing in front of his house. I learned that his wife had been killed by communists and he had come to the United States recently. He didn't speak English and felt strange in the new country. That's why he sat on the steps alone every day, looking sad and lost.

We saw each other once in a while in the next two weeks. I had no intention of becoming involved. I wanted to wait for my husband. It had been seven years and my friends assured me that he was dead, but I could not accept this reality. When I got the flu in spring, the children couldn't take care of me. He came in every day, bringing me soup and helping me. When I recovered, he offered to take me shopping in his car. I was still very Cambodian in outlook and refused to go with him alone unless we took the children with us. He agreed and I let the children sit in front with him and I sat in the back seat. After all, we were two widowers.

After a few months he asked me to marry him. He spoke with his brothers and I asked my uncle for permission. My uncle told me since my friend came from a respectable family even though he had no money now, he had no objection. We were married in May.

Meta's reaction to my marriage was very negative. All her life we had been close together—only the two of us. She couldn't accept that now she must share me with someone else. My new husband was already depressed because he had lost his wife and children. He loved Meta, but he didn't know how to show her his love. Meta had never seen a man in my life.

I used to think that when things changed in Cambodia I would go back and help my uncle in his political activities. But now that my uncle has died I am reluctant to go back, even though the communists are out of power. I do not trust the situation. I have a teenage daughter and a small boy. I think of their future. Also, to tell the truth, I like it here. America is like a second mother to me. Working with Cambodians here gives me a sense of being useful to my own people while enjoying the American way of life.

I love this country very much because it gave me a new life. But when I am sick I feel the loneliness of an exile. In my country when you are sick, relatives and friends come and stay all day. They cook, they clean house, they feed you. Here everybody is so busy they hardly have time to say hello to one another. I miss the relationship between parents and children. Here young people talk back to their parents. They have their own ways which they learn at school. They are so sure their ways are better. In Cambodia the young tried to learn to be like their parents. We thought they knew better and were wiser. Here the second generation thinks they know so much more than the first. Even in American families in which the parents know all the ways of the society, it seems that youth rather than age is considered the bearer of wisdom.

One's expectations of America are often disappointed. The country offers opportunities, not ready-made-life situations. If you don't know or can't make use of opportunities, life can become very difficult and dangerous. Being from the East, I stress the role of destiny.

I see the old people who cannot learn the language, cannot learn new ways. It is so sad to see them try to understand. I ask myself why is it like this. Not only my country, but all over the world. Why must there be war and killing, uprooting people from their land and their customs. I prayed to Buddha to teach me ways to help stop wars. There is so much hurt and pain, especially among the women who seem to have little to do with the causes of disruptions of life but end up to be the majority of those in exile.

I see it in myself. I know I have been lucky to get away, to learn, to adjust, to survive. But I have paid a price. Inside, I am damaged. Like a broken vase that has been mended, I will never be whole and healthy again. I went to a psychologist who gave me a test. I had to draw things from which he could determine my state of mind. My depression was 120 percent. An ordinary American would have scored 60 or 80 on this test.

But all in all I think women can cope better than men with the disruptions caused by exile. They can gather up their strength and push forward, all the time trying to find some joy within the family or in friendship or in their discoveries. In my own case, even though I have suffered, I have not lost my sense of adventure or capacity for fun. My husband finds it impossible to relate to this society. I come home and look in his eyes. He is so sad. I want to go dancing, to meet new people, but one look at him, hunched over at the kitchen table, tells me that it is not possible. I feel so sad for him knowing there will never be happiness in his life. He simply cannot deal with the new world.

My job involves listening to the problems of others all day. The problems are not new, only the details are different. Some women suffer more than others. But it is all the same pain and sorrow. Cambodian women are at first so afraid to go outside by themselves. They have no education. But it is a joy to see them break out and try to help themselves.

I try to tell the husbands they must take turns with their wives caring for the children so that they can go to school and learn English. They tell me "She is a woman, she does not need to learn English." I know to succeed I must appeal to their selfishness. I say to them, "Don't you see if she doesn't learn the language, you will have to go with her every time she goes shopping or to the doctor's office?"

I am only a small human being. I can only help them help themselves. I remembered the proverb Give a man a fish and he will only eat for one day. Teach him how to fish and he will never be hungry. There was a woman whose husband left her with three small children. I encouraged her to go to school. She kept refusing. Finally she told me, "Do you think I can go to school? I who come from such a poor mountain family?" I said, "Listen to me. Do you know the elephant?" I knew very well she knew the elephant. She lived where there were plenty of them to see. I said, "Have you been to the circus? Have you seen the elephant dance? That's only an animal. You are a human being. How can you say you can't learn?" She said she was scared, she was slow to learn. Later she became the first in her class. She had learned in her culture that a woman can never amount to much.

I celebrate the Cambodian New Year in April. I go to temple. We believe that the spirit of our ancestors comes to the temple to visit with us. We sit on the floor and ask for forgiveness. Children buy nice clothes for their parents. They prepare a bath with perfumed oils and bathe the parents. We clean the house. In Cambodia my stepmother had been very young—too young for me to salute her. But she could sit at the same level as my father. The third day of the new year I used to tell my father my major mistakes. My father would get up and say, "I forgive you." Then I was assured a long, peaceful life. Then we all went to the temple together and on coming back we ate a variety of delicious dishes together. Meta won't bathe me, but I can still make her sit on the floor and tell me her mistakes. Meta learns from many children, some Americans, some from other countries.

I became a citizen in 1986. Immediately I voted in the primary election. I was very excited. They gave me a party at the office. Everyone was very happy for me. The best part for me was the voting. I thought I was now part of the great wheel governing the country.

When I started work in the United States I had a suit that I had found in a cardboard box in the church, I had shoes bigger than my foot, and a coat that made me look like a circus clown. I am proud of having made decisions for myself. When I was a child, they babied me. I wasn't sure I could take care of myself. I learned how to struggle and how to survive. I am proud that I made no major mistakes. Mistakes could have meant walking on a land mine, getting stuck in the communist-controlled country, or losing my daughter. But my power of decision-making is only part of the story. In the end, being a lucky woman, as my uncle had predicted, had something to do with it.

My sister arrived in the United States in 1988. Soon she was looking for a job and I made her wear the old pink suit for luck. It worked once again, as I knew it would. As for my family and my people, I don't have money to give them in their need, but I can give them my skill and knowledge and teach them how to live in the United States and how to understand and love this country.

# FATIMA AHMED IBRAHIM

# Arrow at Rest

*The first time I saw Fatima she wore a gauzy black-and-white* toab *over a black sweater and slacks and high-heeled black shoes. She has a small, round face, with large black eyes that change their expression often, from profound weariness to fiery excitement in the course of our conversation. She tells her story with great gusto, concentrating more on the public, rather than the personal, and it becomes clear early in the conversation, that being a pioneer "struggler" for women's rights in a Muslim society, is an unusually agonizing reality. For her, "the personal is political."*

*Fatima's slight and fragile frame becomes taut and powerful—she seems larger and taller—as she recounts her battles. Having heard that she had just won the United Nations Human Rights Award, and knowing something about her decades of struggle and confrontation with successive, brutal governments, I was unprepared for her gentle demeanor and her low, husky voice, and puzzled by her reputation as a powerful advocate of women's rights. Like an arrow at rest that appears to be a plain piece of wood and steel, one cannot get the whole fiercely effective nature of such a woman unless one sees her in action: the arrow pulled hard and let go, penetrating the target with power and accuracy. I try to picture Fatima at home in the midst of the political turmoil in her country, standing up to a military dictator, registering a complaint against a president, mobilizing a crowd—playing her part.*

*Fatima tells me, "I am strong and fear nothing in politics, but in my private life, with my family, I am weak and vulnerable. I think of my family, their health and well-being, not of my own. If I see them ill or injured, I easily faint, even though I never waver, let alone faint, when I confront a tyrant." I begin to understand this duality in her nature when I see the quiet sadness in her eyes as she talks of her yearning for her home and family—a sadness that changes into a fierce strength when she begins to recount her reaction to the police who would not allow her to leave the country.*

*Fatima is not swayed by fashionable theories and expressions. She has lived and worked with the women on whose behalf she speaks. She knows that a true leader must stand close enough to her followers to feel the warmth of their support. To stray too far from them is to render herself useless to them and drained of all strength. She honors their beliefs and wills herself to believe with them, yet she speaks up when she senses the need for change.*

I WAS BORN in Khartoum, the capital of Sudan. When I was three years old, my family moved to Omdruman, one of the three cities built at the point where the Blue Nile and the White Nile come together. It is a beautiful site for a city. You can see the two rivers meet and move in two parallel lines into the horizon, never merging.

I was the third in a family of three sisters and four brothers. The families of both my parents came from the north of Sudan. The father of my mother was assistant to the father of my father, who was a judge. The families had close relations. When my grandfather moved to another city on the White Nile, my mother's father remained in Khartoum and became headmaster of the first school there. He had progressive ideas that affected the way he brought up my mother. When she was a child, there was no school for girls in Khartoum. Her father enrolled her and her sisters at the boy's school he headed. He had a large library and encouraged his children to read and to discuss issues. He brought tutors to the house to give them additional training at home and sent them to the missionary school after they finished their elementary education. My mother was one of the first Sudanese girls to learn English. When she was in the third year at the missionary school, her uncle who was more traditional in his views, using a prerogative of the older member of the extended family, arranged for her to marry a wealthy older man in order to stop the progressive upbringing my grandfather had planned for her. She was, of course, very unhappy and soon fell ill. My grandfather helped her get a divorce. Soon she married again, but since she was a divorced woman and an educated one at that, her second husband's family treated her very badly. She was divorced once again. Finally, she married my father, who was a family friend, a frequent visitor, and a well-educated man.

My father was a college graduate. He had chosen teaching as his profession. Although he was proficient in English, he refused to teach it because he disliked the British and their colonialist policies. Instead, he taught Arabic and religion.

My mother and father kept a large library of religious and literary books. Both were very interested in politics, and although they did not participate in political activity directly, they kept abreast of current events in the country. We grew up in a highly politicized atmosphere.

Our house was an ordinary middle-class home, with no special features or luxuries. There was a men's section, where father's friends and visitors were received, and there was the women's section, where we took our meals, slept, and sat together to talk. My parents had their own room with a double bed. The rest of us slept in the single beds that lined each of the other rooms. There were chairs in these rooms as well and we sat around and talked or read or played games in the same spaces where we slept at night. Mother always emphasized cleanliness. We kept the rooms in our house impeccable and ourselves and our clothes spotlessly clean. In our childhood, when there were no toothbrushes, she taught us to brush our teeth with a special leaf that expanded to become almost brushlike. It was an aromatic leaf that left a wonderfully fresh aftertaste.

We took our meals on the veranda. In the mornings we had tea with milk, and beans, yogurt, cheese, or eggs. Sometimes we had meat or liver. We all came home from school and work to take the midday meal at around two-thirty. This was the most elaborate meal of the day. There was often a stew made with meat and vegetables and a salad of lettuce and tomatoes on which we sprinkled salt and pepper and lemon juice. The food was served in large trays. We ate with our hands from the bowls placed around the tray, using pieces of bread to wrap bits of meat and vegetables into neat morsels. There was not much conversation during meals. After the mid-day meal we rested a while until the heat of the afternoon had passed. In the late afternoon, my mother often engaged us in a favorite game of the family. We sat around the room in a circle. She would recite a line of poetry from memory. The person sitting next to her answered with another line that began with the last letter of the line she had recited. The next person in the circle followed with another line, starting with the last letter of the previously recited poem. We could not use a poem that had been recited already. When someone whose turn it was could not remember a new poem beginning with the right letter, they would be excluded from the game. On and on we went, saying our favorite lines out loud. Most of us knew most of the poems and whispered along with the one whose turn it was. We spent many hours memorizing lines of poetry and took pride in knowing poems that ended in unusual letters, making it difficult for the next person in line. I can close my eyes and see the eager faces of my sisters and brothers and a host of visiting relatives as they recalled the much-repeated lines of poetry.

As a child I hated to do the chores that were specifically assigned to women, especially the work in the kitchen. I thought it was unfair that my brothers could read or play while my sisters and I had to perform our duties as girls. My family were generally progressive and open-minded, but society forced certain roles on women that could not be avoided easily. In our house, men and women ate together—an unusual phenomenon in Sudan, but the best part of the house was for the men and the poorer, uglier parts for the women. My father was the undisputed boss, but he loved my mother very much and she knew how to treat him so that she could share the power in the household. They sat together often, he read her religious texts, she read him the daily papers. She knew how to protect her territory and her rights without making him lose face publicly. As a religious authority, he was under careful scrutiny and subject to pressure from the Islamic extremists. It was important for her to protect his position while guarding her own. She always supported our educational activities and pressed my father to allow us to choose and to engage in projects that interested us, even when they were controversial.

My childhood recollections are generally happy ones. One painful experience, the memory of which has haunted me through the years, is my circumcision. My older sister and brother were being circumcised according to tradition and the family decided to include me, even though I was only three years old. The ceremonies are quite elaborate and involve a coming-of-age celebration. The preparation of the many dishes goes on for days. The house is decorated. The child receives beautiful presents and new clothes and she is made much of by the family. All close relatives and friends are invited to the ceremony. A hole is dug in the ground and a small rug is spread by the hole and the girl child is placed on the rug with her legs held apart and her hips at the edge of the hole. As the midwife approaches, the guests cheer and ululate and sing in a loud voice. The child begins to panic, but before she can move, the midwife's wrist moves swiftly and the child's face contorts in disbelief at the excruciating pain as the clitoris and the labia are cut swiftly. The pieces and the blood fall into the hole and are quickly covered with soil. The child's shouts merge into the singing and cheering of the crowd. The girl's legs are pressed together and tied tightly. The cheering continues. For seven days the midwife comes everyday to untie the legs and clean the wound. She sometimes uses the seed of a plant called Garrad, which she grinds into a powder and applies to the wound to help it heal quickly. The pain does not stop with the healing of the wound in childhood. Since the opening of the vagina is sewed together to leave only a small hole, the size of one's little finger, the first experience of intercourse is extremely painful. At childbirth, the opening is cut open so that the baby can pass through and is sewn again afterward. The physical pain leaves a terrible memory, but it is considered no different from any operation a child might have. Since it is believed to be a beneficial ritual, conducted in the spirit of community and with love from parents and family, it is not as psychologically traumatic as it might have been. Although it is not a requirement of Islamic practice, it is believed to be so by the masses. Women consider it a cleansing operation, beneficial for a woman's health and well-being. It is hard to find a husband for a girl who has not been circumcised.

Because of my mother's intervention, my father allowed me to attend secondary school after I finished intermediate school. My experience at the school motivated me politically. The British headmistress eliminated science courses from our curriculum. We had to pass the standard Cambridge examination in order to qualify for entrance to the university. Without taking science courses, we would have a difficult time passing the examination. We asked her to allow us to study the sciences. She told us that as black women we did not have the intelligence to learn these subjects. "Besides," she reminded us, "the mission of this school is to train good housewives." A number of my schoolmates were motivated by this experience of racism to fight against British colonialism. I reacted by starting a wall newspaper. We also wrote a letter to the city newspaper, describing our predicament. The letter was passed on to the headmistress, and she reacted by immediately dismissing all of us. We were preparing for the examination and missing our classes could take away our chance of passing the examination and the possibility of attending the university. We decided to put all our efforts into preparing for the exam in order to prove to the British woman that we were intelligent and capable enough to pass. We had exceptional results. Sixty percent of us were accepted.

Throughout my childhood and adolescence, my mother was an important presence in my life. She was a tall woman with light skin and three thin, parallel lines cut into each cheek, giving a lovely symmetry to her face. I remember her sitting with the Quran in her hand, reading quietly to women from the neighborhood or members of the extended family. One of the lessons I learned from her has become a mainstay of my philosophy in life. When I was a young girl I completed a class organized by the Red Crescent. I received nicely framed first-class certificates in nursing and first aid—with beautiful calligraphy. I brought them home and hung them on a wall. One day as we sat talking with my mother, we heard a child screaming. We ran out and saw my younger brother sprawled on the ground with his elder brother's bicycle on top of him, the chain embedded in his leg, and blood spurting out from under the chain that had cut deep into his flesh. I took one look and fainted. My mother fetched water and sprinkled it on my face and held a bottle of perfume under my nostrils. When I came to, she ran outside and stopped a passerby and guided him to lift the bicycle from the boy's leg. She took my brother to the hospital to treat his wound. When she returned, she sat down next to me and said warily, "Fatima, I tried my best to educate you and raise your awareness and teach you the best of your culture. I supported all your activities and was proud of them. But what is the use of your first-class certificate of nursing, if the first chance you get to use your learning you faint? Instead of helping me, you became a burden. Fainting is more dangerous than a wounded leg. I had to leave your brother to bring you to consciousness." She then took down the framed certificates and broke them against her knee. "These are only for show and pretense if they don't bring you wisdom and strength."

After high school, I wanted to attend art school, but even with my mother's support, I was unable to obtain my father's permission. For a time I studied journalism on my own. My gradual involvement with the women's movement led me to realize the importance of initiating a journal for women. The first organization for women, established in 1947, had failed because the founders, inexperienced in community organizing, had limited membership to educated women of the capital. By 1952, having learned from the previous experiment, a new group of younger women, myself among them, joined a number from the original organization to form the Sudanese Women's Union. The new organization was based on an expanded membership and a network of branches throughout the country.

I decided to publish a journal that would provide us with a forum to discuss women's issues. Several women helped me and we sold our gold to obtain the necessary capital for this venture. In the first issue of the journal which we called the *Sudanese Women's Voice* we set forth our beliefs. We said we do not consider men our enemies. We do not consider Islam our opponent. We refuse to accept the Western model of liberation as our blueprint, nor do we recommend copying men's behavior as a means of reaching emancipation and equality. We expressed our respect for the positive traditions of our culture. We demanded political, economic, and social rights for women, equal opportunities for employment, and an equal role for women within the family. We conveyed our belief that women's rights must be seen within the context of the welfare of the family and the community and must be sought on the basis of our sociocultural roots. We held that feminism is indigenous to our culture, and full equality can be reached on the basis of our own religious and cultural precepts. We knew we must reassure our people that we did not mean to change

the basic tenets of our traditions. We stressed the beauty and rightness of our national costume, the *toab*.

In the same year, the Egyptians and the British, who had been
ruling Sudan, signed an agreement that gave the country its independence. In 1954 for the first time we had a Sudanese government. We
were jubilant, thinking now that we had our own government, there
would be more attention paid to the problems of the people. A group
of us prepared a proposal for the betterment of the condition of
women, including measures to improve education and health and
maternal care and presented it to the new prime minister. But the new
government showed no response. We realized that replacing white
faces with black in positions of power does not automatically benefit
the masses of women.

We decided that reformist activities, such as establishing literacy
classes, doing charitywork and the like, would not by themselves
bring about substantial changes in the condition of women. In order
to transform the society, we had to change the political infrastructure. We decided to continue these activities in order to receive
the support of certain groups of women who were interested in them,
but we resolved to concentrate on obtaining the right to vote. We
changed the constitution of the organization to reflect our newly
gained awareness. It now included our demands for full participation
of women in social and economic development of the country, and a
whole list of other demands that went beyond "traditional" concerns
of women. We emphasized that it was necessary to change the traditional role of men and women in the family if we were to have full
participation of women in the work force. We demanded, among
others, accessible and dependable childcare facilities, the right to
divorce, increase in the minimum age of marriage, and limitation of
polygyny. But our main concern was to achieve political participation
in order to give women the power of their votes.

There was an immediate and strong backlash from the Muslim
Brothers and other conservative Muslim groups. They began a campaign of slander, accusing us of loose morals and Western tendencies.
We responded by quoting verses of the Quran and the various *hadith*
in support of our claims of equality, stressing our belief in our
religion.

In 1958, pressured by the Americans, Prime Minister Abdulah

Khalil handed his power over to a military government. The women's organizations went underground. The *Sudanese Women's Voice* continued to be published because I, as the editor in chief, personally held the license. The journal was the first to publish political cartoons. One of the first showed a child, scowling, with a caption that read "Even you are disgusted?" The minister of interior called me in and complained about this cartoon and another that clearly depicted the president and the minister himself. He asked me why I was attacking the government. I answered, "Why do you think these drawings are of you or the president? Are these drawings the way you see yourself?" He said, "You are a fragile woman. Your strength is in your tongue." He called his assistant and ordered the closure of the journal, but asked him to give me all the privileges of journalists. When we reopened the journal a year later, its circulation increased from 7,000 to 17,000.

The political movement against the military government continued. Trade unions played a very important role by organizing a series of strikes that eventually paralyzed the government. Our organization was the only women's group that was part of the coalition of forces that formed the opposition. In 1964, when the military refused to obey orders to open fire on the strikers and demonstrators, the mass uprising succeeded in toppling the military government.

Women achieved the franchise in 1964. In the first general elections, which took place in 1965, I ran for office and was the first and only woman elected to a parliament of 365 men. I had chosen to uphold an image of myself as a traditional, respectable, family-oriented Muslim woman in my private life. This image gained me the credibility that allowed me to be radical and outspoken in my public life. I also took on topics and issues which showed that women are knowledgeable and interested in a variety of fields. Other delegates, even those not sympathetic to women's demands, came to me for support, voted with me, and publicized their votes in order to gain the women's vote. We stated our goals reasonably and suggested pragmatic strategies for working toward them. Within a few years, real and important changes came about within the law: women gained access to a variety of professions, becoming judges, police officers, doctors, engineers.

I was very active in the Women's Union and in the Communist

party and the trade unions. I moved in various worker's circles and political activist groups. I met the man who became my husband in these meetings. We worked well together and shared the same ideals. I was too involved in public service and activism to be interested in personal attachments. I decided to marry this man because he was a friend and a partner and a colleague. What we felt for each other was respect, trust, and comradery, rather than love. I have never had time for love. He was a good struggler for human rights and a respectable trade unionist. Our marriage followed our friendship. At the outset, we worked out the context of our marriage contract. We committed ourselves to honesty, to giving each other space to think and work and be. We agreed to be soulmates and allies.

We were married in 1966. There are many rituals connected to marriage in Sudan, all based on subordination and objectification of women. From a month prior to the wedding, the bride is kept indoors, out of the sun. Her skin is daily massaged with aromatic creams and scrubbed so that layers of roughness are gradually removed. Her toenails and fingernails are colored with henna into a dark burnt-orange. The soles of the feet and hands are hennaed in elaborate patterns. She is fed to fatten her if thin and starved to reduce her weight if she is plump. At the end of this period, the perfumes are almost internalized to produce an aroma, special to a Sudanese bride. A considerable sum is given as a dowry. For the celebration, she is dressed in flimsy garments and performs a provocative dance she has practiced for weeks before the occasion. It is called the pigeon dance, because the movements with the chest thrust forward, neck held back, and arms spread out at the sides, resemble a bird in flight. She gyrates her body in sensual movements. The ceremony is usually celebrated with a grand feast.

I decided to use the occasion of my marriage to set an example for emancipated women. I refused a dowry, which I consider putting a price on a woman. Instead of the feast for relatives and friends, I decided to have a simple ceremony but include all my constituents and colleagues and friends. We published the invitation to the wedding in the newspaper and held the celebration in a park. We served only soft drinks and fruits and sweets. Thousands of people came to our wedding. I sat beside my husband on a stage constructed so that the crowd could see us. I no more thought of dancing than my husband did.

In May 1969 there was another coup d'état and a military regime came to power. The generals sent for the women leaders and asked for our support. We negotiated with them about our demands and they initially agreed to our terms, but when we began discussing various specific items, they reneged on their original agreement.

We invited the president, Jaffar Numairi, to open an international conference we had organized on literacy. We hoped that he would use the occasion to give support to women's demands. We were shocked to hear him say that he opposed the demands of feminists because they were propagating imported Western ideas that were incompatible with our Islamic culture. Following his speech, I went to the podium and said, "It is symbolic that the president who is dressed top to toe in imported Western clothing assigns the label 'foreign' to the indigenous demands of Sudanese women, all of whom happen to be dressed in the *toab*. Since he chooses to renege on his promise of support for our programs, we are left with no choice but to withdraw our support from his government." When he was leaving, I accompanied him and a number of his ministers to the door, but he did not look back or say good-bye. At a prearranged reception he gave for the participants of the conference that evening, I was seated on his left. He told me, "Fatima, you have broken the protocol. You should not have responded to my speech, and it certainly was inappropriate to confront and criticize me in a public international forum." I said, "Mr. President, I am a street fighter. I know nothing about protocol. I will speak up against anyone who negates women's rights at any gathering where he expresses such ideas." He smiled and said, "They asked me to have you arrested right there and then, but I refused because you are a courageous woman." He did not speak to me again. I felt that this was a foreboding and a threat.

In November 1970 the Sudanese Women's Union held its general conference in order to elect the president and the secretary-general. A recent split in the Communist party of Sudan, the largest communist party in Africa—following which some had joined Numairi and others had stayed in the opposition—spilled over to the Women's Union, even though we tried hard to keep the women's movement united. In spite of the machinations of the splintering factions, I was elected president of the union.

In April 1971 our organization was banned and Numairi established his own government-sponsored women's organization, giving it a name similar to ours to confuse the international organizations with which we were connected or affiliated. The government's measures became harsher each day and their tolerance for opposition decreased. In the same year they arrested my husband, who was the secretary-general of the Federation of the Trade Unions. They picked him up on his way to a union meeting. A colleague at the Communist party who had joined the ranks of the Numairi supporters after the split sent me a message through my brother, saying that the only way to save my husband was to take my two-year-old son and personally appeal to the president in his office. I told my brother I would never agree to such a thing. My husband would rather die with his head held high than to be alive with eyes downcast because his life was owed to his wife's beggarly appeal to the dictator. I would never beg the killer not to kill. My husband and I had discussed the dangers of our situation and our expectations of one another if one of us was arrested. Days before he was arrested, he asked me to go to my father's because he didn't want the government to use me to force him into demeaning himself or his cause. We had decided together that we wouldn't allow them to use one of us to humiliate us both through the other.

They tortured my husband for three days and on the third day, when they realized he was dying under torture, they held a ten-minute "trial" after which they executed him. Executions were usually held at dawn. My husband's life hung by a thread. Fearful that he might not last the hours till dawn, they executed him at two o'clock in the afternoon in order to avoid public knowledge that he had died under torture.

They arrested me at the same time they killed him, almost to the minute. They kept me under house arrest for two and a half years. When I was released, I organized a demonstration with other wives and children of the executed men and demanded to know the charge against them. Following the demonstration, I went to the supreme court and asked the chief justice to register a complaint against the president for the murder of my husband. I knew he couldn't do anything, but I wanted to register my complaint, pay the fee, and have it on the record for history.

They arrested me again, and this time they took me to a prison outside the city where they held murderers and other criminals. I was left in a room full of men. The guard gave me his chair and I slept sitting up in that chair for three nights. There was nowhere to wash and little food. Soon I was so ill that they had to move me to the hospital. Before leaving for the hospital, I shook hands with all the prisoners and told them that my husband had been killed because he held society responsible for the way people like them were treated. Society created conditions that forced them into criminal behavior. He had died for the idea that people should have decent education and employment and housing.

Eventually I recovered and was released. In the next sixteen years, I continued my activities with the Sudanese Women's Union. The Women's Union was working underground and I was in and out of jail regularly. But throughout the whole period, I kept my political work and my home life in balance. I made sure that I had enough time to spend with my son. I helped him with his homework and told him about my own preoccupations and activities. Wherever I went, even when I attended meetings that were secret, I told him about it. I wanted him to know me and know my goals. I also made sure that my reputation was well protected, because it was important in my work and also because I wanted my son to be proud of me. I never rode in a car alone with a colleague, nor attended a meeting in a house where no woman was present. I made sure to come home from any activity in the early evening. I knew what I was doing, and I trusted my colleagues fully, but I didn't want rumors and innuendo to harm my image or my son's faith in me. During all these years, the Sudanese people supported me in every way. They sent me money and toys and clothes for my son. He had so many toys that he often distributed them among other children. Even now that I am in exile, Sudanese women send me *toabs* so that I have many and can go on wearing different ones and not have to wash before I have time to.

In 1983 the Islamic Front joined Numairi's government, and its leader became his deputy. They put *Sharia* law into effect and declared Numairi the imam, placing opposition to him on a par with opposition to God. They set up the military emergency courts, called

*Kheymeh,* or tent courts. These were set up on street corners and in schools all over town. They made immediate decisions about alleged crimes and carried out the punishment on the spot. Adultery was a common charge. In order to charge a woman with that it was enough to find her, fully clothed, standing next to a man who was not next of kin to her. The penalty was eighty lashes, a fine of a hundred pounds, and a year in prison. Cases of adultery were publicized widely, causing many of the women charged with this to commit suicide rather than tolerate the shame brought to their families. The real aim of this policy was to force the men to keep their wives, daughters, and sisters segregated within the home.

In 1983 I applied for an exit visa to go to Europe for medical attention. They refused at first, but finally agreed because of pressure from Amnesty International. But when I went to the airport, the security guards took my passport and refused to allow me to leave. I shouted my objection to their behavior, taunting them for being afraid of a sick, frail woman. I called them lackeys of a thieving president, who with his wife and brother were robbing the people of their livelihood. I forced my way into the transit area and told passengers who were leaving the country that I am being held back by force and asked them to contact the newspapers and the media in the countries of their destination and tell my story. Hearing this, Numairi ordered that I be taken to the military court, flogged, and put in prison for the rest of my life. He had pronounced my sentence before I was tried. When they took me to the court, I was amazed to see the thousands of people who had surrounded the courthouse. When my son walked to me and put his arms around me, the crowd shouted, "We won't allow them to kill your mother as they killed your father." The judge and the representatives of the army and the police were sitting in judgement. My doctor testified that I would not survive flogging. The general secretary of the lawyer's association sat next to me and whispered advice, but he was not allowed to defend me. He had held a consultation with my lawyer and my brother-in-law and decided that my defense should be made on the grounds of insanity. When the acquittal was being read, I tried to stand and declare my objection to being classified as "insane," but my son held me back, and my lawyer said, "If you do this I will have to believe that you are in fact insane." So I kept quiet and was released. The judge told my brother-in-law not to take me home because people would follow and demonstrate. I was taken to a friend's house outside the city to avoid continuation of the demonstrations on my behalf.

The political atmosphere in the country grew more tense. Women were mobilized against the emergency military courts and the breach of their human rights. There was increasing dissatisfaction and unrest. At the end of March 1984 they expelled the military regime. Sadik El Mahdi, of the Umma party, came to power. The Umma party was a conservative group, but, in the tradition of the extended family and the expanded social network that connects people together in Sudan, we found it possible to work together across dividing lines of political ideology. Sometimes there are members within a family who belong to extreme opposite margins of political parties, but they can reach across these differences and work together because of other ties that bind them. This phenomenon can be used as a base for a rudimentary democracy and utilized to encourage tolerance and to build coalitions.

When El Mahdi came to power, once again there was the possibility of political activism. Women who had participated in the revolt and had been in the front line of the struggle were again able to organize their networks. The Supreme Council called representatives of all groups to the palace and we worked together to prepare a program of reconstruction based on the concept of equality, non-discrimination, and peace. We noted that any force that supports the military to come to power in Sudan would be considered the people's enemy. We sent copies of the statement to the United Nations and to other regional and international groups.

We tried to build a common front representing the whole political spectrum from the left to the right. We discussed our mutual oppression as women and the need to work together for the shared goals of equality and full participation.

In 1989 I was on an official visit abroad when I heard that a coup d'état had taken place in Sudan, bringing to power an army officer and member of the Islamic Front, Omar El Basheer. El Basheer's was a fundamentalist government, supported by the Islamic Republic of Iran. One of its first acts was to impose the Iranian style *hejab* on women. There was a wave of resistance to changing our national dress, the *toab*. The government was forced to limit the compulsory use of the *hejab* to government offices and schools. But even in those spaces, women insisted on wearing the *hejab* under the *toab*.

Conditions in Sudan grew worse. Inflation ran out of control and the infrastructure of the country deteriorated. Shortages of food and fuel became endemic, and public transportation all but disappeared. Civil liberties were suspended.

Early on, President Basheer publicly announced that he would welcome criticism of his regime and consider suggestions about public policy. I met with my colleagues, and we decided to take advantage of this statement and prepared a memorandum listing our demands. We considered sending a delegation to present the document to the president, but I volunteered to go alone so that if he decided to arrest the perpetrator, I would be the only one punished. As I had expected, they arrested me. But they used a new system of imprisonment. I was asked to go to the headquarters of the security forces each morning and stay there without food or water until dark when I was allowed to return home. I was not a prisoner by the usual definition of the term, but I was paralyzed and my movements were limited, as if I had been in jail. They told me I was not arrested because I presented the memorandum criticizing the president's policies but because I signed it in my capacity as the president of the Sudanese Women's Union, an outlaw organization.

Later that year I applied for an exit visa for reasons of health. I was finally allowed to leave in 1990. I went to London, where I continued to speak out against the regime in Sudan. During the Conference of the International Democratic Federation of Women in 1991, the Arab delegations nominated me for president and I was elected. I applied for political asylum in England and with the help of Amnesty International I was given asylum.

In the last two years, I have had time to think and review my life's activities. In view of the events in Eastern Europe, I reconsidered my commitment to socialism. I have concluded for myself that socialism failed in many parts of the world because it was not interpreted and implemented correctly. Another grave mistake was denial of God and religion, which are the mainstay of many people's moral and spiritual existence. Learning from past mistakes should help us work toward a world in which there is an equitable distribution of the necessities of life, full participation of the people in determining their destiny, and

justice and the rule of law. Those who have raised the flag of socialism in the past have often not *believed* in socialism but used it to gain
riches for themselves. At the end of my soul-searching, I am still a
communist, but one who believes in Islam and in democracy. I have
always kept my political beliefs separate from my work within the
women's movement. I have learned that in order to succeed in the
women's movement we must organize the grassroots. To do that we
must include diverse views and lifestyles. Women will follow no
leader unless they come to believe in her sincerity and in the efficacy
of her ideas and proposals, and in her commitment not to impose her
politics upon them.

My life in exile differs, I think, from others. I have, in a sense,
chosen exile because it offers me a better chance to work for my
people. Exile is the place I have come to in order to continue my
struggle. My home, in reality, is where I can struggle for my people. If
I had stayed in Sudan and remained silent and safe, I would have been
a stranger to my own nature and a true exile. I consider my stay
abroad temporary. It is difficult to continue my day-to-day existence.
My life is extremely limited financially and socially. My physical
surroundings are oppressive to me. I miss the bright sun to which I
awoke each day at home. The gloomy weather in England is a symbol
for me of the present state of things. I am convinced that some day
soon the clouds will pass and the sun will come out. The change in the
conditions of my country, which is bound to come, will reveal new,
bright horizons for us. I yearn for news of my country, and when I
hear of the scarcity of food and see the drawn faces of the starving
children on television, I am filled with guilt. Food sticks in my throat
and I am unable to swallow. I cannot sleep at night. I lie down in bed,
but my mind travels home. I am not anxious for the dawn.

My work with women used to be the most energizing part of my
day at home, but here, even though I am engaged in the work of the
Federation, it is less fulfilling, because I feel my ideas and opinions are
different from most of the others. They want to concentrate on rape
and violence and sexual choice. I am concerned with these issues, but
I am much more aware of the problems of simple survival. What
priority can sexual choice have to a woman whose child is dying of
hunger in her arms?

The loneliness of exile is the most difficult part of my life these days. I miss the warmth and closeness of family, friends, and colleagues. At home, one's house was always filled with people, who came at any time, and who were always expected and always welcome. Here no one knocks at one's door. Everyone is in a hurry and there's little time for offering hospitality to strangers.

Like a plant pulled from its soil, its roots withering in the cold air, I am out of my element in the West. My son graduates from the medical school of Khartoum University this week. I am hoping he will be allowed to visit me. His presence will bring me warmth and light and he will be home and country for me.

# Feminist Issues: Practice, Politics, Theory
## Alison Booth and Ann Lane, Editors

Carol Siegel
*Lawrence among the Women: Wavering Boundaries
in Women's Literary Traditions*

Harriet Blodgett, ed.
*Capacious Hold-All: An Anthology of
Englishwomen's Diary Writings*

Joy Wiltenburg
*Disorderly Women and Female Power in the Street
Literature of Early Modern England and Germany*

Diane P. Freedman
*An Alchemy of Genres: Cross-Genre Writing
by American Feminist Poet-Critics*

Jean O'Barr and Mary Wyer, eds.
*Engaging Feminism: Students Speak Up and Speak Out*

Kari Weil
*Androgyny and the Denial of Difference*

Anne Firor Scott, ed.
*Unheard Voices: The First Historians of Southern Women*

Alison Booth, ed.
*Famous Last Words: Changes in Gender and Narrative Closure*

Marilyn May Lombardi, ed.
*Elizabeth Bishop: The Geography of Gender*

Heidi Hutner, ed.
*Rereading Aphra Behn: History, Theory, and Criticism*

Peter J. Burgard, ed.
*Nietzsche and Feminism*

Frances Gray
*Women and Laughter*

Nita Kumar, ed.
*Women as Subjects: South Asian Histories*

Elizabeth A. Scarlett
*Under Construction: The Body in Spanish Novels*

Pamela R. Matthews
*Ellen Glasgow and a Woman's Traditions*

Mahnaz Afkhami
*Women in Exile*